GLOBAL *Cinderellas*

PEI-CHIA LAN

GLOBAL *Cinderellas*

Migrant Domestics and

Newly Rich Employers

in Taiwan

DUKE UNIVERSITY PRESS

Durham and London 2006

© 2006 Duke University Press
All rights reserved
Printed in the United States of America on acid-free paper ∞
Typeset in Scala by Keystone Typesetting, Inc.
Duke University Press gratefully acknowledges the support of the
Chiang Ching-kuo Foundation, which provided funds toward the
production of this book.

Library of Congress Cataloging-in-Publication Data
Lan, Pei-Chia
Global Cinderellas : migrant domestics and newly rich
employers in Taiwan / Pei-Chia Lan.
p. cm.
Includes bibliographical references and index.
ISBN 0-8223-3730-4 (cloth : alk. paper)
ISBN 0-8223-3742-8 (pbk. : alk. paper)
1. Women domestics—Taiwan. 2. Women—Employment—Taiwan.
3. Women migrant labor—Philippines. 4. Women migrant labor—Indonesia.
5. Alien labor, Philippine—Taiwan. 6. Alien labor Indonesian—Taiwan.
7. Filipinos—Employment—Foreign countries. 8. Indonesians—Employment
—Foreign countries. 9. Women—Taiwan—Economic conditions.
10. Women—Taiwan—Social conditions. I. Title.
HD6072.2.T28136 2006
331.4'81640460951249—dc22   2005028233

For my parents,

Wang Ho and Lan Chih-Ching

CONTENTS

LIST OF FIGURES AND TABLES

It was a gorgeous afternoon in the summer of 1999. I had just finished my fieldwork in Taiwan and returned to Chicago for dissertation writing. Feeling overwhelmed by organizing piles of interview transcripts, I took a break to do the laundry. My neighborhood was a racially mixed area where Mexican vendors sold snacks on the street but newly renovated condominiums near the lake shore were attracting growing numbers of yuppie residents. While I was walking to the laundromat at the street corner, a middle-aged white man passing by tossed me a question: "Do you know anybody who can take care of my mom?" Hit by this out-of-the-blue inquiry, I stood there, confused, speechless, and then humiliated and angry. It reminded me of the moment experienced by Audre Lorde in 1967: She wheeled her two-year-old daughter in a shopping cart through a supermarket in New York. A little white girl riding past in her mother's cart called out excitedly, "Oh, look, Mommy, a baby maid!"

The historical legacy of racialized domestic service remains, only involving expanding sources of labor supply and multilayered divisions of labor in the contemporary world. I crossed the Pacific Ocean to pursue a degree endorsed by the Western academia, while many women and men from Southeast Asia are working in Taiwan as domestic or construction workers to improve the welfare of their families. My study on international labor migration generated from my academic interest and political concern, but it had also resonated with my personal experiences. I had never studied race and migration until these topics became an ingrained part of my life. The terms "women of color" and "migrant worker" describe the lives not only of Indonesians and Filipinas in Taiwan but also mine in the United States. I became a "Third World woman" after landing on the alien continent of a racialized landscape. I struggled to perfect my English accent so that American students could not find excuses to complain about me as their foreign teaching assistant. These parallel trajectories indicate the very hierarchical order of globalization, which constrains as well as enables our agency and desire. Despite the diversity in destination and purpose, people's movements across borders have become a primary narrative of identity formation and a critical site of power struggle.

Many people have contributed their time and energy to this book. The most important, yet unnamable, contributors are those Filipina, Indonesian, and Taiwanese women who generously opened their worlds to me. I hope this book does justice in interpreting what they have experienced, although no monograph could produce anything as vibrant as their life stories woven with sweat, tears, and laughter. My debt to those migrant friends is beyond the scope of research. These courageous women taught me how to face hardships with love and faith; their passion and endurance comforted my restless soul.

This book started as a dissertation I finished in the Department of Sociology at Northwestern University. Carol Heimer, my advisor, sharpened my arguments and smoothed the prose in her careful reading of the early drafts. The other committee members, Gary Alan Fine and Orville Lee, also provided valuable support and advice. A postdoctoral scholarship in the Center for Working Families at the University of California, Berkeley, brought me in contact with a collegial and inspiring community. Arlie Hochschild and Barrie Thorne demonstrated an ideal of feminist scholarship with theoretical creativity as well as political commitment.

Many wise minds and warm hearts have guided me in the lengthy process of revision. Michael Burawoy, Pierrette Hondagneu-Sotelo, Nana Oishi, Gul Ozyegin, Rhacel Salazar Parreñas, Chuang Ya-chung, and Tseng Yen-fen read the whole manuscript. Several others commented on various drafts of particular chapters: Michele Ford, Karen T. Hansen, Margaret Nelson, Christena Nippert-Eng, Aihwa Ong, Ann Orloff, Charles Ragin, Raka Ray, Saskia Sassen, Sun Ruei-suei, and Wu Cheng-chong. Some portions of the book have appeared in the journals of *Asian and Pacific Migration Journal*, *Gender and Society*, *Identities: Global Studies in Culture and Power*, *Social Problems*, and the anthology *Global Woman*. I thank the editors and reviewers for their helpful comments. I also appreciate audience feedback from my presentations at numerous conferences and workshops.

My fieldwork in the Filipino community would not have been possible without full support from Sister Ascension Lin and Sister Wei Wei. I am also indebted to the hospitality of the Tinambunam family, Remy Borlongan, Luz Tacca, and the staff at Kaibigan and Kopbumi during my field trips. I have greatly benefited from the labor of several excellent assistants: Lo Jung, Chang Tin-wuan, Thum Chen-jie, Chang Hui-lan, and Chang Chao-ya. Friends also supplied information and other assistances: Chen

Chao-ju, Chen Yi-ju, Chen Wei-chih, Janet Custodio, Shirlena Huang, Huang Yu-lin, Lynn Rivas, Shen Hsiu-hua, and Wu Chin-ju. Majorie Schaffasma, Greggor Mattson, Robyn Taylor, and Martin Williams polished my writing along the way. I am grateful to Reynolds Smith at Duke University Press for expert editorial guidance and to Kate Lothman for editorial assistance while this book was in production.

I thank the institutions that provided financial support for this project over the years. I received dissertation fellowships from Northwestern University, Chiang Ching-kwo Foundation, and the Institute of Sociology at Academia Sinica in Taiwan. I also received travel grants from the Center for International and Comparative Studies at Northwestern University and the Program for Southeast Asian Area Studies at Academia Sinica. The second phase of fieldwork and the writing process was sponsored by the National Science Council in Taiwan. The International Institute for Asian Studies in the Netherlands hosted my visit in the summer of 2005.

My sociological roots in Taiwan have allowed me to maintain dialogues between Western theoretical canons and local ethnographic knowledge. I thank Shieh Gwo-shong, who showed me the wonder of field studies in my early twenties and continued to inspire me with his scholarly commitment. I appreciate the support of my colleagues in the Department of Sociology at National Taiwan University. The previous chair Chen Dungshen went to great length to support junior faculty like me. My lunch and beer partners, Tseng Yen-fen, Su Kuo-hsien, Wu Chia-ling, Lin Holin, Lin Kuo-ming, and Ko Jyh-jer, save me from solitude in academia with their cheerful personalities and intelligent conversations. Many other dear friends have accompanied me in Chicago, Berkeley, and Taipei during the past few years. Special thanks to Liu Hwa-jen and Hong Li-chien, who offer attentive ears when the Pisces part of me is falling into the blue ocean.

Finally, this book is dedicated to my parents. My mother, Wang Ho, grew up in an agricultural family in Taiwan and raised her five children on her own without ever hiring any help. My father, Lan Chih-ching, left his hometown in Canton and migrated to Taiwan as a war refugee in 1949. The political turmoil and ensuing cold war stopped him from visiting his family until forty years later, when he kneeled down in front of his mother's tombstone. They have been teaching me to appreciate the simple life, a silent lesson that took me years to recognize. I am, yet, still learning.

A NOTE ON STYLE

This book uses the system of Hanyu pinyin for the Romanization of Chinese. Yet the names of places and people are spelled according to Tongyong pinyi (a modification of the Wade-Giles pinyin), a system hitherto adopted by the government of the Republic of China (Taiwan).

In the texts and references, I render Chinese names in the native order of family name first and given name without a comma, in cases where original publication was in Chinese. Otherwise, the Western convention is followed.

Norma was born in 1967 in a small village in the Philippines. She went to college for two years, but had to drop out after the sudden death of her father. To mitigate her family's financial difficulties, she departed for Singapore—the first time she had ever left the Philippines—to meet one of her sisters, who had been working in domestic service. Norma worked for a Singaporean family and took care of their two children for five years. During this period she met her husband, a Filipino migrant factory worker. After Norma got pregnant, they both returned to the Philippines and got married. For two years, they lived together in Manila and had another child. Her husband worked as a tricycle driver and Norma took care of the children at home. However, the meager family income worried Norma, particularly in view of forthcoming expenses for her children's education. She decided to work abroad again.

In 1997 Norma borrowed money to pay for an opportunity to work in Taiwan. Alone this time, Norma became a transnational mother and the primary breadwinner in her family. She left her two children in the care of her youngest sister, to whom she pays a monthly allowance. Norma is now saving money to sponsor her husband to come to work in Taiwan. However, as the placement fee for factory workers has risen as high as us$4,000, her savings could barely make the down payment. Taking care of her employer's newborn baby, Norma could not go home during her first two years in Taiwan. She said with a sigh, "My daughter always asks me when I am going home. I keep telling her next Christmas." She finally convinced her employer to let her take a one-week vacation and went home with a lot of toys and gifts, including a Barbie doll, a DVD player, and a new Nokia mobile phone. Norma was not sure about her migratory path after Taiwan, wishing only that her family could be reunited in a few years and that they could open a *sari-sari* (small grocery store) on the outskirts of Manila.

Pei-jun was born in Taipei in the same year as Norma. With a university degree, she worked in an international bank and was recently promoted to manager. After getting married, she and her husband moved in with his parents. Though she consented to live in the traditional three-generation residence, Pei-jun was determined to continue her career after she became a mother. However, childcare became a thorny issue since her job required frequent overtime and did not allow her to pick up her daughter from day care on a regular schedule. Her mother-in-law volunteered to be the caretaker but Pei-jun felt uncomfortable with this suggestion. She was worried about her loss of autonomy in this arrangement and foresaw arguments with her mother-in-law about child-rearing matters.

Hiring a Filipina or Indonesian maid had become common practice among Pei-jun's colleagues and friends. Like most Taiwanese employers, Pei-jun was at first quite nervous about leaving her child with a foreigner. Growing up without hired help, she was also concerned that her child might become spoiled in the care of a maid. She finally decided to hire one but then had to spend some time convincing other family members. Her mother-in-law considered it a waste of money—"Why bother? I can watch your daughter for free!"—and her husband viewed it as an intrusion on his privacy—"So I can no longer walk in my underwear at home?" The employment finally took place after Pei-jun offered to pay for the maid out of her own salary. With the assistance of the Filipina worker, Pei-jun no longer had to fight with her husband over the division of housework or to worry much about the filial duty of serving her parents-in-law. More importantly, she was able to spend some quality time with her daughter after a long working day.

Globalization brings together the lives of Norma and Pei-jun, along with many other Filipina, Indonesian, and Taiwanese women. The migratory route from Southeast Asia to Taiwan reflects a regional pattern. The increasing prosperity of East Asia and the Gulf countries since the mid-1970s has stimulated substantial international migration within this region. Today, out of the 175 million people who reside outside the country of their birth, an estimated 50 million are in Asia (United Nations 2002). Amid the multifarious paths of international migration, contract migration of semi-skilled and unskilled workers has become salient in this region. It is estimated that the stock of temporary migrant workers in Asia, with or without legal documents, reached 6.1 million by 2000 (Battistella 2002).[1] About one third of this migrant labor force is feminized (Yamanaka and Piper 2003). The two million women are concentrated in particular occupations, including the entertainment industry, health services, and especially domestic service.

Migrant domestic workers mostly come from the Philippines, Indonesia, Sri Lanka, Thailand, and Vietnam and depart for Hong Kong, Singapore, Taiwan, Malaysia, and the Middle East (Heyzer et al. 1994). Since the early 1990s, Taiwan has become a popular destination for Asian migrant workers. In spite of stringent government controls on employer qualifications, the number of Taiwanese households employing migrant domestic workers has expanded rapidly in the last decade. Currently about 130,000 foreigners are legally employed as domestic helpers or caregivers. Nearly 70 percent of them are women from Indonesia and the Philippines, with the remainder from Vietnam, Thailand, and Mongolia (CLA 2004).

Migrant domestic workers are global Cinderellas. I use this metaphor to illuminate the complexity and paradoxes in their migratory trajectories: their relationship with employers is a combination of physical intimacy and social distance, and the impact of their migration is a juxtaposition of emancipation and oppression. Migrant women work overseas to escape poverty and stress at home; they also embark on the journey to expand life horizons and to explore modernity. After crossing national borders, they are nevertheless confined within the four walls of their employers' households. At work they act with deference, consistent with the role of a maid; only during days off are they able to put on makeup, jewelry, and short skirts. Recruited to serve as the surrogate family and fictive kin of their employers, migrant domestics are, however, treated as disdained aliens and disposable labor in host countries. Although migrant women may partially achieve the goal of upward mobility in their material lives back home, Cinderella's happy ending remains in the realm of fairy tale for many who are trapped in the circular flow of international migration.

WHEN MADAMS AREN'T WHITE

The gendered division of household labor has been a crucial concern of Western feminism since the 1960s. Women scholars of color later challenged the universal claim of "Woman." The topic of domestic employment in particular exposes differences and inequalities among women. As Judith Rollins (1985: 6–7) remarks, "In no other work arrangement is it typical for both employer and employee to be female." Frequently the relationship between these two women is not "a bond of sisterhood" but "a bond of exploitation" (Romero 1992).

The images of black mammy and primitive servants are often linked to the grim histories of slavery and colonialism. Yet the field of domestic employment has even expanded in the contemporary era of globalization. As Shellee Colen (1995: 72) says, "migration and domestic work are part of an international solution to women's problems within a world economic system." The integration of the global economy has simplified the gendered household burden for more privileged women by complicating the racial and class divisions of domestic labor on a global scale.

Women who can afford to hire market surrogates are able to enjoy the emotional rewards of motherhood while elevating themselves to the status of "mother-manager" (Rothman 1989). Migrant domestic workers, however, are forced to leave their own families behind in exchange for financial gains. These "mother-domestics" struggle to sustain their own family bonds and mother their own children with assistance from family members or local domestic workers. Globalization has triggered the formation of what scholars call "the global nanny chain" (Hochschild 2000) or "the international division of reproductive labor" (Parreñas 2001).

In this "new domestic world order" (Hondagneu-Sotelo 2001), the destinations of migration are no longer exclusively toward core countries in the North. Demand for migrant labor, both in the productive and reproductive spheres, has emerged in newly rich countries in the South, including the oil-rich Gulf countries and the "newly industrialized countries" (NICs) of Asia. Rather than producing a simple dichotomy between white employers and workers of color, the multi-tiered flows of international migration expose inequalities among women in the global South. The emergence of "colored madams" vis-à-vis "colored maids" deconstructs the notion of "Third World woman"—a category assumed to be homogenous in earlier Western feminist scholarship (Mohanty 1991; Ong 1994).

Who are these employers who hire migrant domestic workers? Saskia Sassen (1992), in her study of the global cities of London, New York, and Los Angeles, argues that the growth of middle-class professionals employed in producer services has generated increasing demand for personal services provided by recent immigrants, employed either as janitors who clean public offices or as maids and gardeners in private households. Similarly, the expansion of the service-based middle class in lower-order global cities in Asia, such as Hong Kong, Singapore, Kuala Lumpur, and Taipei, creates a demand for domestic service. The new rich of Asia emerged in the 1980s—a time when prolonged recession and low growth rates depressed markets in the West. The rapidly developing Asian economies became markets flooded with imported products like McDonald's, mobile phones, and luxury cars (Robison and Goodman 1996). The purchase of migrant domestic service became another marker for Asian employers' recent achievement of middle-class status (Chin 1998).

A burgeoning literature has explored this recent phenomenon.[2] Some works focus on the policy and social contexts of sending countries: for instance, Nana Oishi's (2005) study of the complex motives of emigration in a comparative project and Michele Gamburd's (2000) examination of the impact of migration on family relations in Sri Lanka. Others look at the overseas lives of migrant domestic workers, including Christine Chin's (1998) study in Malaysia and Nicole Constable's (1997a) ethnography about Filipina maids in Hong Kong. Despite these rich findings, there is still no solid connection between the macro analysis of political economy and the micro politics of identity formation. And most studies collect only one side of the story, from either workers or employers, overlooking the complex dynamics of employment relationships.

To address these shortages, I have designed this research to include the perspectives of both Taiwanese employers and migrant domestic workers. In this way, the relationship between employers and workers is approached as a dynamic and interactive process subject to negotiation and contestation. I situate the levels of analysis not only in the domain of household dynamics but also in broader social and cultural contexts, including the politics of nationalism and racialization, the restructuring of class relations, and the transformation of family lives. Further, I turn to the process of boundary making as a way of connecting macro and micro, the global and the local, and structure and agency.

DOMESTIC SERVICE IN THE PAST

The trade in women as domestic servants in Taiwan long predates the arrival of migrant workers. In the Ching Dynasty (1644–1911), affluent households usually purchased and owned a number of slaves, and brides brought one or more *chaboukans* (Hoklo: girl slaves) to be part of their dowries.[3] The Japanese colonial government abolished the trade in human beings in the early 1920s. Domestic service then became an occupation in which *shijonins* (Japanese: servants) are free to sell their labor in exchange for wages and often food and lodging. Despite the gradual growth in the number of domestic workers, the service was still a privilege accessible only to Japanese officials and a small number of Taiwanese landed gentry.[4]

The sector of domestic service expanded more significantly after 1949, when the Kuomintang regime retreated from China with approximately one million followers. Some wealthy Mainlander expatriates brought their servants along to Taiwan; the others experienced difficulty in finding local servants after relocation.[5] The strata of domestic employers also included Taiwanese double-income nuclear households. Urbanization drew educated women to seek employment in teaching, nursing, and other white-collar occupations in Taipei (You 1995). Living far away from their mothers-in-law and other extended kin, employed women had to seek help for childcare; housework was still strenuous given the limited availability of modern household facilities at that time.[6] These employers, who were rural migrants themselves, recruited single girls from their hometowns to work for them.

For these teenaged girls, working as a maid in Taipei was glamorous compared to farm labor at home; this working experience was viewed as a temporary passage before entering a marriage. Their relationships with employers tended to be highly personalized. Although employers and workers were not necessarily related, they called each other "auntie," "cousin," or "sister." Employers relied on social networks in their hometowns to recruit known workers they trusted; in the meantime, the workers' parents entrusted the employers to be surrogate parents and moral guardians for their daughters in Taipei. The employers usually remitted wages directly to the parents and the daughters received only a small allowance while residing in the city. Recruitment based on migrant networks was gradually replaced by the mushrooming private agencies in the 1960s. Most private agencies were concentrated behind Taipei Railway Station, conveniently accommodating the flow of migrant labor from rural areas.

After Taiwan's industrialization opened a variety of waged jobs for women, domestic work was no longer the only option for young girls to start a new life away from patriarchal families. Single young girls, who were alleged to be cheap and docile labor, were targeted as ideal workers for the export labor zones (Kung 1983). Owing to the improvement of household economy and the extension of public education, an increasing number of Taiwanese households could afford for their daughters to attend senior high school or college. As a result, the major source for domestic workers shifted from single girls to middle-aged *obasans*, who are mostly married or widowed women.[7]

Unlike single young rural migrants, most *obasans* have families living close by and prefer not to reside with their employers. They serve as day workers, who only go to their employers' houses during the day, or part-timers, who clean and maintain several houses on a daily or weekly basis. Day workers are paid by a fixed monthly rate and their job assignments are specific.[8] Part-time cleaners are paid by the number of hours they work.[9] Fewer and fewer Taiwanese workers are willing to take on a live-in job in spite of the rising market wage.[10]

The tradition of domestic servants in Taiwan was not as common as it was among Chinese families in Hong Kong (Constable 1997a) or colonial Malaya (Gaw 1991). Yet the romantic ideal of loving and loyal women servants exists in the minds of contemporary Taiwanese employers, even if they actually never had servants in their family histories. The employers' nostalgic mourning for the disappearance of "ideal servants," analogized as family members based on village ties, contrasts sharply with their feeling of dissatisfaction with today's Taiwanese domestic workers, *obasans*. In the portrait sketched by employers, *obasans* are difficult to deal with, calculating about working hours, selective about job assignments, and demanding about wages and raises; their cleaning services are substandard, their childcare styles are out-of-date, and they lack professional skills and work ethic.

In fact, some of these complaints against *obasan* day workers concern the workers' attempt to rationalize domestic employment and to safeguard their private lives from the employer families. In comparison with *obasans*, live-in migrant workers are, in the words of an employer, "somewhat closer to the old time servants." In other words, Taiwanese employers seek live-in migrant workers to approximate the ideal of domestic servants in the past—they are more obedient, deferential, and personally subordinated; they are paid at a lower rate but offer live-in services that cover an unlimited variety of domestic tasks.

Scholars two decades ago predicted that the occupation of domestic servants should become obsolete with the commodification of household service and the introduction of new household technology (Chaplin 1978; Coser 1974). The prediction proved premature. The old fashion of live-in domestic service did not diminish in the process of modernization but has revived and even expanded with the facilitation of modern states and global capitalism. Migrant labor provides a solution to the quandary of contemporary Taiwanese women positioned between patriarchy and modernity.

TAIWAN-PHILIPPINES-INDONESIA LINKS

This book focuses on the links between three major actors in the system of Asian migration: Taiwan, the Philippines, and Indonesia. These three "Third World countries" have taken different paths in the global economy during the last few decades. Taiwan shifted its status from a recipient of economic aid from the United States to a major U.S. trading partner after its rapid and successful industrialization.[11] The Philippines, once a leading economy in Asia, has suffered from political turmoil and economic depression since the 1980s and has become the second largest source of migrant labor in the world. Indonesia, a new Asian tiger whose economic boom tumbled during the 1997 financial crisis, has expedited the export of its nationals to smooth the problems of labor surplus and rising unemployment.

In 1992 Taiwan's government granted work permits to "domestic caretakers," who are employed to care for the severely ill or disabled, and later released a limited number of quotas for the employment of "domestic helpers" by households with children under the age of twelve or elderly members above the age of seventy. Today the government has stopped releasing quotas for the employment of domestic helpers, but it places no quota restriction on the employment of foreign caretakers.[12] Many households thus apply for caretakers with forged medical documents but actually give them housework or childcare duties. Since the distinction between the categories of "domestic helper" and "caretaker" is ambiguous, I use the term "domestic worker" in this book to cover both terms.

Unlike that of most labor-receiving countries, the history of Taiwan lacks a lasting tradition of slavery or a prevalent practice of domestic servitude. Disregarding the small number of transient skilled migrants, the population was relatively ethnically homogenous until the inflow of labor and marriage migrants in 1990s.[13] The introduction of migrant workers has triggered a degree of fear and prejudice among the public. How do Taiwanese perceive these darker-skinned foreigners, especially when they are placed in private households (assumed to be a haven of intimacy) and take care of children (the most precious asset of the family)? This question leads us to explore the racialization of migrant domestic workers in both institutional and discursive realms. Taiwan's government has enforced restrictive immigration policies, including prohibiting foreign contract workers from transferring employers or seeking permanent residence. Popular discourse depicts Southeast Asian migrants by way of conflicting stereotypes: they are "the dangerous savage" associated with criminality and backwardness as well as "the ideal servant" naturally suited to dirty work and deferential conduct.

Taiwan's case is also significant because it reveals the concurrent transformation in class stratification, gender relations, and family patterns among the new rich in Asia. Most domestic employers in Taiwan are first-generation employers who grew up without a maid or babysitter at home. They are the so-called new middle class, consisting of professionals and the owners of small and medium-sized businesses (Chu 1996). They have built their wealth on the integration of an export economy into the capitalist world system. They advance their status and improve their well-being by leading a metropolitan lifestyle, which ties into the transnational flow of goods and labor, such as imported cars, overseas travel, and, now, foreign maids.

Taiwanese employers are also first-generation career women. Their mothers and mothers-in-law quit their jobs to become full-time homemakers after getting married or after the birth of their first child, but the daughters and daughters-in-law yearn for a different life. The contemporary version of middle-class womanhood is inscribed with the discourses of gender equality, career achievement, and couple egalitarianism. Caught between traditional ideals and modern values, these younger generations of Taiwanese women seek labor-market solutions, in particular the newly available migrant domestic worker, to outsource housework, childcare, and the duty of serving parents-in-law. Despite this, they continue to be torn between the demands of a full-time career and the cultural ideologies of motherhood, housewifery, and filial piety.

Compared with the pairing of First World employers and Third World workers, the hiring of migrant domestic workers in the global South involves more ambiguity and contestation in the power geometry of employment relationships. The encounter between Taiwanese newly rich employers and Filipina downwardly mobile migrants, in particular, is theoretically interesting in this regard. For example, a Hungarian domestic worker once summed up her Canadian employers by saying, "They think you are as stupid as your English is" (England and Stiell 1997). By contrast, one college-graduated Filipina domestic worker in this research said of her Taiwanese employers, "They have more money but I speak better English!"

Filipina women have dominated the global domestic labor market because of their English-language skills and relatively high levels of education. It is not unusual to find middle-class, college-educated Filipinas working overseas as maids and caretakers. This case presents several puzzles for sociologists: How do Filipina workers validate their upward mobility while performing the socially stigmatized work of maids in the host country? How do Taiwanese employers establish their hierarchical status as employers when the maids correct their grammatical mistakes in English? And how does the household setting become a globalized terrain for both employers and workers in affirming and contesting difference and inequality?

Indonesian women have been late in joining the flows of international migration, but they have gradually outnumbered their Filipina competitors in several Asian host countries, including Taiwan, Singapore, and Hong Kong. How do we make sense of this transition, especially in relation to the racialization and stratification of migrant domestic workers? This is another puzzle to be explored in this book. In contrast to the educated, Westernized image of Filipinas, Indonesian women are portrayed by labor brokers as subservient, tradition-bound villagers who better resemble model servants. By comparing Filipina and Indonesian migrant domestic workers, I examine the construction of stratified ethnic others in terms of their distinct recruitment venues, representations, and working conditions.

By focusing on encounters between migrant domestic workers and Taiwanese employers, this book examines how people identify themselves vis-à-vis "others" across national and social divides. I use the theoretical lens of *boundary making* to connect a macro analysis of structural forces with a micro investigation of interpersonal dynamics. The construction of social boundaries—drawing lines between "us" and "them"—not only requires the political-legal regulation of citizenship and national borders but also involves symbolic struggles and local negotiations in the daily interactions between employers and workers.

WHY DO BOUNDARIES MATTER?

Boundaries, according to Michèle Lamont (1992: 9), refer to "conceptual distinctions that we make to categorize objects, people, practices, and even time and space." Social boundaries are constituted on multiple levels—the cognitive, interactive, and institutional. On the mental level, we perceive the world through making distinctions in everyday life.[14] On the institutional level, social classification, such as racial taxonomy in national censuses or occupational schemes devised by professional groups, embodies the symbolic politics of domination and resistance. Privileged social groups tend to safeguard boundaries and consolidate the status quo by excluding others. Other groups seek inclusion by making the boundaries permeable or reconstructing alternative boundaries.

More importantly, it takes *work* in everyday practices to weave institutional divisions and cognitive classifications. Christena Nippert-Eng (1996: 7) defines the concept "boundary work" as "the strategies, principles, and practices we use to create, maintain, and modify cultural categories." My approach to boundary making is in line with a power-sensitive theory of *practice* that looks at "people's everyday actions as a form of cultural politics embedded in specific power contexts" (Ong 1999: 5). Consciously or not, we engage in boundary work to cultivate tacit knowledge or embodied habitus (Bourdieu 1977) that frames our understanding of selves and others. This social act is fundamental not only in the reproduction of cultural repertoires but also in the perpetuation of social inequalities.

Why do I think that the theoretical lens of boundary making offers a critical perspective on the globalization of domestic service? This concept offers a framework of relational positioning for us to comprehend the subjectivities of women across social divides; it also highlights the exercise of human agency and the dynamic process of identification.[15] More specifically, there are three interconnected reasons why boundaries matter in the social division of domestic labor and the cultural politics of migration. First, the performance of domestic labor is a central site for the construction of gender boundaries in articulation with other social inequalities. I use the concept "the continuity of domestic labor" to describe the structural mechanism that positions women similarly yet unevenly in the organization of domestic labor. Second, the relocation of migrant women into the host country and family has intensified the racialization of foreign workers as stratified others. Their cross-border movements have also complicated the landscape of class stratification on a global scale. Finally, home has become a meeting place for global inequalities and social differences. In everyday life, both employers and migrant domestic workers are cultivating spatial boundaries that make concrete the existence of social boundaries.

Negotiating Gender Boundaries in the Continuity of Domestic Labor

Judith Gerson and Kathy Peiss (1985) introduce the concept of gender boundaries to emphasize the flexibility and permeability of gender divisions instead of the static idea of gender roles.[16] Jean Potuchek (1997) reformulates this concept by defining gender boundaries as markers that divide "men" and "women" as two sharply distinct categories. The construction of gender boundaries is a dynamic system subject to individual negotiation. Potuchek also uses empirical data to establish that breadwinning is a salient gender boundary that differentiates male employment from female employment.

As breadwinning is essential to the construction of manhood, womanhood is grounded on the institutions and ideologies of domesticity and motherhood. Domestic labor, which refers to a range of labor activities that maintain the daily subsistence and social reproduction of family,[17] is a strategic site for the construction of gender boundaries. For women who hire a domestic worker and women who are employed as one, reality departs from this gender norm. Both groups of women leave their children for waged employment and deviate from full-time homemaking and mothering. Despite crossing this boundary, they continue to subscribe to gender conventions by negotiating the meaning of womanhood and the practice of motherhood in family routines. I found striking similarities as well as differences in the lived experiences of "maid" and "madam," both driven by the feminization of domestic labor as a mechanism of structural continuity across the public and private spheres.

Scholars tend to study unpaid household labor and paid domestic work as separate subjects, ignoring their articulation and embeddedness: the gender battle over housework at home is influenced by the availability of domestic service in the market, while those service providers are often wives and mothers themselves. A flawed dichotomy between "maid" and "madam" blinds us to the multiple positionings of women and the fluidity of their trajectories; it overlooks the fact that women may commute between maid and madam or occupy both positions at the same time. We need new ways of conceptualizing domestic labor that "transcend the constructed oppositions of public-private and labor-love" (Glenn 1994: 16).

To fill in this theoretical gap, I view unpaid household labor and paid domestic work not as separate entities in an exclusive dichotomy but as structural continuities that characterize the feminization of domestic labor across the public and private spheres.[18] When recruiting nannies or maids, employers often request information on their experiences of mothering or housekeeping in their own households as an assurance of their capability for paid domestic work. Conversely, a woman who has worked as a domestic worker is often considered by her mate to have better wifely and motherly potential. Individual women, during their life course, may engage in diverse forms of domestic labor that are nevertheless consistently constructed as women's work.

Domestic labor is socially seen as "naturally feminine" and as such becomes unskilled and unpaid work. The economic devaluation of household labor is rationalized by the compensation of its moral value, the myth of "labor of love." A similar interchange between emotional value and monetary value is used to rationalize low wages among care workers. The social belief that love and care are demeaned by commodification drives neoclassical economists to argue that care workers receive low wages because of their receipt of emotional compensation as an intrinsic reward of their jobs (England and Folbre 1999). In other words, both unpaid household labor and waged domestic work are feminized work possessing moral merits and yet undervalued in cash.

I look at the feminization of domestic labor as a structural continuity to engage with feminist literature on two major points. First, the conception of continuity breaks down binary thinking and highlights *similar* patriarchal constraints women face given their distinct social positions. The gendered division of domestic labor never disappears by simply being replaced with class and national inequalities. Female employers and domestics, with mutual assistance, seek liberation from the role of housewife; and yet both remain to grapple with gender norms and boundaries. Second, the continuity of domestic labor demonstrates a *differentiated* construction of womanhood within a system of interlocking social inequalities, and it provides a means for women to exercise agency by shifting across multiple positions embedded in the organization of domestic labor.

Not only is domestic work considered a woman's "calling," women of particular ethnic groups are viewed as more naturally suited to it. The racialization of particular ethnic categories is associated with specific constructions of womanhood (Anthias and Yuval-Davis 1992). Based on a historical study of American housewives and domestic workers between the two World Wars, Phyllis Palmer (1989) argues that white women acquired distinct versions of womanhood in opposition to women of other races and classes. White "madams" were good women associated with purity and domesticity, while "colored maids" were dirty, sexualized, bad women.

Female employers, fearful of being usurped by their market surrogates, safeguard their womanhood by enforcing the maid-madam boundary. The binary distinction between maid and madam, as well as the polarized construction of womanhood, requires constant confirmation through the division and interpretation of domestic duties. Women employers deliberate on what kinds of labor are socially acceptable to transfer to commercial agents without diminishing their status as "the lady of the house" (Kaplan 1987). Mothers also develop a stratified division of mothering labor between themselves and their nannies to maintain the spirituality and morality of their motherhood (Macdonald 1998; Uttal 1996). When female employers attempt to carve out a rigid boundary between themselves and domestic workers, they are simultaneously participating in the imagining of class and ethnic differences.

For migrant women, the risk of transgressing gender boundaries lies in their status as transnational breadwinners. Although they pursue similar full-time employment as male migrants do, migrant women nevertheless need to confirm gender boundaries by achieving "good" mothering from afar. As Pierrette Hondagneu-Sotelo and Ernestine Avila (1997) have argued, migrant fathers fulfill their family obligation simply by playing the role of a distant breadwinner who supplies stable remittances, but migrant mothers must expand the definition of motherhood by developing the belief that they can best fulfill their maternal responsibilities through being a breadwinner overseas. With their husbands back home feeling deprived of the masculine identity of breadwinning, Rhacel Parreñas (2005) found that migrant women tend to reinforce gender boundaries by overacting the "super mom" performance as if to compensate for their physical absence from the family.

Both Taiwanese female employers and migrant domestic workers are engaged in what Deniz Kandiyoti (1991) calls "patriarchal bargaining," a concept that describes how women devise various strategies to maximize security and optimize life options when facing various forms of patriarchal oppression. Later chapters in this book borrow this term to explore how women bargain with local patriarchal relations and gender boundaries with distinct strategies. Some women ease the gendered duty of domestic labor by hiring a maid, but others escape gender constraints at home by becoming one.

Mapping Racialized and Class Boundaries in the Age of Migration

Contemporary scholarship has refuted the validity of "race" as a biological fact or natural category. Acknowledging the constructive nature of racial classification, scholars suggest that we use the concept "racialization" to describe the social process of categorization and otherization. This process makes group relations appear as if they were natural and unchangeable, hence reducing and essentializing differences (Miles and Torres 1999: 5).

In the context of international migration, foreigners or migrants—outsiders to the politico-cultural community—become the major target of racialization. Around the globe, we have witnessed the prevalence of political discourses that rationalize the exclusion of outsiders based on "cultural difference." Although racialized boundaries are traditionally constructed on the basis of physical and genetic attributes, racial taxonomy often conflates with culture-based "ethnic groupings" (Anthias and Davis 1992: 12). In the words of Étienne Balibar (1991: 21), this new racism is "racism without races"—the dominant theme is no longer biological heredity but the *naturalization* of cultural differences.[19]

It is important to note that not all foreigners are subject to the same degree or kind of racialization. To most French people, the term "immigrant" means Algerians even though the Portuguese constitute a larger immigrant group in France. In Japan, "foreign worker" refers to only manual laborers from poor Asian countries, excluding other significant ethnic groups such as Koreans, Chinese, Europeans, and North Americans (Lie 2001: 18–19). These phenomena demonstrate that the process of racialization is structurally tied to class stratification and the division of labor in the world system.[20] And the construction of racialized boundaries reflects the cultural imagination of the other in a given society—some groups are considered to contain historical or cultural affinities and hence the potential to become part of "us," while other groups are marked as essentially different and as such excluded from the project of acculturation.

I raise the concept "stratified otherization" to emphasize the *relational* construction of racialized boundaries. Racialization is not merely a dichotomous construction between the self and the other; it creates plural categories of ethnic others associated with stratified layers of cultural imagery. The subject position of migrant workers is situated in discursive and institutional terrains that accommodate ethnic others within the coordinates of class differentiation and national disparity. To concretely depict the process of racialization, sociological research needs to identify where the process takes place, who the carriers are, and what material or symbolic interests are involved. Michael Omi and Howard Winant (1994) have argued that racialization is a political project in which the state distributes different rights and resources according to racial categories. Racialization is also a discursive process that deploys symbols, language, and images to convey group-based stereotypes. In addition, racialized boundaries are reproduced through the application of norms, etiquette, and spatial rules that orchestrate personal interaction (Glenn 2002: 12). This book demonstrates the racialization of migrant workers in three major arenas: policy regulations imposed by the receiving state, recruitment and representation of migrants by labor brokers, and migrants' encounters with employers and local citizens.

The host state tends to favor or disfavor migrants of particular nationalities or ethnicities to uphold diplomatic interests or maintain the ethnic status quo; the policy also contains class bias as it usually grants different rights and benefits to foreign professionals and blue-collar migrants. In other words, the regulations on immigration and citizenship not only delineate a boundary between migrant and citizen but also stratify migrants along the lines of occupation and nationality. State policy, whether intentional or not, has drawn racialized boundaries by categorizing migrants on the basis of stratified foreignness.

Labor brokers, with their matchmaking role, actively participate in the racialization of migrant workers. International labor migration does not consist of random flows but instead organized channels that are often dominated by for-profit recruiters. In order to impress potential employers, labor brokers must present certain racialized discourses about migrant applicants as a display of their market knowledge and professional screening (Bakan and Stasiulis 1995). They also apply racialized stereotypes to naturalize divisions of job assignment and establish nationality-based niches in the segmented labor market. Scholars in Europe and Canada have observed that distinct yet ambiguous stereotypes are associated with domestic workers of different skin colors, ethnicities, or nationalities (Anderson 2000; Pratt 1997).

Migrants' personal encounters with employers and locals do not curtail the social distance between them but often increase a tendency in the host society to erect barriers to the exclusion of outsiders. While disparaging migrant domestic workers as the inferior other, employers confirm their superiority not only on racial terms but also along the axes of gender, class, and nationality. Later chapters in this book will demonstrate how employers cultivate racialized boundaries intertwined with the borders of private domesticity, and how locals fortify spatial fences to marginalize the presence of foreign workers in the urban landscape.

In addition to the transformation of the ethnic landscape, people's movements across borders have reshaped class stratification on a global scale. Drawing on Pierre Bourdieu (1987: 6), I define social class in terms of "similar positions in social space"—social classes as groupings of individuals sharing similar life chances and dispositions. Class boundaries are not fixed lines defined by the possession of economic capital but sites of conflict that take shape in the form of symbolic struggles—different social groups deploy cultural capital and symbolic capital to impose their visions of social order as legitimate (Bourdieu 1984).

Bourdieu's class theory has been criticized for a holistic assumption about an objective social space (Hall 1992: 279) and a structuralist framework conceived in a relatively static fashion (Ong 1999: 89). Echoing these criticisms, my analysis casts light on the constitution and negotiation of class boundaries in transnational arenas. I coin the term "transnational class mapping" to demonstrate the articulation between class and nation on two levels. The first refers to the structural process of *class positioning*. Globalization not only opens up the local market to capital, goods, and labor but also prompts cross-border movement of people for work and marriage. National disparity is converted into class hierarchy in these relations of production and reproduction. The second component of this concept is the consequences of *class becoming*, or, more specifically, the durability or mutability of class boundaries. International migration has created a range of subject positions that allow individuals to negotiate multifaceted class identities across national borders and social settings.

A few studies have offered insights on the contested class identification of transnational migrants. In her study of Hong Kong immigrants in California, Aihwa Ong (1999) found that affluent Chinese deliberately convert their economic capital into the acquisition of cultural capital (a British education, good command of English, and cultural tastes) and "flexible citizenship" (possessing multiple nationalities) to seek social recognition in the new country. Despite navigating multiple political arenas and global trade, these migrants remain subject to the discourse of juridical citizenship and schemes of racial stratification in the new country.

In a similar yet distinct way, lower-order migrants experience contradictory class identification in their overseas journeys. Rhacel Parreñas (2001), in her study of Filipina domestic workers in Rome and Los Angeles, calls this situation "contradictory class mobility." Overseas domestic work brings a simultaneous increase and decrease in labor market status for these migrant women. Despite substantial financial gain, migrant domestics have to cope with their downward mobility when working in this stigmatized occupation. Their experience of class dislocation emerges from the unequal development of regions in the large forces of globalization.

The circumstance of "transnational class mapping" not only shapes the class identification of migrant workers, but also impacts the identities of those who do not move but are tied to globalization in one way or the other. Newly rich Taiwanese confirm their class mobility through the consumption of migrant domestic services. However, the superior status of some employers can be challenged by the foreign "maids" who speak better

English, a linguistic capital endorsed with colonial supremacy and global legitimacy. In other words, the employment of well-educated Filipinas by the Taiwanese new rich presents a global conjuncture in which class boundaries are ambiguous and subject to contestation.

Cultivating the Boundaries of "Home" and "Family"

Spatial images such as "distance" and "territory" are often used to depict social differences and similarities that have no physical existence but are experienced as if they did (Zerubavel 1991: 15). Space is also implicated in the process of otherization in a material way. David Sibley (1995: 77) argues that "spatial purification" is a key feature in the organization of social space. People fortify spatial segregation in the built environment to make concrete the existence of social boundaries, thereby avoiding trespass and consolidating the exclusion of minority groups. The private home is particularly a "strongly classified, purified space"—order and boundary maintenance are essential features of domestic space and family life (90, 94–95).

"Home," according to the *Oxford English Dictionary*, refers to "the place where one lives, especially with one's family." The contemporary notions of home and family are products of particular social and historical configurations. The division between production and reproduction in capitalism has led to the modern definition of home as a private haven sheltered from the chaotic public world (Lasch 1977). Family life marked by intimacy is socially viewed as a "backstage area" that harbors secrets and behaviors accessible only to insiders (Skolnick 1992).

However, domestic employment challenges the dichotomization between workplace and home, public and private, and local and global. A "private" home becomes a "public" workplace for migrant domestic workers, who are outsiders in the family and even aliens in the host society. Not only are nonfamily laborers placed in the homes of employers but the families of migrant domestics are forced to live in separate residences. These disjunctures between "family" as a circle of intimacy and "home" as a physical residence demonstrate two facets of the phenomenon "globalization at home." For both employers and workers, home becomes a "meeting place" that articulates a network of social relations and cultural understandings linking with the global world (Massey 1994: 154).

This book examines how employers and workers redefine and reconstitute spatial boundaries in response to the disjunction between family and home in their lives. Their spatial practices of constructing home and family are implicated in their negotiation of class, ethnic, and gender identities. I view the boundaries of "family" and "home" as shifting, elastic frames that are contingently defined and situationally constructed in everyday domestic lives.[21] The performance of domestic labor, in particular, is a crucial activity for the maintenance of family ties and the reproduction of private domesticity. The most salient example is that women make use of food to organize family members and to "construct a family" in daily meals (DeVault 1991).

Taiwanese employers invite migrant women into their homes to keep their family life in order, but, ironically, they often distrust the sanitary condition or moral reliability of migrant domestic workers. The presence of "disdained aliens" at home intensifies the tendency among employers to safeguard the domestic territory from the perceived pollution and danger in the outside world. In the meantime, employers must negotiate the boundaries of family to accommodate the intimate presence of migrant domestics. Female employers, in particular, are in charge of the invisible work of constructing flexible family boundaries. They mark boundaries in everyday household practices, including the distribution of food, the ritual of eating meals, and the layout of home space. Although domestic workers are often analogized as family members, employers only do so to ensure the quality of emotional labor or to smooth anxiety in fusing the public with the private. Workers are excluded from the front regions of the family life by the invisible walls of class and racialized boundaries.

Migrant domestic workers encounter the transformation of family boundaries in two senses. Their departure from home leads to the formation of a transnational family. Migrant mothers struggle to rewrite the family boundaries via the transnational circuits of affection, care, goods, and money. At the same time, their entry into the households of employers introduces family analogy and kinship metaphors. Migrant caregivers maintain relationships with their wards in which emotional investments often come in tandem with the forfeiting of labor rights. As Mary Romero (1992: 130) warns, this situation tends to "blur the distinction between paid and unpaid housework and weaken workers' ability to maintain contractual agreements."

Migrant workers also negotiate the meanings and references of "home"

—where they reside physically (a place of residence) and where they feel at "home" psychologically (a place of belonging)—in their transnational journey. Some scholars describe the milieu of migrant workers as a "provisional diaspora" (Barber 2000), in which they "inevitably envision some kind of an end/return to homeland" (Huang, Teo, and Yeoh 2000: 393–94). However, many returned migrants experience an ambivalent feeling of "homelessness" after living abroad for extended periods, a situation that raises their incentive to stay overseas permanently (Constable 1999; Yeoh and Huang 2000). During the migratory journey that often spans multiple host countries, migrant workers manage to create a sense of home by connecting to the diasporic community.

To summarize, the employment of migrant domestic workers is a public-private, local-global matrix that demonstrates complex identity politics and boundary work in the context of global migration. Taiwanese employers invite migrant women into their homes for labor transfer but guard the intimate circle from them; migrant domestic workers cross national borders only to experience the constraints of social boundaries. When examining the articulation of class, gender, and racialized boundaries, we not only explore the complex identity politics in the age of migration but also demonstrate how global inequalities are sustained and contested through the production of local boundaries.

TALES OF THE FIELD

Postmodern scholars have challenged the interpretive authority of the ethnographer by revealing the cultural and social situatedness of research and writing (Clifford and Marcus 1986). Here I sketch my research process and describe my research locations (see Appendix 1 for more details about the methods). My social positioning and biographical background framed my epistemological lens of observation and understanding (What did I see? How did I know?), and channeled the inflow of data mediated by my interactions with the informants (How did they perceive my positions and respond to my questions?).

A reflexive analysis of research relations as power relations not only deconstructs the ethnographic authority but also reveals the larger historical and social contexts in which researchers and informants are located (Groves and Chang 1999). Numerous vignettes in my research process demonstrated that my ethnographic knowledge and interview data are embedded in "the micropolitics of the research interactions and the macropolitics of societal inequality" (Lal 1996: 197). These tales of the field echo the major theme presented in this book, boundary making and identity formation at transnational encounters, exactly because I came across multiple social boundaries in the fieldwork and such subject position allowed me to observe, experience, and comprehend these issues in depth.

Going Home to Study Foreign Maids

After a few years of residence in the United States for graduate school, in July 1998 I returned to Taiwan to start fieldwork on this project. I approached employers for in-depth interviews through snowball sampling. It was not difficult to locate informants since almost everyone in my personal networks, including my family, knows someone who hires a foreign maid. My sister and her husband both work six days a week and spend more than ten hours per day at work and commuting. They "borrow" a Filipina maid from their friends to clean their apartment every other week, so they can maintain a clean place without sacrificing their precious sleep on Sundays. Even my mother, a full-time homemaker in her early sixties, was urged by a relative to hire a migrant worker: "It's time for you to get some rest! Hiring a foreign maid is very cheap now anyway."

When hearing about my research, many employers (men in particular) hesitated for a few seconds and then remarked: "Um, interesting. Why did you decide to study this topic?" Their responses revealed that domestic work is often considered a trivial and feminine issue in contrast to high-profile, masculine issues such as production and development. I later "upgraded" my topic by presenting my concerns as "foreign labor policy" or "policy solution to childcare and eldercare," so some interviewees would feel that talking to me was not a waste of time but something of public value.

Only four pairs of migrant domestics and their Taiwanese employers participated in this research. I deliberately avoided interviewing both parties from the same household for ethical and practical reasons. Some employers voluntarily "offered" their maids to be interviewed by me. When I saw the workers nervously sitting in the corner waiting for me, a stranger who was functionally an extension of their employers, I had to decline the interview opportunity. A few times I reminded the employers to gain consent from their workers about my interviews. These employers went to the kitchen (where the workers usually were when we were talking in the living room) and often returned with a surprised look, telling me: "Wow, you are right! She really doesn't want to be interviewed!"

I avoided the above situations because I did not want my interview to become a job assignment that a worker could not refuse. Nor did I want to be in an embarrassing sandwiched position that could hinder a worker from building trust in me if she saw me as "the employer's friend." For example, Rosemary was the first Filipina worker I interviewed, referred by her employer, Fang-Ping.[22] Both of them later tried to retrieve information from me about the other party: Rosemary urged me to figure out if her employer would renew her contract next year, and Fang-Ping asked me if I detected any sign that Rosemary might run away by the end of her contract.

After I met Rosemary for the interview, I sometimes joined her Sunday outings with her friends. Rosemary once happily showed Fang-Ping some pictures she took on Sundays, in which I was smiling in a group of Filipinas. Fang-Ping then called me and said: "Well, Rosemary just showed me some pictures. I'm just wondering . . . what were you doing with them?" Behind her tone of concern and confusion was an implicit question: "Why was this U.S.-trained Ph.D. hanging out with *them*, those Filipina maids?"

As a Taiwanese researcher of middle-class background, I gained easy access to potential interviewees, and most employers implicitly assumed that I would think and act like them. Such assumption, albeit often incorrect, facilitated my data collection because the employers felt comfortable to share their views with someone alike. Nevertheless, I was emotionally troubled on hearing remarks of racism or class prejudice from some of my national fellows. And sometimes I felt like an accomplice to the oppressive system when I sat there listening to these employers and could not find a way to argue against them in a skillful, polite manner. Being a feminist, I am also hesitant to view the market transfer of domestic labor as only a selfish act of female employers. My subject positions as such, to some degree, shaped the way I launched my sociological inquiry. Rather than to quickly blame female employers for their class and ethnic privileges, I seek an empathetic understanding of the structural circumstances and gender relations that situate their actions, attitudes and opinions regarding domestic work.

A Taiwanese in a Migrant Community

The other part of my data emerged from field observation and in-depth interviews with migrant domestic workers. I conducted the first phase of fieldwork in a Filipino migrant community between August 1998 and July 1999. Every Sunday, I woke up early, packed my tape recorder, notebook, and camera, and jumped onto the bus to Holy Spirit (not its real name), a church-based nongovernmental organization. There I worked as a volunteer teaching a Chinese class for a few months and assisting in case counseling on labor disputes from time to time. Being invited and accompanied by Filipina migrants, I also frequently attended a variety of their social outings, including shopping trips, birthday parties, disco dancing, karaoke, picnicking in parks, and hanging out at fast-food restaurants.

In the second phase of fieldwork (from September 2002 to October 2003), I expanded the scope of research to include Indonesian domestic workers. Getting access to Indonesian migrants was more difficult than reaching Filipina migrants. The first reason was that Indonesian migrants do not form communities in bounded settings like Filipinas do in churches. I had to locate interviewees at Taipei Railway Station, where Indonesian migrants often hang out on Sundays.

Secondly, my new identity as a university professor proved to be more of a burden than a privilege during my encounters with Indonesian migrants. In my earlier fieldwork with Filipinas, I was still a graduate student living on a meager fellowship; my monthly stipend was not substantially higher than the wage of a migrant domestic worker. Then I was about the same age as many Filipinas (late twenties), and there was not a huge gap between me and college-graduated Filipinas. For example, one Filipina who took a sociology course in college asked me, "What you are doing is called 'immersion,' right?" She went on to share with me the experience of her professor doing fieldwork in a gay community.

Indonesian migrants, by contrast, were younger (most in their early twenties) and their average education was lower (high school). Both factors enlarged the social distance between them and me, a thirty-something professor (although I still deviated from the image they had of "a professor" because of my gender, age, and looks). Besides, Muslim Javanese, raised in culture sensitive to status hierarchy, were inclined to see me as "someone above" and treat me with distance and deference. It took some time and extra effort for me to establish relations with Indonesian informants across the visible status gap.

My identity was always a matter of curiosity among migrant women. The most common assumption was that I must be someone's employer. When I shook my head to this suspicion, the question usually followed along these lines: "So, you are a broker? No? Journalist? No? Then why are you here?" Some migrants guessed that I might be working together with other migrants and asked me, "Which factory are you working in?" It seemed that the Taiwanese who may have been present in their lives were either co-workers or those who sought control over or information about them.

In the beginning, I detected subtle messages that signaled their distrust about my presence as Taiwanese. Once we went to a lunch buffet, a popular weekend feast for migrants to eat whatever they want (in contrast to the budget control in their employers' houses) without going through the trouble of ordering Chinese food. A Filipina migrant, Norma, put some apples and cupcakes in her bag. Another Filipina pushed Norma's elbow to remind her of my presence. Partly to ease her friend's discomfort and partly to cover up her act in front of me, Norma said in a joking tone, "Don't worry. She knows that I am bringing these home for my boss's children!"

Their distrust in me gradually gave way to friendship and mutual dependence. I was their linguistic and cultural translator when communicating with taxi drivers or bargaining with street vendors. They were my travel guides who led me to migrant enclaves hidden in the corner of the global city. My Taiwanese identity shifted from a curse to a blessing. I repeatedly received compliments conveying "you are so down-to-earth, not like other Taiwanese. They are snobbish!" I was not simply a friend but a *Taiwanese* friend. Oftentimes other Filipinas mistook me as an employer and remarked to my Filipina companions: "You are so lucky! Your employer speaks good English!" My friends would answer them with a proud smile: "She's not my employer! She's my friend!"

Their appreciation of me, a Taiwanese *friend*, often turned into a public display. I became the most popular model in their pictures taken to send to their families in Indonesia or the Philippines. Some Filipinas even mailed their pictures taken with me to their American pen pals and wrote on the back, "This is my Chinese teacher from Chicago." A few times when we went to karaoke clubs, I tried to obscure my identity in the full house of migrants. My migrant friends, however, insisted that I should sing a Chinese song, because, they said, "We want people to know that we are proud we have a Taiwanese friend with us!"

In their eyes, I was more than a Taiwanese because of my U.S. connection and English fluency. As much as I was interested in their lives in Taiwan, migrant workers were curious about the details of my life in the States. Filipinas in particular were drawn to the American dream as a legacy of the colonial history. They could not understand why I would return to Taiwan after finishing my degree instead of finding a job or a husband in this promised land. There was even a rumor circulated in the community that I had been naturalized to become a U.S. citizen. Some said to me with a mischievous grin: "Do you need a maid in Chicago?" "When are you going to find me a husband in America?"

My affiliation with the United States not only increased my popularity among migrant workers but also dissociated me from "ordinary" Taiwanese, as they perceived. As it is, migrant women felt at ease when joking with me about their Taiwanese employers. After ridiculing their employers for poor English performance, they often gave me a compliment, "But your English is good. You sound just like an American."

During my fieldwork I was mistaken for Filipina or Indonesian several times. When I shared a taxi with some migrants, most Taiwanese drivers were amazed to hear me speaking Chinese and asked,"How did you learn to speak Chinese?" After I explained my nationality, they usually responded with an even more surprised look: "Then why are you hanging out with these people?" A few times in the church or at the train station, some Filipinas asked my companions in Tagalog: "How come that Filipina keeps speaking English?"

I did not pass as a Filipina or Indonesian for reason of any similarity in my physical features. This was confirmed by my experience during my visits in the Philippines and Indonesia—most people on the street could recognize my status as a foreigner long before I started speaking limited phrases of the local languages in a funny accent. Neither was my "passing" the result of being such a great participant observer that I could fool people in the field with a fake identity of an insider. The reason was rather that, by being with Filipinas or Indonesians, a group of a different race, class, and nationality from mine, I became one of them socially. In other words, I transgressed the boundary between "us" and "them."

Yet one moment in my fieldwork clearly revealed the externality of social boundaries that ultimately define my status as an outsider in the migrant community.[23] I went to interview a Filipina worker, Elvie, in a small village in mid-Taiwan. Elvie and another Filipina resided with two elders, and the adult children lived in another house nearby. My visit happened after Elvie had put her wards to bed, so we could sit on the couch with bare feet chatting over some snack I brought. Then Elvie mentioned that in the previous month her friends had come over to visit her in the house and her young employers were quite discontent about it. Hearing this, I sat up, concerned that my visit might cause her any trouble. Elvie continued eating her peanuts and said easily, "Don't worry—you are one of them!"

OVERVIEW OF THE BOOK

Chapter 1 presents the policy contexts and institutional mechanisms that organize the migration links between Taiwan, Indonesia, and the Philippines. I argue that migrant workers in Asia are circulating in a "bounded global market," constrained by contract bondage, debt burdens, and territorialized regulations. Chapter 2 examines the racialization of migrant workers by media outlets and recruitment agencies. Labor brokers, through various marketing discourses and recruiting strategies, present Indonesian and Filipina women with distinct stereotypes and stratified job entitlements.

Chapters 3 and 4 unpack demand and supply for migrant domestic services and examine how women on both ends of the class spectrum negotiate the boundaries between maid and madam. Chapter 3 discusses how Taiwanese women hire surrogates for housework, childcare, and care for the elderly, while safeguarding their pious, wifely, and motherly images. Chapter 4 explores how migrant women transform the meanings and practices of motherhood and marriage when crossing national borders and gender boundaries.

Chapters 5 and 6 delve into the power dynamics and identity politics in the daily lives of migrant domestic workers. Chapter 5 looks at the geography of exclusion and incorporation at home and in the city. Despite stringent surveillance at work, migrant workers empower themselves through the use of mobile phones and their collective presence on Sundays. Chapter 6 demonstrates that both employers and workers develop a range of approaches in negotiating social distance from the other party and in reconstituting the boundaries between the public and private spheres.

The conclusion revisits the theme of boundary making by presenting ambivalence and discontinuity in our mental maps as well as the landscapes of social inequality. I end with some policy implications for the enhancement of equality across the ubiquitous social divisions in an increasingly globalized yet more divided world.

 A BOUNDED GLOBAL MARKET

I was there [Chiang Kai-shek International Airport] by myself. I was very nervous because that's the first time I went abroad. It was very strange. I was standing there, holding my passport tightly in my left hand and grabbing my jacket with my right hand. We bought that jacket from the broker. It has the name of the company and many colors. It's like our ID, you know? So the broker can find us in the airport. A lot of Chinese came by with a [piece of] paper with names. They looked at your passport and checked if your name was on their list. If you are not, they just left and didn't say a word. Or they just murmured in Chinese. They didn't bother to say excuse me or sorry or whatever. I stood there for one hour! At least six men from other agencies approached me. It was very strange, very scary. They finally found me. We drove one hour and half on the highway. I saw no people on the road and I was afraid they would bring me to the woods or somewhere. They brought me to a place to stay for one night. I thought I would sleep in a hotel. But I slept in a garage! I slept there and went to the hospital [for the medical exam] the next morning. After that, I waited for three hours to meet my employer . . . In the [pre-departure] seminar, they talked about the airport map and other stuff, but I forgot all of them. We didn't listen. We just want to go. We don't mind about our contract. We just think about money, our salary. We just think, "be courageous, you have to face whatever." We don't know anything. We only have guts.
—Vanessa, a Filipina migrant domestic worker.

Every day thousands of men and women like Vanessa arrive in the airports of Taipei, Hong Kong, Singapore, and Kuala Lumpur, throwing themselves into the flows of international migration and an uncertain future in the global economy. This chapter examines state regulations and other institutional mechanisms that organize the import and export of migrant labor. I focus on the formation of foreign labor policy in Taiwan, but I will also compare it with the situations in other Asian host countries and introduce the policy contexts of outward migration in the Philippines and Indonesia.

Instead of a premature celebration for the downfall of national sovereignty in a deterritorialized world, I found that migrant contract workers in Asia are situated in a bounded global market. The integrated regional economy has accommodated a large volume of labor migration across countries. This global labor market, built on transnational links of labor brokers and bilateral relations between state agencies, is simultaneously confined by the territorialized regulations enforced by both sending and receiving governments. Immigration policy serves the goal of charting national boundaries through regulating the porous borders; furthermore, it is an institutional project that constitutes and redefines social boundaries along class, ethnic, and gender divides within the nation.

LABOR MIGRATION IN ASIA

Asian labor has been a major source of international migration for decades. However, there have been dramatic changes recently in the volume and direction of migratory flows in the region. Since the 1960s there have been substantial streams of emigration, mainly of students and skilled workers, from East and Southeast Asian countries to North America and Australia. Asian migrants later moved increasingly to Gulf countries after the oil boom in the mid-1970s. In the 1980s and 1990s, rapid industrialization by East Asia's "four tigers"—Taiwan, Singapore, Hong Kong, and South Korea—produced a switch in these countries from net emigration to net immigration. These countries have become major destinations for migrant labor from Southeast Asia and South Asia (Skeldon 1992).

The globalization of production has resulted in a rapid acceleration in international trade and finance as well as a restructuring of the international landscape. Scholars use the concept "the new international division of labor" to describe the multi-tiered spatial division of labor (Frobel et al. 1980). While global cities in core countries function at the apex of investment flows, lower-order global cities on the semi-periphery act as control nodes to sustain the global economy. These circumstances have stimulated two kinds of migration flows in East Asia (Findlay et al. 1998). The first involves highly skilled professionals, managers, and service providers from core Western countries; they wear suits and carry briefcases to their air-conditioned offices in high-rise buildings located in business and finance districts. The second flow consists of low-cost Asian workers, who sweat in factories and construction sites, pick up garbage, and mind children behind the façade of the glamorous global city.

As Saskia Sassen (1999: 155) summarizes, "migration is not simply an aggregation of individual decisions but a process patterned and shaped by existing politico-economic systems." International migration is not an exogenous process shaped merely by the poverty of sending countries and the wealth of host countries. National inequality needs to be activated as a push-factor for migration through organized recruitment, neocolonial bonds, government agreements, and so on. In the following pages, I examine the roles of three major gatekeepers in the Asian system of international migration: sending states, labor brokers, and host states.

First, the direct involvement of governments in promoting international migration is a major feature that distinguishes the Asian system from its counterparts in North America and Western Europe (Massey et al. 1998: 191). Many states of origin actively facilitate and channel the export of their nationals as profitable commodities. Several Asian governments, for example those of the Philippines and Indonesia, have established special labor export agencies within their national bureaucracies to regulate flow, handle recruitment, train potential migrants, and promote their workers to receiving countries. The deployment of migrant workers is sometimes facilitated by formal bilateral agreements, such as those between Indonesia and Malaysia, the Philippines and Saudi Arabia, and Vietnam and Taiwan.

Many sending states have established special financial programs to attract substantial remittances sent by their overseas nationals, such as offering tax breaks, setting up banking facilities in receiving countries, subsidizing interest rates on deposits remitted home, and requiring the remittance of a fixed share of earnings into government-controlled accounts (Athukorala 1993; Massey et al. 1998). The governments can also extract significant profits during the emigration process, including charging fees for processing travel documents and predeparture briefings, mandating life and accident insurance, and regulating the licensing of recruitment agencies (Abella 1992: 270).

Commercialization is the second distinct feature of the Asian migration system. Intermediaries in Asia are different from those in North America. There, migrant workers are entitled to acquire permanent status, and contractors usually emerge within ethnic communities ("bottom-up" intermediaries). But in Asia the contract workforce is constantly replenished with new blood, and employers and workers alike lack sufficient information about the other party. They must therefore rely on private agencies as intermediaries. The agencies can thus appropriate a significant cut from the process of recruitment and placement (Martin 1996; Okunishi 1996).

For a fee, private agencies provide a range of services to migrants, including smuggling across borders, clandestine transport to internal destinations, matching with employers, counterfeit documents and visas, arranged marriages to local citizens, lodging, credit, and so on (Prothero 1990). Most Asian sending countries have adopted measures that permit the growth and proliferation of private recruitment agencies. State-to-state direct hiring gradually gave way to commercial recruitment, which prevails in the political milieu of deregulation and privatization.

The last and most salient feature of Asian migration is the strict regulations enforced by hosting governments. The majority of migrant workers in Asia are employed on temporary contracts and are prohibited from immigrating or naturalizing. Historically, more strict modes of labor migration have existed, such as indentured workers (the "coolie" system) who were recruited, sometimes by force, to work in plantations of European colonies or the United States during the second half of the nineteenth century. Indentured workers were bound by strict labor contracts for a period of several years and subject to rigid discipline and poor wages (Castles and Miller 1993).

Today, "guest worker" contracts are still a common mode of employment for recruiting migrant workers across borders. They are especially predominant in European and Asian countries that lack a history of immigration or an ideology that favors permanent settlement (Massey et al. 1998: 5). In Europe, the scheme of guest worker is prevalent in spite of national variation in methods of incorporating migrants (Soysal 1994). European welfare states find it difficult to deny migrant workers their entitlements to economic and social rights. In some countries, noncitizen migrants are also granted the right to vote in local elections. Migrant workers, in theory yet not always in practice, are eligible for some kind of "membership without citizenship" (Brubaker 1989).

In Asia, more restrictive immigration policies are enforced on the basis of state concerns about geographic constraints, population densities, and nationalist agendas. Quota controls, work permits, and levies are widely adopted to control the volume and distribution of migrant workers (Cheng 1996). No immigration is granted for unskilled workers in any Asian host countries so far; the Singapore government even prohibits residency to migrant workers married to Singaporean citizens.

As Michael Walzer (1983: 58–59) describes, the market for guest workers is created based on the political premise that migrants as a group constitute a disfranchised class: "Without the denial of political rights and civil liberties and the everpresent threat of deportation, the system would not work." Through prohibiting migrant workers from permanent settlement and family reunification, host states externalize the cost of renewing labor to the economies and states of origin (Burawoy 1976). Such an arrangement allows the host countries to enjoy the labor power of migrants while they are young and healthy. They are, however, sent back home after they age, fall ill, or suffer injury.

TAIWAN: RICH DRAGON, INVISIBLE NATION

Taiwan has attracted global attention for its rapid and successful economic development over the last few decades. Its "economic miracle" was grounded on millions of small- and medium-sized enterprises that exported labor-intensive manufactured products (Shieh 1994). In the 1990s Taiwan's economy went through a relatively successful phase of industrial upgrading and economic restructuring. Since 1995 it has been the third-largest computer hardware supplier in the world, behind the United States and Japan. In 2001 it was the sixteenth-largest trading country in the world; its per capita GNP reached US$12,621, the twenty-fourth highest in the world.[1] Taiwan has maintained stable economic growth, surviving the Asian financial crisis in the late 1990s, and has continued to be a major destination for migrant workers from Southeast Asia.[2]

Taiwan is a latecomer in the Asian market of international migration. In October 1989 the government, for the first time, authorized foreign workers to work legally for a national construction project. Two years later the release of work permits for migrant workers expanded to the private sector, starting with specific industries such as construction and labor-intensive manufacturing. In May 1992 the legislature passed the Employment Service Law, which provided a legal basis for the recruitment and regulation of foreigners.

The number of migrant workers did grow rapidly over the succeeding decade, but that growth stabilized under the influence of employment regulations. The current number of documented migrant workers exceeds 300,000—about 2.5 percent of the national workforce. Most jobs are concentrated in low-skill positions, or the so-called Three D jobs (dirty, dangerous, and difficult).[3] The total number of migrant domestic workers by the end of December 2006 reached 153,785, the highest figure yet.[4]

Why did Taiwan open its labor market to foreign workers in the early 1990s? Why was this timing much later than that of neighboring countries such as Singapore and Hong Kong, which started recruiting foreign workers as early as the late 1970s? And why has Taiwan's government imposed more stringent regulations for hiring foreign maids compared to the latter two countries? Why did the government select migrant workers of particular nationalities? How is it that Taiwan shut the door on ethnic Chinese, unlike Japan, which prefers the recruitment of *nikkeijin* (descendants of Japanese immigrants in Brazil and Peru)? What are the other factors that determine the uneven regulations that exist for different categories of foreign worker? The following discussion solves these puzzles and delves into the formation of Taiwan's foreign labor policy.

Shortage of Labor and Care

The entry of migrant workers into Taiwan emerged primarily as a response to a labor shortage, or, more exactly, a lack of cheap labor for Three D jobs that were not held in high favor by most Taiwanese. Because of the rise in local wages and competition from China and Southeast Asia, Taiwanese labor-intensive industries had been losing their competitive advantage in global markets since the mid-1980s. To ensure surplus accumulation, these small-scale capital units had to either relocate to countries with cheap offshore labor or recruit low-waged migrant workers to factories in Taiwan.

The domestic service sector has also suffered from a growing shortage of labor. Since the 1990s it has become increasingly difficult to find local domestic workers—mostly middle-aged *obasans*. Local women are not at all interested in live-in jobs, even with high wages. Migrant labor therefore provides a financially affordable solution to market demand for house-work, childcare, and care for the ill and elderly. These augmenting de-mands result from recent transformations in household patterns and gen-der relations in contemporary Taiwan.

Dual-income households have become the dominant family model with the growth of women's waged employment in the last few decades. While industrialization has provided job opportunities for both men and women, its relative importance has been greater for women, who serve as a cheap labor force for export-oriented, labor-intensive manufacturing in-dustries.[5] The feminization of the labor force is even more obvious in the service sector, where the number of workers has surpassed the number in the manufacturing sector since the mid-1980s. In 2004 over 47 percent of Taiwanese women above the age of fifteen were gainfully employed; the percentage of labor participation is more significant among educated women in urban areas.[6] Dual-income families have become a social norm as well as the outcome of economic necessity given rising housing prices and living expenses in urban areas.

In the meantime, the nuclear household has become the primary resi-dential pattern. Current generations of young married couples express the expectation of living separately from their parents, especially among youn-ger, well-educated wives, as well as among those who have arranged their own marriages. According to an official survey in 2000, about 55 percent of Taiwanese households were nuclear units; three-generation cohabita-tion, mostly on a patrilocal principle, described about 15 percent of urban households and 22 percent of nonurban households (DGBAS 2002).[7] Al-though the proportion of parents living alone has been increasing, there remains a social expectation that sons, especially the eldest, should take care of aging parents. Institutional care is associated with the stigma of filial failure. According to another survey, only 7.5 percent of Taiwanese above the age of sixty-five live in nursing homes; 28 percent live alone or with their spouses, while the majority (61 percent) still live with their chil-dren (Ministry of the Interior 2002). Caregivers for young children and the elderly are therefore in serious demand. Nuclear households require assistance for childcare when cohabiting extended kin are no longer avail-able. Adult children seek nonfamily caregivers for their aging parents either to sustain separate residences or to outsource part of their filial duty in three-generation households.

In many ways, regulations for foreign contract workers in Taiwan were copied from the policies of its neighbors, Hong Kong and Singapore. Nana Oishi identifies a particular immigration model shared by newly indus-trialized countries (NICS): "The state responded promptly to labor market needs and opened their immigration gate for foreign domestic workers as a means to push local women into the labor force. In other words, accept-ing migrant women was clearly a part of the state industrialization plan" (2005: 32). In comparison, Taiwan's government opened the gate for mi-grant workers one and a half decades later and it has regulated the entry of migrant contract workers in a much more cautious way.[8] The Council of Labor Affairs (CLA) has adopted a quota control and points system to con-trol the quantity of migrant workers and their distribution. The qualifica-tion for domestic employers is not based on household income (unlike Hong Kong and Singapore) but on the "urgent need" for care as defined by the government.[9]

This comparison reveals similarity and difference between Taiwan and the other two NICS. On the one hand, Taiwan's government shares an economistic view that the outsourcing of domestic labor would improve the participation of Taiwanese women in the labor market. On the other hand, this policy is still bound by the conservative gender norms that define the woman's primitive roles as wife and mother (Lin 2000). The employment of foreign maids is strictly limited to dual-income house-holds, where a woman's "calling" is in conflict with waged employment. Regulations for hiring a caregiver for the elderly or the sick are much more relaxed than regulations for hiring a domestic helper. The govern-ment confers insufficient legitimacy and secondary urgency on the market transfer of housework and childcare. A CLA official interviewed by Lin Chin-ju (2000: 104–5, my translation) clearly expressed this perspective: "Foreign maids could help take care of the elderly, but we still hope that children can be taken care of by mothers, rather than leaving them to foreigners."

The introduction of migrant domestic workers has created controversy and debate in the public forum. Conservative groups are concerned about the impact of foreign workers on social order and the quality of childcare. Feminist scholars and organizations contest that this policy would not enhance the employment of Taiwanese women as the government wishes but only consolidate the gendered division of domestic labor (Lin 1999:

13–14). All of this demonstrates that market forces of supply and demand are only part of the machine that shapes foreign labor policy in Taiwan. The formation of immigration policy weaves together social values and cultural discourses associated with the understanding of membership in a given country (Brubaker 1992; Soysal 1994). In the following discussion I look at three other factors that underline the scripts of immigration policy in Taiwan: maintaining the ethnic status quo, upholding diplomatic interests, and the stratifying of migrants along class divides.

Making Aliens Visible

East Asian countries, including Korea, Japan, and Taiwan, are said to be unusually ethnically homogeneous compared with other parts of the world (Castles and Davidson 2000). It is not by accident that these countries maintain strict immigration policies, including a framework of citizenship primarily based on the descent principle (*jus sanguinis*) and rigid regulations concerning the permanent settlement and naturalization of foreigners. Both Japan and South Korea have prohibited the entry of unskilled foreign labor, while opening a side door to foreign workers admitted in the form of "trainees" (Oishi 2005). None of the governments encourages employment among local housewives or the recruitment of foreign maids. It was not until November 2002 that the South Korean government started admitting foreign domestic workers, but the number of workers is still limited and employers can only hire Chinese citizens of Korean descent (Lee 2005). This situation changed only recently when Korea finally decided to accept unskilled foreign labor in August 2004.

Japan has maintained an ethnocentric framework in recruiting overseas labor. As with Taiwan, Japan in the late 1980s saw a growing number of unauthorized migrants from the Philippines, Bangladesh, Pakistan, South Korea, Malaysia, and China in response to shortages in unskilled labor in manufacturing, construction, and service industries. However, instead of legalizing non-Japanese guest workers, in 1989 Japan revised the immigration law to create a visa category of "long-term resident" to accommodate the employment of noncitizens of Japanese descent. By the mid-1990s an inflow of more than 200,000 Brazilians of Japanese origin (*nikkeijin*) had been recruited (Yamanaka 2003). Most of them were male. The only exception for female migration to Japan is in the category of entertainers—mostly young, single women from the Philippines. The recruitment of foreign women for domestic work is yet to be permitted by the government.[10]

Like Korea and Japan, Taiwan's immigration policy is partly driven by concern for maintaining the status quo in a country of relative ethnic homogeneity. However, the government has made quite a different decision on the sources of foreign labor. During the initial period of recruiting foreign workers, the then-president of the CLA, Chao Sho-buo (1992: 145, my translation), expressed his concerns in a public speech: "Look at the current situation facing black people in the United States. They were in fact 'foreign workers' at first . . . The race problems in the United States today resulted from the introduction of foreign workers . . . Taiwan is such a small and populous country . . . We have to consider this very carefully."

Public concern centered on the consequences of recruiting "ethnic others" into a society which "never had any experience of living together with a great number of foreigners in our country" (Chao 1992: 144). This xenophobic mentality is nevertheless not applied to Overseas Chinese (*huaqiao*). The principle of citizenship in Taiwan, officially called the Republic of China, has been based primarily on *jus sanguinis*. Overseas Chinese played a critical role in the establishment of the Republic of China, and they were allowed to participate in national representative bodies in the mother country (Cheng, L. 2003: 88). In honor of blood ties, ethnic Chinese in other countries were formerly eligible to apply for ID and Republic of China passports.

To recruit Chinese workers from the People's Republic of China is nevertheless a different matter. Such possibility has been heatedly debated during deliberations on the Employment Service Law. Some legislators leaned toward the Chinese rather than Southeast Asians based on the existence of a shared language and cultural commonness. Other legislators, however, cautioned that there would be severe consequences if an open-door policy applied to people governed by a regime hostile toward Taiwan. The debate directed attention to a thorny question: Are mainland Chinese "foreigners" or not? This category of people, characterized by cultural proximity and political opposition, presented an anomaly in the ethnonationalist classification of "us" and "them."[11]

The government finally decided to maintain a closed-door policy toward Chinese workers, with the exception of contract fishermen, who would not be permitted to set foot on land. Tseng Yen-fen (2004: 33, my translation) describes the underlying logic: "In most societies, the 'problem' is unsuccessful acculturation among immigrants, but in Taiwan, the attitude toward Chinese workers is quite the opposite: We are worried that it would be too soon, too easy for them to become 'us,' unlike foreigners who just come and leave."

In contrast, the differences between Southeast Asians and Taiwanese in culture, language, and physical features are assumed to be more evident. Therefore, the employment of Southeast Asian migrants keeps the membership boundary between "us" and "them" more intact. The visibility of ethnic differences also facilitates the host state to monitor these ethnic others and to naturalize their subordinate status as temporary and disposable labor.[12]

Foreign Labor Diplomacy

As early as the beginning of the 1980s, some Southeast Asians entered Taiwan as tourists and overstayed their visas. The estimated number of undocumented foreign workers in the late 1980s exceeded 50,000 (Tsay 1992). The legalization of migrant labor in 1989 should be read not only as a response to capitalist demands for cheap labor but also as a turning point in border control—total exclusion became limited and regulated inclusion. The new opening, however, was restricted to four countries only: the Philippines, Thailand, Indonesia, and Malaysia, all members of the Association of Southeast Asian Nations (ASEAN). Other countries, such as Sri Lanka and Bangladesh, whose citizens were also working illegally in Taiwan before 1989, were excluded.

This contrast indicates that the selection of sending countries takes into consideration not only geographical distance and cultural affinity but also political and economic interests associated with building transnational links. The most obvious example is Malaysia. Although Taiwan's government included it as a sending country, the actual number of workers recruited from Malaysia per year is no more than one or two dozen. This is not surprising, because Malaysia itself has suffered from significant labor shortages, and its average wage is no lower than the wage offered to migrant contract workers in Taiwan. The inclusion of Malaysia as a possible source of migrant labor is rather symbolic, serving as a diplomatic means of bilateral cooperation in tandem with the investment of Taiwanese capital in Malaysia.

We cannot fully understand Taiwan's foreign labor policy without situating it in the lengthy struggle the state has had with ambiguous nationhood in the international community. Taiwan has faced severe difficulties in restoring diplomatic relations with most countries in the world because of opposition from the People's Republic of China. As Wang Horng-Luen (1999) observes, Taiwan presents a "political oddity"—in every sense it qualifies as an independent country, but its national title, "the Republic of China," is virtually unrecognized and this seriously obstructs its participation in the world polity. For Taiwan's government, the administrator of an "invisible nation," economic power becomes one of the few resources it can maneuver in its struggle for recognition on the global scene.

Taiwan's government has resorted to a policy of "economic diplomacy" —or, less diplomatically, "checkbook diplomacy"—to encourage investment of Taiwanese capital in selected countries in exchange for bilateral relations. In 1994 then-president Lee Teng-hui announced a "Going South" policy that encouraged investment in Southeast Asia. This policy was not only a solution for relocating labor-intensive industries but also a means to develop political ties with four ASEAN countries. In 1997 the amount of direct foreign investment (DFI) from Taiwan ranked fourth among all countries in Malaysia, sixth in Indonesia and Thailand, and ninth in the Philippines (Lee et al. 1999).

To a great extent, the connection between capital outflow and labor inflow explains how these four ASEAN countries were chosen by the government as sources of migrant labor (Tsai and Tsay 2001). The entry of foreign capital can also facilitate the export of labor overseas. For instance, some migrant workers currently employed in Taiwan had previous working experience in Taiwanese-invested factories in their home countries. By being familiar with Taiwanese investment in their hometowns, locals gained direct experience with the wealth of the island. In addition, some Taiwanese business owners who invest in Southeast Asia recruit workers from their foreign branches to their factories in Taiwan. Their social networks in the sending countries also assist them in recruiting domestic workers for their own or their friends' homes.

The recruitment of foreign workers is another government instrument for pursuing diplomatic bargains with sending countries—the media have even coined a term for it, "foreigner labor diplomacy." In July 1999 Manila unilaterally cut air links with Taipei;[13] one month later, the POEA (Philippine Overseas Employment Administration), in an official memorandum to the CLA, referred to Taiwan as a province of the People's Republic of China. These diplomatic crises led to a six-month suspension of Filipino migrant worker recruitment. Later, in September 1999, the CLA announced that Vietnam had become the fifth sending country for migrant labor after a bilateral agreement for direct hiring was signed between the two countries. The CLA has also raised the possibility of expanding sources of migrant labor to include Panama, Guatemala, and Honduras, chosen on the basis of "diplomatic concerns."[14]

In August 2002 the CLA suspended recruitment of Indonesian migrant workers based on the allegation that of all migrants, Indonesians had the highest rate of "running away" from contract employers. This ban, meant as a temporary warning, continued to be enforced over two years because of the fraught relations between Taiwan and Indonesia. In December 2002 Taiwan's president, Chen Shui-bian, was scheduled to pay a private visit to Indonesia (an instance of so-called vacation diplomacy). This plan was canceled because the media disclosed the information and the Indonesian government openly opposed the visit. Taiwanese media described the incident as a "serious humiliation of the dignity of Taiwan's nationhood"; Annette Lu, Taiwan's vice president, retorted in public, "Indonesia owes us."[15] The Ministry of Economic Affairs then put on hold a project establishing an export-processing zone (EPZ) in Indonesia. And legislators urged the government to "take revenge" against the Indonesian government by replacing Indonesian workers with labor from "more friendly" countries.[16] The ban was finally lifted in December 2004. Shortly after that, the CLA announced a freeze in the recruitment of Vietnamese workers because of their rising number of runaways.

In April 2003, in the midst of the SARS epidemic, the Thai government was reported as saying that it would not welcome Taiwanese tourists because of SARS.[17] This stirred up nationalist sentiment among the Taiwanese public, and the CLA once again raised the possibility of banning Thai workers in protest. These policy maneuvers have actually done little to serve the diplomatic cause; sudden, arbitrary changes in the recruitment of foreign labor have only incurred higher costs for both the workers and the host society. For instance, with recruitment opportunities denied to Indonesian migrants, some have organized sham marriages in order to work in Taiwan.[18]

Stratifying Foreignness

Immigration policy not only determines who is eligible for entry into national territory but also stipulates who may be included within the symbolic boundaries of the nation by regulating access to civil rights (Satzewich 1991). This section looks at Taiwan's regulations concerning the economic, social, and civil rights of foreign workers. The government not only enforces distinct rules on the rights and benefits of citizens and noncitizens but also creates class stratification among migrants.

Foreigners working in Taiwan are broadly divided into two categories, each with distinct regulations involving work permits and health matters. Work permits for white-collar migrants, including professionals, managers, and teachers, are granted on an individual basis and are not subject to quota control. There is no limitation on length of stay in the country and migrants are eligible to apply for permanent residence or citizenship after residing in Taiwan for a certain period. The other category encompasses workers in more menial forms of employment, including seafarers, domestic helpers, caregivers, factory workers, and construction workers. These migrant contract workers are not entitled to permanent residency and they are also deprived of the right to circulate in the local labor market.

Although the descent principle has dominated the regulation of citizenship in Taiwan, the passing of two new laws in response to recent increases in transnational marriage and professional migration has resulted in an alternative. The Immigration Law issued in May 1999 entitles foreigners to permanent residency after residing in Taiwan with legal employment for seven years. And, according to the Law of Nationality revised in 2000, foreigners may apply to be naturalized after legally residing in Taiwan for five years and if they possess "sufficient property or professional skills, which enable him (or her) to make a self-reliant living or a living without worry."[19]

These laws intentionally exclude foreign contract workers from access to naturalization, because they are prohibited from working in Taiwan longer than six years and are not considered to possess "sufficient property or professional skills." CLA officials have repeatedly said that one of the crucial principles in the foreign labor policy is to prevent the transmutation of labor migration into immigration. In the beginning, the government mandated that the maximum duration of a migrant worker's contract would be three years (two years plus a one-year extension) and that each worker could work in Taiwan only once. This strict regulation has increased training costs for Taiwanese employers and the incentive for migrant workers to overstay their visas. To address these problems, the recent version of the Employment and Service Law, promulgated on 21 January 2002, allows migrant workers with "a good record" to reenter the country and work up to six years (which includes both contracts).

In addition to controlling the quantity of migrant contract workers, the government has also enforced surveillance of their physical "quality." Every migrant worker has to pass a medical examination before entering Taiwan and is required to have a periodic checkup.[20] The exam includes a chest X-ray, blood tests for syphilis and hepatitis B, a surface-antigen test, a blood test for malaria, a stool test for intestinal parasites, an HIV-antibody test, and a psychological evaluation. If a migrant worker fails any of these checks, he or she is repatriated immediately. But such medical surveillance is not evenly applied to foreign professionals and teachers.[21]

The bodies of migrant women, which have the capacity to produce "alien" offspring, are subject to the state's "medical gaze" (Huang and Yeoh 2003). Until recently, if a woman was found to be pregnant during a checkup, she would be repatriated. Some female migrant workers resorted to abortions to avoid being deported. The rising abortion rates among Filipina migrants have become a concern for the Catholic Church. Taiwan's media have also reported cases in which babies were allegedly abandoned by their migrant mothers. After local and international NGOs had expressed persistent concern about violations of human rights, the pregnancy test was lifted in November 2003 to comply with the Gender Equality in Employment Law, in force since March 2002. A female migrant worker still has to take a pregnancy test when applying for a job and entering the country, but the test is no longer included in the periodic checkups.[22]

The marginality of migrant contract workers is defined not only by their temporary status but also by their immobility in the labor market. The CLA dictates that a migrant worker can work for only one employer. No transfer is allowed except under the following conditions: if the employer goes bankrupt, closes down, or cannot pay wages to the worker; if the care recipient of a migrant worker dies or migrates to another country; or if a worker is abused by the employer or illegally placed with an employer different from the one contracting his or her services.[23] These stringent regulations were relaxed only recently. Now a migrant worker who terminates her or his contract with an employer by mutual consent is legally entitled to relocate with a new employer, but in actual practice this new policy is still unclear.

By depriving migrant workers of the right to freely circulate in the domestic labor market, the government aims to monitor the whereabouts of these ethnic others. This measure deprives workers of their trump card—"voting with their feet"—thus helping employers stabilize the relations of production and aggravating inequality in the worker-employer relationship (Liu 2000). In consequence, migrant workers, tied to a contract of personal subordination, have little bargaining power and must tolerate any hardship or mistreatment.

In principle, the rationales of classism and meritocracy dominate the legal-political regulations of labor recruitment and immigration in Taiwan. Yet the stratification scheme on the basis of occupations often parallels the national divides among migrant workers. This is no coincidence but mirrors the very hierarchical system of global economy. Semi-peripheral economies such as Taiwan welcome the relocation of managers and professionals from Japan, Europe, and North America whose trajectory of migration is in tandem with the inflow of foreign capital. Similarly, the flows of low-class migrant workers from Southeast Asia are in structural parallel to the offshore relocation of Taiwanese capital. Poor countries on the periphery serve the newly rich Taiwan as the destinations of capital outflow as well as the sources of cheap replacement labor.

THE PHILIPPINES: A NATION OF MIGRANT HEROES

Today the Philippines is the biggest labor-exporting country in Asia and is ranked second in the world after Mexico. As of December 2003, the number of Overseas Filipino Workers (OFWS) was estimated to be 7.7 million; the population of the Philippines is some eighty million. Forty-three percent of these emigrants were on temporary contracts, 68 percent of which were placed in Asia.[24] The remittances sent by OFWS are the Philippines' largest source of foreign exchange, contributing US$7 billion to the national economy in 2003.[25]

Labor emigration in the Philippines is rooted in its colonial history. Spanish colonial rule started in the middle of the sixteenth century and lasted until the Spanish American War in 1898. The United States declared political authority over this archipelago until Philippine independence in 1946. The colonial and postcolonial associations with the United States facilitated and encouraged labor emigration throughout and after the period of U.S. sovereignty. As early as 1909, Filipino men were recruited for sugar plantations in Hawaii. After immigration acts in 1921 and 1924 barred Asian immigration to the United States and restricted European immigration, farmers and canneries along the Pacific Coast turned to Filipinos to solve the labor shortage. The U.S. navy also recruited large numbers of Filipinos during World War II. Many of them earned U.S. citizenship for their wartime service and brought their wives to the United States. Filipino migration to the United States after 1965 came to be dominated by white-collar professionals, nurses in particular, because of the shortfall in medical personnel in inner cities and rural areas (Choy 2003; Espiritu 1995).

The stagnant Philippine economy has stimulated its nationals to seek jobs overseas. Following a growth period between 1952 and 1969, industrialization slowed for reasons of political corruption and internal conflicts. During the 1960s, the Marcos government implemented an economic plan that depended heavily on U.S. war efforts in Vietnam. When the war was over, the Philippines was left with an infrastructure ill-suited to local needs (Espiritu 1995: 19). The economic situation continued to deteriorate and increased an already gigantic foreign debt. By the early 1980s, inflation averaged 32 percent and two-thirds of the population lived below the poverty line (Constable 1997a: 31–32).

In 1974 the Marcos administration initiated the "labor export policy," known as the Labor Code of the Philippines. Announced as a "temporary measure" to ease massive unemployment and bring in foreign currency, this policy nevertheless became "permanently temporary" in the following decades (Asian Migrant Centre 1992c, cited in Constable 1997a). Through government-to-government handling, thousands of Filipino workers participated in construction projects in the Middle East. Shutting out existing private agencies, the Philippine government was formally in charge of the Overseas Employment Program and enforced mandatory remittances from overseas workers.[26] The post-1978 policy is marked by privatization of migration. The government relinquished most recruitment activities to private agencies, maintaining a regulatory and supervisory role carried out by POEA and the Overseas Workers Welfare Administration (OWWA). After Corazón Aquino came to power in 1986, her administration continued to recognize and exploit the financial contribution of OFWs. Instead of enforced remittance, the bureaucrats adopted more subtle measures such as raising import taxes on the appliances that migrant workers brought home.[27] The government also conferred the status of "new heroes" on OFWs, aligning their experiences with the homecomings of the national liberators Rizal and Ninoy Aquino (Aguilar 1999).

The primary destinations of labor emigration in the Philippines have gradually switched from North America and Europe to West, East, and Southeast Asia. Among the land-based OFWs deployed from 2001 to 2004, 46 percent of them were located in the Middle East, 41 percent departed for East and Southeast Asia, and only a small number went to North America (1.7 percent) and Europe (6.7 percent). Taiwan has become a major host country for Filipino migrants since the mid-1990s. In 1998 it was the second-most-popular destination for newly hired migrants from the Philippines, next to Saudi Arabia, and in 2004 it was the fifth major destination, after Saudi Arabia, Hong Kong, Japan, and the United Arab Emirates.[28]

Filipino workers have occupied a dominant position in the global labor market because of their proficiency in English and level of education. Both male and female OFWs are well-educated: over half have completed college or have at least taken some college subjects, and one-third complete secondary education (NCRFW 1993). But the large outflow of experienced, skilled, and professional human resources constitutes a brain drain that poses a threat to development in the Philippines (Alegado 1992).

Annual changes in the numbers of overseas Filipino workers have pointed to a growing trend toward feminization. Women constituted only 18 percent in the 1980 outflow of OFWs, but that percentage rose to 36 in 1987 and 69 in 2002.[29] Most women are employed in service occupations such as housemaid, caregiver, and entertainer. Domestic work accounted for one-third of overseas female deployment in 2002,[30] despite the fact that most Filipina migrants were educated and skilled workers.

Some demographic characteristics of Filipina migrant workers deviate from the profiles of male migrants. The majority of migrant women are in their late twenties and early thirties, younger than their male counterparts, who are mostly in their thirties and forties.[31] Official statistics provide no details about the marital status of OFWs. One survey showed that the majority of Filipina migrants were single (56 percent) while 37 percent were married.[32] In contrast, a much larger proportion of male migrants were married (71 percent), and only 27 percent were single (NCRFW 1993). The differences suggest that the decisions to migrate are embedded in the gender roles and ideologies in the Philippine family. Also, migrant women tend to face greater difficulties than their male counterparts in building or maintaining a family during their overseas journey.

Labor migration in the Philippines fluctuated in reaction to several crises in the 1990s. The Gulf War in 1991 resulted in the repatriation of 30,000 workers, mainly from Kuwait. Overseas deployment declined by 13 percent in 1995 after the hanging of Flor Contemplacion, a Filipina domestic worker found guilty of murdering a Filipina coworker in Singapore. To mitigate the public outcry over this case, the Ramos government banned deployment to Singapore for a short period. The Congress passed the Migrant Worker and Overseas Filipino Act (RA8042) in 1995 to announce its intention to ensure the welfare of migrants. But legal protection has proved to be nothing but a symbolic measure, and the halo of "national hero" only glows when politicking takes place.[33]

INDONESIA: FEMALE PILGRIMS TO MODERNITY

Indonesia, the fourth most populous nation in the world, entered the international labor market later than the Philippines. The number of TKI (*tenaga kerja Indonesia*, or migrant Indonesian workers) has nevertheless expanded rapidly in the last two decades. Kathryn Robinson (2000: 250) argues that the recent explosion in Indonesian migration exhibits features of the "new" migration (Castles and Miller 1993), characterized by globalization, acceleration, and feminization. It is estimated that more than 2.5 million Indonesians worked overseas in legal or clandestine venues, which account for 3 percent of the national workforce (Hugo 2002a: 19).

The trend of international migration from Indonesia has changed significantly since the 1980s. Before that time, labor outflow was limited, and almost half of it was to Europe, especially the Netherlands, the former colonial ruler (Nayyar 1997). The oil boom in the 1980s attracted labor from West Java to the Middle East, mostly to Saudi Arabia. In the 1990s, Southeast and East Asian countries became popular destinations for a flight of Indonesian migrants. Malaysia, in particular, hosts the largest

number of Indonesian workers who arrive via official or irregular channels.[34] The gender and occupational placements of Indonesian overseas
workers vary by receiving country: men usually go to Malaysia as planta-
tion workers and drivers, while women are placed as household maids in
Saudi Arabia, Singapore, Hong Kong, and Taiwan.

Transmigration from crowded Java to outer islands has long been proposed by politicians to ease the problem of overpopulation. The Dutch
colonial government first adopted this policy, and Suharto carried it on
as an instrument to strengthen political stability and national integration
during the New Order period.[35] Only until mid-1980s did the Suharto
regime start to regulate the international deployment of migrant labor
(Tirtosudarmo 1999). This "repressive-developmentalist" government
(Feith 1980) attempted to facilitate economic growth by opening up the
economy to foreign investors, creating new forms of waged employment,
and adopting an instrumental attitude that linked the labor market with the
flow of international labor (Robinson 2000). In 1983 the Department of
Labor and Manpower (Depnaker) established the office of AKAN (*Angkatan
Kerja Antar Negeri*, or Labor Movement Between Countries) for the coordi-
nation of international labor migration. In 1988 the Labor Minister passed
Decree No. 5, which set out the procedure for sending labor overseas.

Although remittances from overseas workers do not amount to a source
of foreign exchange as large as that in the Philippines, the Indonesian
government has recognized that export labor is a handy solution to the
problem of labor surplus. In the Guideline for State Policy (*Garis Besar
Haluan Negara*, or GBHN), a general policy framework that is outlined
every five years, the government has set targets for the numbers sent
overseas since Repelita III (1979–84). Repelita VI (1994–99) set a target
of 1.25 million overseas workers, but 1.46 million were deployed. The
target for Repelita VII (1999–2004) was more than doubled to 2.8 million
(Hugo 2002b: 178). The financial crisis of 1997 and the ensuing economic
decline increased the pressure to engage in international labor migration.[36] Locals turned to overseas employment to cope with the income lost
from unemployment and underemployment, coupled with the rising cost
of commodities following the depreciation of the rupiah (Hugo 2000).
Recognizing the importance of remittances to the national finances, the
government declared its overseas workers to be "foreign exchange heroes"
(*pahlawan devisa*).

Religion has also played a significant part in migration links between Indonesia and Saudi Arabia. Muslim Javanese work abroad to make money as well as to make a pilgrimage to Mecca. Some work agreements even state that employers must fund their workers to go on the haj at the end of their work contracts (Raharto 2002). If Saudi Arabia can be seen as a destination for Muslim pilgrims, then newly rich Asian countries might be seen as a capitalist version of Mecca, hosting an increasing number of Indonesian migrants making a secular pilgrimage to modernity.

Taiwan has been a popular destination for Indonesian migrant workers except for the two-year period of government ban (from August 2002 to December 2004). The number of Indonesian migrant workers in Taiwan grew with amazing speed: in 1991 there were only 10,000 Indonesian workers, but the number reached over 90,000 in 2001. Most Indonesian migrants in Taiwan are women from East Java, and the majority of them are placed in private households. Parallel to the increase in Indonesian housemaids was a decline in Filipina migrant workers. A similar transition also occurred in Hong Kong and Singapore. The share of Filipinas among all foreign domestic workers in Hong Kong decreased from 85 percent in 1995 to 72 percent in 2000, while the number of Indonesian migrant domestic workers tripled. In Singapore, Indonesian migrants only amounted to 20 percent of foreign domestic workers in 1995, but one recruitment agency has estimated that about 70 percent of newly hired foreign domestic workers are now from Indonesia (Ogaya 2003).

Indonesia has become a major source for housemaids across Asia. Women have dominated the official outflow of labor migrants in the last two decades. Domestic service accounted for 70 percent of overseas jobs between 1984 and 1989, and 60 percent between 1989 and 1994 (Hugo 2002b: table 13.2). Almost 95 percent of migrants engaged in domestic service were women (Nayyar 1997: 11). Surveys of Indonesian female migrants found that they tend to be in their twenties or early thirties and have relatively low levels of education. Migrant women tend to be single or divorced, with the exception that married women are predominant among housemaids in Saudi Arabia (Hugo 2002b: 164, 174).

According to Kathryn Robinson (2000), the Indonesian government's current support for female labor migration stands in sharp contrast to its cultural scripts and political discourses about women. Indonesian official gender ideology "naturalizes" a particular form of the patriarchal family as a foundation of the nation; the assumed patriarchal power in the family legitimizes the authoritarian system of government. In the GBHN for Repelita III (1979–84), women were defined as "reproducers of the next generation of workers." It was not until 1993 that the GBHN recognized women as workers whose value was no longer based solely on fertility; they were redefined as a "human resource," with the economic potential to benefit national development.

The fact that Indonesia is the only Islamic country in Asia that allows the recruitment of women as housemaids overseas has nevertheless made some Indonesians uncomfortable, particularly social elites. In 1997 the then Minister of Women's Affairs urged the government to ban the export of housemaids because women, as the pillars of the nation, should be treated with respect (Ananta 2000). Twice, in 1980 and 1986, the government placed a ban on sending domestic servants to the Middle East in response to prevalent cases of rape and abuse, including one case in which an Indonesian household worker was sentenced to death for murdering her employer in Saudi Arabia. These bans were lifted only a few years or months after their imposition (Raharto 2002). Nana Oishi (2005) has pointed out that in Asia the emigration policies for female migrants are more value-laden—driven by social values and moral concerns—than policies for male migrants.[37] Indonesia is no exception to this. Women must be at least twenty-two years old to work abroad, and they need to present letters of permission from their father or husband upon application. The state policy of emigration is torn between the moral discourse of "protecting" women and the economic interest of promoting them as better servants than migrant women from competing countries.

BROKERING LABOR IN THE GLOBAL VILLAGE

"The world is becoming a global village! Globalization is making the deployment of workers much easier," a Filipino labor broker excitedly told me in his Manila office. During our meeting, I heard frequent footsteps of Filipina applicants passing by the door to meet a recruiter from a Taiwanese agency. My mind was also distracted by the television set on his desk that was monitoring a training course held in the next room—a group of Filipinas were learning how to dance in preparation for working as entertainers or club dancers in Japan.

In the Asian system of contract employment and circular migration, both employers and workers rely on private agencies as intermediaries. Placement agencies in Taiwan, in cooperation with recruitment agencies in sending countries, provide services including recruiting, interviewing, and videotaping applicants, matching up qualified ones with employers, processing workers' documents, assisting in the signing of contracts, arranging transportation and medical examinations for workers, and providing translation and training for workers.

Taiwan has a notorious reputation for the size of placement fees charged to migrant workers. Based on my investigation in 2004, the average fee paid by a Filipina domestic worker for placement was NT$90,000 to NT$110,000, about one third of which (45,000 pesos) would be paid to the Filipino agent, with the remainder paid to the Taiwanese agent via wage deductions.[38] The fee imposed on Indonesian and Vietnamese domestic workers was even higher: something from NT$140,000 to NT$160,000. The worker may pay nothing or make a down payment at home, with the fee collected through monthly wage deductions for the first twelve to fifteen months. The job offers in construction and manufacturing cost even more than domestic work.[39]

The placement fees are equivalent to between five and ten months of the migrant's wage in Taiwan, and this charge has been rising constantly over the last decade. The emergence of exorbitant placement fees in Taiwan has a great deal to do with the supply-demand imbalance in the migrant labor market. Taiwan is one of the most popular destinations for migrant workers because of its relatively attractive wages. The minimum-wage regulation has made the average wage offered to migrants higher than that in other Asian receiving countries.[40] Yet opportunities to work in Taiwan are relatively scarce owing to quota controls. Labor brokers are therefore able to appropriate a significant cut from the process of recruiting and placing workers.

Some Taiwanese agencies have bought out firms in sending countries to minimize transaction costs, an economizing strategy that internalizes market competition as a vertical organizational hierarchy (Williamson 1981). Because both the Indonesian and Philippine governments outlaw foreign-owned agencies, these Taiwanese agencies purchase management rights and register under the name of local owners.[41] In addition to demanding payment through placement fees, labor brokers extract profits from workers through mandatory purchases, such as nursing uniforms, books or tapes for instruction in Chinese, or hats or jackets with the company logo (so that workers can be easily recognized at the airport).

Although Taiwan's government has set a maximum placement fee that can be collected from a migrant worker, placement agencies usually invent "service fees" to conceal the actual fee imposed.[42] Some placement agencies require workers to sign a receipt before leaving for Taiwan to disguise wage deductions as money that the worker has "borrowed"—for instance, a loan "for my family's immediate expenses while waiting for my salary here in Taiwan." Workers are usually told by recruiters that job offers in Taiwan are valid for two or three years. In fact, their contracts are renewed annually. Those who fail to extend their contract after one year rarely have their placement fees refunded.

During the first year of the contract, migrant workers receive only partial wages after the subtraction of the placement-fee deduction and "forced savings" (NT$3,000–NT$5,000; a deposit held to prevent workers from "running away"). The three-year stay in Taiwan is divided into three phases: the first year is to pay the debt, the second year is to balance the costs, and the third year finally nets a profit for the worker (Lee 1995).

The reason that placement agencies hold different attitudes toward their two sets of clients (employers and workers) owes partly to Taiwan's migration policy. A migrant worker is allowed to work in Taiwan only once or twice, but the quotas used by employers are renewable. Quota, as an abstract capacity of recruiting and replenishing workers, becomes an even more valuable commodity than migrant workers themselves. The procedures of releasing quotas and granting admissions have provided a breeding ground for bribery and corruption. Taiwan's newspapers have uncovered several scandals in which employers mobilized political networks to increase quotas, or placement agencies paid off CLA officials to expedite the bureaucratic procedure for granting admissions.[43] In this highly regulated market, quotas have become profitable commodities that can be bought and sold between employers and agencies, and between qualified employers and unqualified employers.[44]

Another commodity that can be bought and sold in the recruitment process is personal documentation. To circumvent the rule of working only once (which later became twice), many migrant workers reenter Taiwan with forged passports. They are called "ex-Taiwan" by fellow migrants.

In some cases, returning with a false name is acknowledged or even encouraged by employers, especially domestic employers who wish to keep employees they have grown accustomed to instead of recruiting and training new ones. Many "ex-Taiwan" migrants "borrow" the name of their sisters or cousins who have decided not to work overseas but who are willing to lend them their legal identities. Others, through recruitment agencies, purchase names of people they have never met.

The passport represents the state's documentary control of the movements of people in a bounded national community (Torpey 2000). Yet the passport, a tag of membership bestowed by the state of origin, is also a document of personhood required for one's entrance into and circulation in the global labor market. Metropolitans seek passports from different countries to facilitate their business and social ties across national borders (Ong 1999). In contrast, lower-status migrants obtain multiple passports from their home nation to recycle quotas and repeat entry into destination countries. In Indonesia and the Philippines, where many nationals cannot afford to travel abroad unless working overseas, the passport becomes a commodity that can be bought and sold between locals and overseas migrants. Although counterfeit passports indicate a failure in national sovereignty, sending governments often turn a blind eye to covert violations to facilitate labor export. These practices reveal how migrants maneuver institutional channels of nationhood and citizens to improve their prospects in the bounded global market.

MARGINAL AND BOUND LABOR

Taiwan's migrant labor policy can be characterized as a strange mix of strong intervention and weak regulation. Although the government has actively intervened in the recruitment of migrant workers, the regulations are often poorly enforced. For instance, the CLA has set rigorous terms for employer qualifications, especially regarding the hiring of domestic helpers, but categorical abuse is commonly reported. Migrant caretakers are often assigned multiple tasks and even extra work outside their households.

According to the Employment Service Act, migrant workers have rights and are entitled to rights and benefits as stipulated in the Labor Standards Law, including a minimum wage, maximum working hours, weekly and annual leave, and health insurance.[45] However, the policy is motivated less by the desire to safeguard the welfare of migrants and more by the appeasement of trade unions. Universal labor standards help protect the job security of Taiwanese workers by reducing the gap between the cost of hiring a local worker and a migrant worker. The pressure from local unions explains why Taiwan's government has been hesitant to remove migrant workers from the coverage of the minimum wage, even in the face of widespread complaints among employers.

The legal protection of migrant workers is, after all, more a symbolic statement than a set of enforceable measures. The CLA has in fact failed to supervise actual working conditions or provide effective legal assistance. Many migrant workers receive partial benefits only, having no health insurance or paid vacations. They are often given unfavorable assignments, such as night shifts and the use of hazardous equipment in substandard conditions. For instance, Anru Lee (2002) found that Thai workers in a textile factory were assigned to double shifts and paid at a fixed rate (the minimum wage) that was lower than the wages for local workers paid on a piece-rate system.

A riot broke out on 22 August 2005, in which about one hundred Thai migrants working on Kaohsiung's mass rapid transit railway project protested against stringent labor management. They were banned from smoking, drinking alcohol, and using mobile phones in the very crowded dormitory. These workers also complained about wage docking and underpayment; they received only 46 hours of overtime pay for the 100 hours of overtime they worked each month.[46]

The primary feature that distinguishes migrant workers from local workers is the bondage of contract employment. Many Taiwanese employers report that the total expenses for hiring a migrant worker, including food, boarding, and the employment stabilization fee, are only slightly lower than for hiring a local worker. Nevertheless, migrant workers, who have little bargaining power and are eager to earn money during their limited stay, grant their employers enormous flexibility in organizing the pace of production.

Burdened by substantial debts, migrant domestic workers tend to agree to work on Sundays in order to earn extra income and to save on expenses. Said two informants: "If I go out, I lose money. I need more money to pay the broker." "I didn't have even one single day off the whole year! But I didn't want to, either. How can I have my days off? I don't have money at all!" Workers also agree to work overtime to demonstrate their loyalty and diligence to their employers to ensure the renewal of their second-year or third-year contract. For example, one Filipina worker explained to me why she voluntarily gave up her days off during her first eleven months: "I want to take the time to show my employers I will be good . . . I want to win their trust."

Activists lament that open confrontation and the assertion of rights rarely happen among migrant workers in Taiwan and wonder why those workers don't take action (Lee 1995). I asked this question at a focus-group discussion with migrant workers, and the answers of those gathered for the meeting centered on the financial burdens of debt and placement fees: "Placement fees tie our arms from fighting." "We still have 'five-six' to pay at home!"[47] "We are afraid if we speak out, we will be sent back home. We don't want to spend money on placement fee again. We rather stay in Taiwan, at least making money."

Bound by financial shackles, migrant workers must tolerate hardship and mistreatment at work. The employer of Maya, a Filipina domestic worker, offers her no health insurance, in violation of Taiwanese law. Maya had to see a doctor at her own expense for an ankle injured by overwork. I told her that she should ask her employer to pay for it. She said: "No! If she knows I am sick, she will send me home!" She went on to explain why she endured such hardship and avoided confrontation with her employer:

> In the beginning, I often cried on the phone when I talked to my friend. My employer didn't like it. She said, "I don't like to see you crying. It's bad luck for Chinese." They shouted at me a lot. Before, I was very sensitive, but now [*looks tough and serious*], my heart is like a stone.
> *Why do you choose to be quiet, not to fight?*
> We are afraid the employers will send us home. After forty days [the trial period], you can only get 20 percent of your placement fee back. But, some brokers are *mukhang pera*, "money face." They don't give it back to you.

Living under the jurisdiction of employers, most migrant domestic workers exercise overt resistance only when a contract's termination is inevitable. Open confrontation mostly happens toward the end of a contract or when employers attempt to terminate a contract. Without the opportunity to switch employers, some migrant workers choose to "run away" from their contractual employer (Lan, forthcoming).

The Taiwanese state is greatly concerned about the problem of "runaway" migrants, which constitutes a challenge to its sovereignty. Without acknowledging the structural predicament of runway migrant workers, the CLA attempts to mitigate the problem by holding employers liable for an escape. Each employer is required to deposit a sum equivalent to a migrant worker's two-month salary as a bond and to pay a monthly levy.[48] The fee is designed to subsidize government expenses for managing migrant workers and retraining local workers. If a migrant worker disappears from the custody of her or his employer, the latter is still obligated to pay the fee every month until the worker is caught or the contract expires. Another more serious punishment to the employer entails temporarily freezing the quota associated with the "runaway" worker so that the employer cannot hire a replacement.[49]

For the sake of monitoring, the government imposes strict regulations on the transfer of employers among migrant workers and places the workers in the custody of employers as a way of externalizing management costs. Accordingly, preventing migrant workers from running away becomes the primary concern of employers, leading to control strategies such as compulsory deposits, personal surveillance, and moral custody (discussed further in chapter 5). However, such measures only exacerbate labor exploitation and personal subordination, thereby pushing workers toward "running away" from harsh working conditions.

A BOUNDED GLOBAL MARKET

A flux of people, facilitated by a variety of networks and agents, is crossing borders on a constant basis. Globalization has nevertheless consolidated the walls of national territories at the same time. Contemporary nation-states, described by Aristide Zolberg (1991) as "bounded states in a global market," continue to assert territorial sovereignty and distribute uneven resources along the divide of citizenship. In addressing the interlocking processes of the "denationalization of economies" and the "renationalization of politics" (Sassen 1996), I argue that migrant contract workers in Asia are situated in a "bounded global market." Despite the formation of a regional market and economy, Asian host states impose a series of legal, political, and economic regulations on migrant contract workers. Through regulating the global flows of labor, the host states control the porous geographic borders and chart the symbolic boundaries of the nation.

Rogers Brubaker (1992), in his comparative study of France and Germany, reminds us that a nation's definitions of membership and citizenship mediate the formation of immigration policy. I further argue that such policymaking not only defines the lines between citizens and aliens but also constitutes social boundaries along class, ethnic, and gender divides. All host countries in Asia have more relaxed and friendly policies toward the integration of white-collar migrants (called "foreign talents" in Singapore) than toward blue-collar foreigners. Class-based preferences create stratified categorization among foreigners parallel to their citizenship and nationality in the hierarchical world system. When comparing foreign labor policies across host countries in Asia, we also find that the modes of incorporating foreign workers fluctuate depending on the ethnic component of the country and the national imagery along ethnic borders.

Policy relating to migrant domestic service reflects a state's understanding of membership on gender terms. Defining a woman's citizenship on the basis of wife/mother or worker determines the extent to which a state welcomes the recruitment of foreign domestic workers. The reproductive role of women also leads to gender-sensitive regulations imposed by receiving states on foreign workers. Migrant women, who have the capacity to produce "alien children," are often subject to medical surveillance, in particular through regulations on pregnancy. Similar gender ideologies shape policies relating to emigration of female citizens in their countries of origin. The sending states face a similar dilemma of promoting women as remittance-producing workers while "protecting" potential mothers in their role as producers of the next generation of nationals.

Finally, state policy has a great impact on the organization of the migration industry and the daily practice of employers. In Taiwan, quota controls enforced by the government have aggravated competition among labor brokers. Migrant workers who are charged excessive placement fees are tied to their nontransferable employers and the loan sharks back home. The financial burden, coupled with uncertainties in the renewal of contracts, contributes to the increasing number of "runaway" migrants. Taiwan's government has not dealt with the root causes of this problem, instead holding employers responsible for monitoring workers' whereabouts. And yet the stricter the measures of personal control the employers adopt, the more likely migrant workers are to choose to escape them. These multilevel practices of labor control, enforced by the state, agencies, and employers, result in a vicious circle that reinforces the exploitation and victimization of migrant workers.

Since 1996 the Taipei city government has enforced a policy dubbed "no garbage on the ground" to improve sanitation in this densely populated city. All households are now required to take out their garbage to be collected by trucks at specified locations and at a scheduled time. Every evening, among the people waiting on the sidewalks for the trucks to arrive, one can easily identify groups of darker-skinned women who gather on the corner, speaking their distinct dialects. Migrant domestic workers are not seen much in public during the week. The garbage collection is one of the few occasions when they can leave the houses of their employers. They briefly chat with their fellow nationals, exchange romance novels with each other, or use a pay phone to call their families. Other people in the crowd have mixed reactions to their presence, from indifference to curiosity, and sometimes even aversion.

This occasion vividly characterizes the double position of migrant domestic workers in Taiwan: they are doing the dirty work and they are treated as disdained aliens. The term *wailao* (foreign worker), widely used in official documents and lay conversations since the early 1990s, has a class and racial signification. It does not refer to *all* but rather a particular category of foreign workers—foreign contract workers coming from Southeast Asia and doing Three D jobs in Taiwan. The fusion of an occupational categorization with an ethnic classification implies that these nationals are "naturally suited" to these dirty, dangerous, and demeaning jobs.

Racialization refers to "a process by which a group comes to be marked by its physical and cultural distinctiveness" (Lie 2001: 18). The marked distinctiveness of foreign workers is not limited to their difference from Taiwanese citizens; their subject positions are also constituted in relation to other categories of foreigners. I raise the concept "stratified otherization" to emphasize the relational construction of racialized boundaries. The previous chapter offered an institutional analysis of the state regulations that divide foreigners into stratified categories: Southeast Asian manual laborers are subject to strict exclusion and racial marking, but white-collar foreigners are welcome to become neighbors and even nationals. This chapter continues to examine the discursive dimension of racialization, in particular, the media representation of *wailao* as the inferior other to be distinguished from the more neutral and general category of "foreigner."

The other aspect of stratified otherization is the construction of racialized differences among migrant workers by national divides. Recently in Taiwan, as well as in Hong Kong and Singapore, there has been a declining recruitment of Filipina domestic workers, followed by an increase in the recruitment of Indonesians. This chapter discloses the hidden reasons behind the distinct images of "smart yet unruly" Filipinas and "stupid yet obedient" Indonesians. Labor brokers not only construct and disseminate nationality-based stereotypes but also produce "professional servants" through the organized practices of recruitment and training. These marketing strategies have great impact: they channel the preferences of prospective employers and shape the competitive dynamics between migrant workers along national divides.

THE OLD AND NEW ETHNIC OTHERS

"I was shocked when I saw her [the Indonesian worker] for the first time. I felt really bad, as if a needle stuck in my heart. I was very uncomfortable. Her skin was so dark, like *shandiren* [mountain people], and her body had a bad odor . . . I was thinking, 'Oh my God, an outsider, a black person, is going to live in my house for two or three years. What should I do?' "

These words are excerpted from my interview with Mrs. Ho, a restaurant owner in her mid-forties, who candidly revealed her negative feelings upon meeting the Indonesian domestic worker she hired. Many employers of her generation or older analogize foreign workers with the derogatory terms associated with Taiwanese Aborigines such as *shandiren* and *fan* or *hoan* ("barbarian" in Mandarin and Hoklo, respectively). Racism is of course nothing new in Taiwan. The discursive construction of Southeast Asian migrants has appropriated antecedent racist narratives placed on the Aborigines, who are now officially categorized as *yuanzhumin* ("original inhabitants"). To comprehend the racialization of migrant workers, it is necessary to historicize the configuration of ethnic others, especially in relation to nationalist discourses in contemporary Taiwan.

The majority of the population in Taiwan is Han Chinese, descending from multiple waves of immigrants from China. They are usually divided into three subethnic categories: the Hoklo, the Hakka, and Mainlanders.[1] About 1.6 percent of the population consists of Aborigines of Austronesian descent who share ethnic and linguistic features with peoples from Hawaii to the east and New Zealand to the south and Mauritius to the west. They inhabited Taiwan for thousands of years prior to Han migration. The industrialization of the last few decades obliterated what remained of a subsistence economy and accelerated migration to urban areas. Most Aboriginal men work in the high-risk construction sector, where job opportunities have been curtailed by the introduction of foreign workers since the early 1990s.

This sketch of the ethnic landscape, as clear as it may seem, actually contains ambiguous boundaries subject to political negotiation and historical reconfiguration. Although there are differences in the customs and sociopolitical experiences in the subethnic categories of Han Chinese, they share a primordial sentiment that the Han is significantly different from the non-Han (Aborigines and Europeans).[2] The imagined unity under the umbrella of Confucian culturalism requires the oppositional existence of the racial and ethnic other. Taiwanese Aborigines, for their part, have long been the objects of the colonial gaze. The Qing literati represented the islanders with the tropes of dehumanization, primitivization, feminization of indigenous men, and hypersexualization of "savage" women (Teng 2004). After considerable bloodshed, the Japanese colonial regime (1895–1945) transformed the uncivilized savages into loyal imperial subjects (Ching 2000). An increased rural-urban migration of the Aborigines took place in the postwar period. Widening cross-ethnic contact, however, exacerbated a feeling of enduring rejection and resulted in a stigmatized ethnic identity among the Aborigines (Hsieh 1987).

The boundary between the Han and the Aborigines, perceived by many as a "racial" distinction, has actually shifted several times throughout history (Brown 2004). The rule of the Qing, as well as its Japanese successor, placed the natives into two categories, "raw barbarians" (*shengfan*) and "cooked barbarians" (*shufan*), according to their political submission to the state and assimilation into Han culture (Teng 2004). Cooked barbarians, also known as "plains Aborigines," adopted much of the Hoklo culture, including the language, and gradually became "sinicized." The marked identity of plains Aborigines slipped into history after administrative changes by the Japanese.[3] Only in the 1990s were this overarching ethnic identity and the political capital that came with it reclaimed by Aboriginal activists and acknowledged by the general community.

The inverse boundary shifting in the 1990s can be situated in a broader context of identity politics against the backgrounds of Taiwan's ambiguous nationhood and its contentious relationship with the People's Republic of China. Then-president Lee Teng-hui successfully crafted a nationalist rhetoric by coining the inclusive concept of "new Taiwanese." This stitched up the fractures among subethnic groups on the one hand, while on the other established the autonomy of a Taiwanese identity vis-à-vis the political and cultural China.[4] In 1994 the Aborigines secured the new official label of *yuanzhumin* after a decade-long campaign by activists. As Melissa Brown (2004: 21) argues, the new narratives of national membership "distance Taiwanese identity from the Chinese nation by incorporating Aborigines in ways that acknowledge Aborigine cultural influence and even matrilineal ancestral contribution." Although prejudice and subtle discrimination continue to have an impact on their everyday lives, the Aborigines have become a principal constituency of the "new Taiwanese" identity in the contemporary discourse and political project of nationalism.

The ethnic landscape in Taiwan also changed substantially in the 1990s in the wake of an influx of foreign workers and marriage migrants (mostly women from Southeast Asia and China). A Taiwanese cab driver interviewed by a TV reporter commented on the gathering of migrant workers on Sundays: "Taiwanese girls are scared of them, as if they see raw barbarians."[5] The analogy of "raw barbarian" struck me, as if he thought that the term "barbarian" was not bold enough to describe the "savageness" of foreign workers. In the eyes of many Han Taiwanese, the Aborigines have become "cooked," "sinicized," and therefore part of "us," in opposition to Southeast Asian migrants, whose cultural origins are "foreign" and whose status as permanent outsiders in Taiwan is institutionally sealed. In other words, after the old ethnic other—the Aborigines—was incorporated into the nationalist rhetoric of the "new Taiwanese" identity, foreign workers became the new ethnic other in the process of racialization.[6]

The derogatory label of "barbarian" was also associated with Europeans in the cultural history of Han Chinese. The ancient literature ridiculed their white complexions as "ash-white" (*huibai*) and considered their heavy hair and red beards as evidence of savagery. Texts in the nineteenth century referred to Westerners as "barbarian devils" (*fangui*) who constituted a serious threat to China with their invasion of the Qing empire (Dikotter 1992). In Taiwan, the Hoklo term for "matches" (*hoan-a-hoe*), literally "savage fire," vividly indicates the ambivalent feelings the locals harbored toward Western civilization. Taiwanese gradually dissociated Westerners from the stigma of savagery in the path of modernization. Moreover, the post–World War II development of Taiwan was built on the political and economic dependency on the U.S. state and capital. Today the Western savage has been elevated to the superior other in the general social perception of Taiwanese.

In the 1990s the discourses of racism and xenophobia emerged to attack the formation of Filipino towns and Thai communities, but Taiwanese residents never released similar anxieties toward migrants from Japan, Europe, and North America. These foreigners, who largely fall under the categories of multinational executives, managers, technicians, and language instructors, are considered human assets who can benefit the economic development and cultural enrichment of the country. Taiwan's media usually refers to white-collar, light-skinned foreigners with the formal term "foreign persons" (*waiji-renshi*), while referring to blue-collar migrants as "foreign workers" (*wailao*). It is as if only the former have a complete identity as human beings while the existence of the latter is reduced to their labor performance. While Taiwanese in the semi-periphery look up to the white superior other, they reproduce the colonial gaze to look down at the dark inferior other.

WATCHING THE DANGEROUS SAVAGE

When the employment of migrant contract labor was first legalized in Taiwan, rampant reports and editorials cautioned against the forthcoming dangers. "Once you open the door, it can never be closed!"[7] "A tornado and a wild fire are at the front door!"[8] Since the arrival of guest workers, the media has continued to apply the discourse of "social costs" to warn against their potential harm to local society. "Low costs for employers, high costs for society: Don't wait until it is too late for the problems caused by foreign workers," said another headline.[9] In September of 1999, a fight broke out between a group of Filipino migrant workers and a group of Indonesian workers at a local factory. After this incident, local headlines used militaristic metaphors to report on the incident, such as "Taiwan cannot turn into a war zone for foreign workers."[10] These representations embody an emerging discourse of social pathology (Wu 1997) that singles out *wailao* as a particular group of foreigners who should be subject to careful scrutiny and effective management.

Local newspapers and magazines often use sensational headlines to cover stories of contagious diseases carried by migrant workers, such as "Parasites: The majority of the carriers are Filipina maids"[11] and "Two more AIDS migrant workers found."[12] These diseases are often associated with the living conditions in Southeast Asia, which are negatively portrayed as "backward," "dirty," and "uncivilized" among the Taiwanese public. During an interview, one Taiwanese staff member of a recruitment agency bluntly conveyed her criticism of the hygiene of Southeast Asian migrant workers:

> They are more backward than we thought. Those from the provinces are beyond your imagination. Once they open their mouths, you can tell that they've never been abroad: heavy English accents, bad sanitary habits . . . Some employers told me that their maids don't even shut the door while using the toilet, or come out of it without having zipped up their pants yet.

Under the media gaze, poor hygiene among migrant workers is not only an indicator of underdevelopment but also an alleged consequence of "having low morals." Southeast Asian migrants are suspected of promiscuity and thus deemed carriers of dangerous sexually transmitted diseases. As one headline warned, "Thai workers into prostitution: Be careful of spreading AIDS."[13] Such representation triggers a public fear that Southeast Asian workers endanger public health in Taiwan. One councilor from Taoyuan County—the administrative area that hosts the largest number of migrant workers in Taiwan—suspects that the rising number of

HIV-positive carriers in this region comes from the presence of migrant workers. Concerned about the "invalid enforcement" of medical checkups among migrant workers, the councilor said, "AIDS carriers could sneak into Taiwan to jeopardize the health of our nationals."[14] One newspaper published a letter from a housewife diagnosed with tuberculosis who complained that, given her "normal life," her disease "most likely resulted from the introduction of foreign workers."[15]

Poverty is another condition that allegedly causes criminal orientation among migrant workers. One headline, "Thai worker killed for NT$1,000," conveys the message that migrants are so poor that they might commit a major crime for a trifling sum of money.[16] By the same logic, migrant workers often become scapegoats in crimes of theft if there are no known suspects. In a number of news reports, Taiwanese farmers who encountered thefts of fruit, chickens, or pigs jumped to the conclusion that "they must have been stolen by foreign workers."[17] Their suspicion was backed up by the rationale that these stolen items are so cheap to buy that only migrant workers would be tempted to steal them.

Migrant workers are also presumed to lack "work ethics," which explains their "temptation" to steal instead of earning what they want. Michèle Lamont (2000b) has argued that moral standards occupy a central role in the construction of racialized boundaries. The majority excludes or discriminates against "the less worthy" minorities on the basis of their cultural and moral failings. During interviews, several Taiwanese employers cited their country's economic prosperity as proof of the moral superiority of hardworking Confucians. In contrast, economic stagnation in Southeast Asia is seen as unavoidable because of the tropical weather, the generic nature of the people ("Filipinos are the descendants of pirates"), and, resultantly, their lack of a work ethic by the standards of modern capitalism.

There were a few cases in which mentally unstable migrant caretakers caused the death of their wards.[18] On 3 November 1999 a satellite television station in Taiwan aired a video in which a Filipina maid was seen kicking a three-month-old baby. This news triggered panic about the potential harm caused by migrant nannies. A stream of articles appeared in newspapers and magazines cautioning readers of the negative influence of migrant caretakers, such as the neglect of children or their arrested development. Although similar mistreatment has occurred under the care of Taiwanese caregivers, employers are more concerned about migrant ones, who are outsiders not only to the family but also to Taiwanese society as a whole. In fact, the average crime rate among migrant workers is significantly lower than the rate among Taiwanese citizens.[19] The events-based media reports and their sensational rhetoric tend to racialize foreign workers by reading the part for the whole. A criminal act by or health problem of an individual is equivalent to a general default of all migrant workers or an inherent defect of all nationals from the same country.

While the image of a violent criminal, such as a murderer, robber, or rapist, is mainly associated with male migrants, the "controlling images" (Collins 1990) of migrant women are related to their bodies and sexuality. Both newspaper and television have pried into the sex lives of migrant workers. A TV magazine ran a special report about the Sunday gathering of migrant workers in the park behind Taoyun Railway Station with a salacious title: "Foreign workers have sex outdoors; X-rated live shows in the park."[20] However, the substance was not based on any firsthand observation but built on anecdotal information and hearsay only. Another media narrative is that migrant women are part-time prostitutes who provide paid sexual service for male migrants on Sundays.[21] The image of the whore carries over into a threat of seducing the male employer and jeopardizing the entire family. The other common media trope regarding migrant women is their falling victim to employers' abuses and sexual harassment. The pictures of abused maids published in newspapers usually show only a bruised body without a face. The target of media voyeurism is the sexualized body of migrant women—the sexually aggressive woman and the helpless victim alike.

The media construction of foreign workers as disdained aliens with poor hygiene and low morals impacts how employers carry out labor control at home. Employers adopt measures of segregation and life management to prevent migrant domestics from "contaminating" the household. Some ask foreign maids to use a separate set of utensils or do laundry separately from the family's clothes. One employer even asked a worker to drink water from a separate bottle and use a separate bathroom. Other employers attempt to discipline migrant workers by "civilizing" their habits. For example, Taiwanese usually bathe in the evening, while most Filipinos take a shower in the morning. Some employers view this habit as "strange," "abnormal," and "unclean" and instruct their workers to change the time that they shower. A simple difference in living habits is interpreted as a sign of backwardness or abnormality, which should be brought in line with the "normal" custom, as defined by employers.

Domestic employers want migrant workers to be "clean" in the sense of personal hygiene as well as moral purity. Incidents of family property being stolen by migrant workers came up frequently in my interviews with employers, regardless of whether they reflected the employer's personal experience or just hearsay. To safeguard family assets, employers keep valuables away from workers, avoid giving them keys to the house, and prohibit them from having visitors. It is very common for employers to "test" a worker's honesty by deliberately leaving money or jewelry around the house or in the laundry.

On some extreme occasions, migrant workers are treated as a dangerous species that is best segregated or distanced from the locals. For example, one elementary school forbids migrant workers from entering its campus on the pretext of "protecting the children's safety."[22] Another way to control migrant workers is to make them visible and marked. According to a news report, one Taiwanese resident at a community meeting suggested that all migrants wear a badge saying "I am a foreign worker!"[23] This bold suggestion was not accepted by others in the meeting, but the government has adopted other, more subtle measures of surveillance. All migrant contract workers must register fingerprints upon their entry and are requested to carry their documents at all times for random police inspections. In the contemporary era, governed by the global discourse of human rights, state projects rarely include blunt measures of racial segregation, yet foreign workers are under organized surveillance by a system of registration and spatial allocation.[24]

Mary Douglas (1966) has insightfully argued that the opposition between purity and dirt is critical in the maintenance of a symbolic order. To avoid pollution and defilement, each society has rituals of separation as well as categorizations of things and people. The purity/dirt schema rightfully depicts the discursive construction of *wailao* in Taiwan. Media reports portray foreign workers as the dangerous savage, trapped in poverty and underdevelopment. At the same time, they project an imagined purity of society, whose public health, safety, and moral order are endangered by the presence of outsiders. The "controlling images" projected on foreign workers—as savages, villains, whores, and victims—may be inconsistent or even contradictory, but together they weave the racialized boundaries between "us" and "them"—between the Taiwanese self and the inferior ethnic others.

A STRATIFIED LABOR MARKET

While *wailao* is constructed as a social collective by the host society at large, it is further divided into subcategories associated with distinct stereotypes premised on nationality-based ethnic categorization. I argue that the migrant domestic service sector in Taiwan is an ethnically stratified labor market, in which labor brokers cultivate and promote ethnic-national stereotypes across migrant groups and position them in different market niches. Anne Loveband (2004a) calls this process engaged in by labor brokers "positioning the product."

The capacity of labor brokers to maneuver the placement process is grounded on the insufficient information of prospective employers. Although there are a few employers who are so cautious that they go to Indonesia or the Philippines to interview applicants themselves, most employers make their choices in Taiwan solely on the information provided by agencies. Each prospect's profile, presented to potential employers, usually includes her bio-data, half-body and full-body pictures, and sometimes a videotaped self-introduction done by the applicant in English or Chinese. Given the paucity of information, many employers choose on the basis of patterned assumptions about the backgrounds or appearances of applicants. For example, dark skin is associated with a "lack of civilization" and plumpness is considered a sign of "laziness." Given the recent introduction of migrant workers in Taiwan, most employers have limited or even no previous employment experiences; consequently, they rely on agency staff to provide knowledge about the labor source they are unfamiliar with.

Among the many conditions of applicants—age, education, religion, marital status, skin color, body type, and so on—recruitment agencies tend to market their "labor products" by nationality. They do so for business reasons under given institutional constraints. As noted in chapter 1, Taiwan's government uses foreign labor policy as a tool of diplomatic bargaining; nationality-based preferences govern the approval or temporary freezing of labor recruitment. In response to the often-changing state

TABLE I. *Percentage of migrant domestic workers in Taiwan by nationality, 1998–2003*

End of Year	Philippines		Indonesia		Vietnam		Thailand		Malaysia		Total
1998	44,559	83%	7,761	15%	N/A		1,030	2%	18	0%	53,368
1999	42,893	57%	27,948	37%	33	0%	3,912	5%	7	0%	74,793
2000	34,772	33%	63,563	60%	2,634	2%	5,356	5%	6	0%	106,331
2001	24,875	22%	78,678	70%	5,221	5%	4,158	4%	2	0%	112,934
2002	21,223	18%	81,490	68%	15,263	13%	2,733	2%	2	0%	120,711
2003	29,347	24%	47,891	40%	40,397	33%	2,901	2%	2	0%	120,598

Source: Council of Labor Affairs, Executive Yuan, Republic of China.

regulations, Taiwanese brokers minimize their financial risks by cooperating with recruiters from multiple countries of origin. They manage the market by carving out different "product lines" along the divides of nationality.

In the past, Filipina migrants dominated the domestic service sector in Taiwan. But they have recently been outnumbered by competitors from other countries. An increasing number of employers, often on the advice of agencies, are replacing Filipina workers with Indonesians and Vietnamese. The proportion of Filipinas among all migrant domestics decreased from 83 percent in 1998 to 18 percent at the end of 2002, while the proportion of Indonesian workers rose from 15 to 68 percent during the same period. The number of Indonesian domestic workers decreased in 2003, because the CLA had suspended their recruitment from August 2002 to December 2004 (see chapter 1). Under such circumstances, some employers turned to labor forces in Vietnam, a source that has been approved by the CLA only since November 1999.

It has become common knowledge among employers, labor brokers, and the public that Filipina workers are "smart yet unruly" while Indonesian workers are "stupid yet obedient." How do we explain the formation of such ethnic characterizations and, correspondingly, the declining and rising employment of these two groups of migrant domestics? National background is a common explanation that people use to historicize the formation of ethnic differences. Indonesians come from a Muslim community under several decades of authoritarian rule, as compared with Filipinas coming from a country influenced by a U.S colonial history of "democratic ideals" (Loveband 2004b). To go further, I emphasize the disparity of educational and linguistic resources between these two groups of migrant workers, which impacts their capacity to negotiate with Taiwanese employers. I also highlight the marketing discourses and recruitment strategies of labor brokers in magnifying ethnic differences between these two groups of migrant workers.

Education and Linguistic Capital

When comparing Filipina and Indonesian migrant workers, we found an obvious discrepancy in their average levels of education. A significant proportion of Filipino migrant workers are college-educated and held white-collar jobs, or even professional positions, in the Philippines, an outcome related to the fact that the United States widely established colleges during its colonization of this archipelago. In 2000 the gross enrollment rate (as a percentage of the population in the relevant age group) in colleges and universities was over 31 percent in the Philippines, a number significantly higher than the 14.6 percent in Indonesia.[25] Compared to the "brain drain" in the Philippines (Alegado 1992), there are far fewer Indonesian college graduates seeking jobs overseas. The average level of education of Indonesian migrant workers in Taiwan is between junior and senior high school.[26]

When I spoke to Filipina domestic workers about their previous occupations, many answered with a deep sigh or in a self-mocking tone. Jorita, a former high school teacher, said, "My friends in the Philippines were making fun about me. They said my instruments before were pen and papers, and my instruments now are knife, blender, and cutting board!" Vanessa, who was a supervisor of a chain bookstore in the Philippines, said: "A friend of mine worked in the government office, but you know what she's doing now [in Taiwan]? She's cleaning chicken every day! I always say I was a manager in the Philippines, and I am a manager in the house now!"

In addition to their more than adequate education, Filipina workers also hold a competitive advantage in the global labor market with their English-language proficiency, another legacy of U.S. colonization. I want to emphasize that language skills cannot be reduced to an individual asset accumulated through personal effort only. To understand the cultural meaning and social value of linguistic capital, we need to place it within the social-linguistic contexts of the Philippines and Taiwan, both of which are embedded in the international "linguistic field" currently dominated by the English language.[27]

The English language was declared the basis of all public school instruction in the Philippines in 1901, three years after the archipelago was taken over by the United States from Spain. The policy was supported by the colonial belief that "a knowledge of the English language was essential for adoption of the American way of life" (Bresnahan 1979: 65). To this day, the domination of English still prevails in government documents and curriculum materials in the Philippines.[28] Educated people use a hybrid language of Tag-lish (a mixture of Tagalog and English) in their daily conversations. English is still preferred in higher education and the professional world, while local languages are considered less intellectual and modernized (Sibayan 1991).

In the post-independence era, the cultural and linguistic heritage of their colonizer ironically becomes the most valuable resource for Filipinos, enabling them to escape the stagnant economy. The high-tech industry in Taiwan prefers Filipino workers to Thai workers because the former can read English instructions on imported machines and equipment. Filipino musicians are widely employed in prestigious hotels in major Asian cities because they can sing English songs well but command a wage much lower than that of North American musicians.

Although the cultural scene in Taiwan bears the imprint of American pop culture, average Taiwanese, even college graduates, do not attain English fluency. This situation has nevertheless changed in recent years given the wide recognition of English as a dominant source of human capital in the contemporary era of globalization. Public elementary schools have recently started offering English courses in order to improve the quality of English education. President Chen Shui-bien even suggested the possibility of assigning English as the second official language after Mandarin Chinese.[29] Public opinion is pushing the government to loosen regulations on the employment of white-collar foreigners in order to meet the growing demand for native English-speaking instructors.

The current generation of Taiwanese parents, who emphasize children's education in line with Confucian beliefs, eagerly invest economic capital to equip their children with the English linguistic capital. Upper-class households hire home tutors to teach their children English, and middle-class parents send children to after-school language centers or summer programs. English has become a vital lever for the young generation of Taiwanese to pursue upward mobility in the global economy. However, hiring a well-educated English-speaking Filipina domestic worker is a double-edged sword for the nouveau riche—it may validate their recently achieved status but it can also undermine their authority over the maid.

Several Taiwanese employers and Filipina workers reported difficulties in communicating with each other in English. This kind of complaint is especially common among employers with a high school education or less. They have to rely on the assistance of a third party, such as agency staff, adult children, or even young children who are enrolled in English classes. Some use an electronic dictionary to mediate their communication with workers.[30] Judy works as a housekeeper for a family headed by a small-factory owner. The eldest daughter, who is currently studying in Canada, is the only family member who can speak English fluently. Judy complained about the difficulty in communicating with her employers: "If I have a problem, I write it down on a letter; my employer brings the letter to the factory. The secretary there can speak a little English. It's very complicated. Sometimes I want to complain [about] something, they just say, 'I am sorry, I don't understand.' "

In Taiwan, Filipina workers with English fluency are often assigned duties beyond the scope of domestic work, which signals a status more advanced than that of "maid." Claudia, with a college degree in pharmacology, proudly told me that she could speak better English than her employers so she was asked to answer phone calls in an upper-class private club:

My employer used to be the vice-president of a women's club. She always brought me to their meeting.

Why? Do you have to serve them there?

No, she just asked me to take phone calls, and told me to call this person, that person. They have many Americans there.

So she wants you to speak English!

Yes, I think so. They have more money, but I can speak better English than most of them [*smiles*].

Tutoring or language exchange is another English-related job requirement that is commonly assigned to Filipina domestic workers in Taiwan. While I was teaching a Chinese course at Holy Spirit, several of my Filipina students complained that they had no chance to practice Chinese at work, explaining, "Our employers like to talk to us in English." "They want to practice English!" Many of their employers requested that they instruct the employers' children in English, as evidenced in the experiences of Olivia and Imelda:

> My boss told me: When they were reading my bio-data, my lady employer didn't like me. She said I looked old and ugly in the picture. But my boss said: "But she is a college graduate, and she has a BA in English! Maybe she can teach us English!"

> They hire us because they want to learn English. Like the children in my house, they go to an American school. They don't speak Chinese to me. They want to practice their English. I know if they hire an English tutor, it will be very expensive. But they hire us for everything and it is cheap!

Although the employment of college graduates might include the side-benefit of a live-in English tutor, it could incur additional costs in communication and management for employers with lower education. Some employers face obstacles in making requests in English to their Filipina workers. Shu-wen, a high school graduate who runs an electronics store, voiced her complaints on this matter:

> Local workers—you ask them; they don't necessarily listen to you. Foreign workers—you ask them; they don't always understand you. She [the Filipina worker] would ask you, "Ma'am, what were you saying?" She was confused and so were you. Every day you are worried about how to express your request [in English]! Sometimes I think: Forget it, I will just do it myself [*smiles bitterly*].

Some Filipina domestic workers consider language barriers beneficial because their employers are thus unable to enforce complex work regulations: "It's good if your employer doesn't know much English, then they cannot ask you to do much work." There are also Filipina workers who manipulate English as means of resisting employers' demands. Mercy worked in Singapore for five years and then came to Taiwan to be employed by a family who own a small factory. She described her trick for lowering her workload:

> Last time my employer told me to clean the factory office, I said, 'What?' Then I kept mopping the floor and pretended not hearing anything. Then he didn't say anything more. Because he didn't speak much English!
>> *But in Singapore you cannot do this. The employer there speaks English?*
> I still could [*smiles secretively*]. I just pretended I didn't understand English!

The linguistic capital and white-collar background of Filipina migrants are in marked contrast to the controlling images of uncivilized others and subordinate servants. Employers feel they have lost face when their Filipina maids correct their English pronunciation or grammatical mistakes. To keep their authority intact, some employers replace Filipinas with Indonesian or Vietnamese workers. One such employer is Rei-hwa, a college dropout and small-business owner. She was not satisfied with the Filipina worker she previously hired (too opinionated, asking for days off, and having a boyfriend). Later she decided to hire an Indonesian worker:

> We want someone naïve, who has never been abroad before. Because those experienced ones, they know how to loaf on the job. We would rather hire someone who cannot read, cannot speak. So I can teach her from zero. It's easier to train someone who is not yet polluted.

In fact, the Indonesian worker Rei-hwa hired was a high school graduate, rather than someone "who cannot read, cannot speak." That exaggerated description of illiteracy refers to English and Chinese specifically. The Taiwanese employers who feel frustrated at communicating with Filipina workers in English are now able to have the upper hand vis-à-vis Indonesian or Vietnamese workers. Unlike their Filipina counterparts, prospective migrants in Indonesia and Vietnam have to learn Mandarin Chinese or Hokkienese to win job orders in Taiwan. As I will detail later, they have to go through a months-long training program before departure overseas. Even after the training, it is still difficult for them to verbally bargain with employers. The dominance of the Chinese language marks the employer's authority and silences the migrant workers during their day-to-day interactions.

The possession of linguistic skills also expands a migrant worker's venues for information and social support. English-speaking Filipino workers have access to a number of English newspapers and radio programs, both of which serve a larger group of English-speakers in Taiwan.[31] By contrast, migrant workers of other nationalities can only avail themselves of the few radio programs in their native languages. Only those who can speak local languages and have access to television at home are able to receive more information about the outside world. In addition, Indonesian workers have few affiliations with civil institutions offering legal assistance or counseling, unlike Filipina migrants, who make contacts through local Catholic churches and church-based NGOs. All these factors contribute to the relative empowerment of Filipina workers versus their Indonesian counterparts.[32]

Stereotyping and Market Niches

In fact, both Indonesia and the Philippines are multi-ethnic countries with heterogeneous cultural landscapes. However, the advertisements of recruitment agencies in Taiwan tend to objectify migrant workers from the same country as a social collectivity with homogeneous characteristics.[33] Recruitment agencies cultivate nationality-based market segmentation for three major purposes: First, through such advertisements and discourses, they convince prospective employers about the importance of professional screening and matchmaking. Second, they provide patterned labor options based on market segmentation to satisfy the diverse needs of employers (housework, childcare, or eldercare). Third, they maneuver these stereotypical images to persuade certain types of employers to replace Filipina workers with Indonesian ones, because the latter offer agencies higher profits and more control in the process of recruitment.

To systematically explore the discursive construction of migrant domestic workers, we browsed ninety-three recruitment agencies' websites found through a Google search.[34] Among them, twenty-nine websites offered nationality-based characterizations. The contents are coded in Table 2.[35]

In these discourses, little mention is made about the historical or social contexts of national variations; some even bluntly use terms such as "in nature" and "born to be" to imply the essential nature of such ethnic characteristics. The racialized images that labor brokers project on migration

TABLE 2. *Descriptions of migrant workers by nationality by Taiwanese labor brokers*

Filipina The Westernized Other		Indonesian The Traditional Other		Vietnamese The Communist Other	
Description	No. of websites	Description	No. of websites	Description	No. of websites
Well-educated	15	Obedient	15	Affinity for Chinese culture	17
Smart	10	Simple-minded	10	Work endurance	10
Easy to communicate	9	Mild personality	8	Mild personality	8
Westernized	8	Loyal	8	Diligent	6
Lively	8	No days off	6	Frugal	6
Autonomous	3	Accommodating	5	No running away under the influence of communism	5
Sensitive to the employers' moods	1	Honest	4	Kind-hearted	4
				Speaks Chinese well	3
				Nice-looking	1
Conscious of labor rights	6	Slow	2	Better not discuss politics with them	4
Difficult to manage	6			Lack of experience; need to communicate patiently	4
Likes to make friends	4			Tends to run away	2
Tends to run away	4				

Source: the websites of 29 recruitment agencies in Taiwan (accessed in October 2003); description originally in Chinese; translation by the author.

workers along national divides embody differential patterns of otherization. Filipinas are viewed as the Westernized other, portrayed as "optimis-
tic, romantic, autonomous"[36] and "outgoing, individualistic, opinionated,
and difficult to manage."[37] In contrast to the Westernized Filipinas, the
stereotype of Indonesians conjures up images of docile women trapped in
rural villages with Muslim conventions. They are characterized as the
traditional other, who is "obedient, loyal, slow and living a simple life,"[38]
and therefore naturally "suited to hard work and no days off."[39]

The discursive construction of Vietnamese migrant workers is more
ambiguous and complex. On the one hand, Vietnam is considered to have
been historically influenced by Han-Chinese culture. Its nationals are
therefore associated with some positive features related to Confucianism,
such as diligence, frugality, and endurance. Racialized aesthetic standards
also shape employers' evaluation of workers' appearances: the fair skin of
Vietnamese women is considered better looking than the darker skin of
Filipinas and Indonesians. Given these assumed racial and cultural affinities, agencies market this new group of migrants as proper servants
suitable for Taiwanese families. On the other hand, the political background of Vietnam stimulates ambivalent stereotypes about the communist other. Vietnamese are imagined to be politically narrow-minded and
ignorant of the outside world because they were "locked behind the iron
curtain," a common metaphor associated with communism in the cold
war discourses in Taiwan. According to Taiwanese agencies, high-handed
communist rule cultivates a disposition of loyalty, or an inclination to
calculate cunningly, among Vietnamese workers. These polarized characterizations lead to quite contradictory predictions concerning the workers'
tendency to "run away."

Abigail Bakan and Daiva Stasiulis (1995: 309, 317) have argued that
stereotyping is endemic to the matching process that defines the parame-
ters of placement agencies. In order to survive and thrive in this volatile
industry, labor brokers must effectively project certain racialized images
as a way of impressing upon their potential clients the need for professional screening. For a similar reason, Taiwanese agencies maneuver
ethnic-national stereotypes to justify the promotion of Indonesian domestic workers, especially by magnifying their differences from Filipina
ones. A vital force behind this promotion is profit. Most interviewed brokers admitted that Taiwanese agencies gain higher profits from brokering

Indonesians than from Filipinas, despite their reluctance to tell me their exact profit share.[40] An Indonesian of Chinese descent who worked as a translator in a recruitment agency bluntly remarked, "They said Filipinos are difficult. It's nonsense. It's only because agencies can make more money off of Indonesians."

Racialized stereotyping often naturalizes divisions of job assignments. In Canada, migrant women of lighter skin are employed for childcare and cooking, while darker women are assigned to housework (Cohen 1987). Similarly, by producing a divide between Filipinas and Indonesians, Taiwanese agencies suggest that employers assign them different tasks. Indonesian workers, portrayed as dutiful, loyal, and accommodating, become candidates for taking care of the elderly and the ill. Yet English-speaking Filipinas are considered better educated, more civilized, and thus more capable of caring for Taiwanese children. In addition, Indonesian workers are often assigned extra work outside the household, such as working in the factory or restaurant owned by their employers. The alleged stupidity and subservience of Indonesian women make them "suitable" candidates for such "double exploitation" (Loveband 2004a).

The racialized boundaries across migrant groups not only carve their separate niches in the labor market but also demarcate hierarchical differences in their status and rights. Labor brokers usually instruct employers to adopt distinct methods of management toward these two groups of migrant domestics. It is feasible to ask Indonesians to give up their day off, but the no-day-off rule is often not acceptable among Filipina workers. The second-class labor conditions of Indonesian migrants are even sealed by labor contracts; before their entry to Taiwan, many have been coerced to sign an article that specifies their agreement to take no days off or only one day off each month. The complaints about wage disparity by nationality are less commonly heard in Taiwan, but in Hong Kong, Indonesian domestic workers tend to receive lower wages than Filipina workers.[41]

The constructive nature of ethnic characterization is made clear by the fact that the controlling images of particular ethnic groups are relationally defined and context-dependent. In Taiwan, Filipina migrant workers are depicted as being assertive and militant in contrast to their Indonesian counterparts. However, Canadian placement agencies associate Filipina nannies with a soft and loving character, as opposed to the aggressive "island girls," West Indian domestic workers (Bakan and Stasiulis 1995). Another example is the "obedient" image of Indonesian domestic workers in the discourse of Taiwanese agencies. This image shattered after an increasing number of them fled from their contractual jobs, finally leading to a temporary suspension of imported labor from Indonesia in August 2002. In fact, when taking a hard look at the statistics, I found that "running away" has never been a phenomenon unique to one particular ethnic group. Filipino migrant workers used to have a reputation for "running away" until the absconding rate among Indonesian workers outnumbered their Filipino counterparts in 2000.[42] This transition happened at about the same time that more employers were replacing Filipinas with Indonesians. After the ban on Indonesian migrants, the replacement Vietnamese workers, once promoted by labor brokers as a newer model of "ideal servants," soon became the "calculating communists" who have had the highest absconding rate among all migrants since 2003.[43] The CLA then announced a temporary freezing of the recruitment of Vietnamese workers in December 2004.

The rising numbers of "runaways" among Indonesian and Vietnamese workers indicate that it is the occupational category of domestic work, rather than a particular nationality of migrant workers, that contributes to workers' tendency to escape from the exploitation of employers. Labor brokers and employers utilize the racialized controlling images to rationalize their high-handed management over Indonesian and Vietnamese workers, but the consequence—"runaways"—ironically subverts the myth of "subservient servants."

Maid to Order

I have so far demonstrated how labor brokers construct and disseminate exaggerated ethnic-national characterizations of migrant workers. Yet the influence of labor brokers is far beyond the discursive level. Many Taiwanese agencies have established offices in sending countries, Indonesia and Vietnam in particular, to minimize transaction costs and to maximize control. Or they seek business partners in sending countries for efficient and enduring collaboration. Through the establishment of a transnational industry, labor brokers on the receiving side are able to integrate recruitment and training into part of the marketing plan. To facilitate the market positioning of Filipina and Indonesian migrants, labor brokers select different venues for labor recruitment and they establish training programs to actively manage the "transformation" of labor power.

Agencies in Indonesia and the Philippines have utilized different venues of recruitment and, as a result, they bring in workers of distinct characteristics. Agencies in Manila not only seek prospective workers in the villages but also use newspapers and even flyers in city neighborhoods to advertise job opportunities. These advertisements are more accessible to urban residents and workers, such as clerks, secretaries, and other low-level white-collar employees, as well as returned migrants who are familiar with recruitment procedures. Those who apply through such channels are more educated and have more contact with urban lifestyles than those recruited in the village. Without much orientation and training, these prospects are ready to land jobs overseas.

Nevertheless, these types of workers are considered "no good" by recruitment agencies in Indonesia. In principle, they prefer villagers to urbanites, personal references (local sponsors) to newspaper advertisements, and "known" recruits to anonymous applicants. The lack of previous experience working overseas is even considered a plus, because these applicants are "unpolluted" and more easily "transformed." In Manila there are only a few training centers that offer short-term courses (in the daytime for a few weeks) in domestic service and care work; prospective workers enroll in these training courses on a voluntary basis in order to improve their odds of getting a job offer.[44] Yet in Indonesia all job applicants have to go through an intensive, live-in training program that takes two to six months.

In other words, the opposition between "smart Filipina" and "docile Indonesian" has been established as a framework from the outset of the recruitment process. They are not average profiles of migrants out of a random sample but result from the purposive actions and selection biases of recruitment agencies. The agencies choose particular venues to recruit workers of "anticipated" and "desired" characteristics in accordance with the stereotyped images associated with these two groups of migrants. To compete with English-speaking, well-educated Filipinas in the global labor market, Indonesian migrants are marketed as a model of "docile servants," whose niche is grounded in their rural background and their subjugation to intensive training, including the learning of the master's language.

PRODUCING "PROFESSIONAL SERVANTS"

"Can you imagine what an Indonesian worker looks like when she first arrives? She wears slippers and carries a plastic bag—not even a handbag! Inside the bag are only underwear and maybe 20,000 Rp in her pocket.

Then she says she wants to go to Taiwan! She was like that at registration, but we *train* her. Now she knows how to dress, she knows sanitation, she speaks Chinese, and she can do things. This is not an easy job."

Mr. Chen, the CEO of a recruitment agency, made this comment while we were sitting in his office in Taipei. Outside the room were a few dozen staff members busily answering phones that seemed to never stop ringing. Along with another three local offices and overseas branches in Indonesia, Vietnam, and the Philippines, his company handles the recruitment of eight hundred migrant domestic workers into Taiwan each year. During the interview, Mr. Chen, without any hesitancy, characterized these Southeast Asian women as backward and uncivilized while he continued to brag about the success of his training program, which could miraculously transform "the disdained other" into "professional servants." In what follows here, I examine how employment agencies produce and materialize the image of "professional servants" through three major processes of "production": recruitment, training, and presentation.

Recruitment

Sitting in his office in Jakarta, Mr. Damo, an Indonesian of Chinese descent, explained to me his company's preference regarding the venues for recruiting workers:

> We used to run ads in newspapers, but it was useless. Those who came were nearby workers and they were just asking. They already had jobs and they were not determined. So advertisement is no use. You have to use sponsors. Village people are different from urban folks. Sponsors have to talk to the family several times; otherwise they would be worried that their daughters are trafficked. You need the reference of known people. In the future, if something happens, they can go to the sponsor. And if the maid runs away, we can go to the sponsor, too. People who come to us themselves are usually those who have been to Taiwan before. We don't like them. We are afraid that she might run away; she might have a boyfriend in Taiwan.[45]

Sponsors, also known as "the head cow" (*niutou*), serve as an important medium in the recruitment process in Indonesia. They are usually local figures respected in a community, such as a village head, a successful local businessman, or even a religious leader (Rudnyckyi 2004: 414). The sponsor finds prospective workers in the village, prepares their documents, expedites the processing of papers with his local connections, and brings them over to the agency in the city. Usually, a prospective worker pays the sponsor Rp 2,000,000 (US$200) for transportation and other expenses. Upon a worker's arrival, the agency gives the sponsor a fee, about Rp 600,000 (US$60) to Rp 1,000,000 (US$100) for each recruit. The prospect usually pays nothing to the agency until she starts working overseas.

Mr. Damo's words demonstrate the benefits of subcontracting the task of head hunting to sponsors. In this way, a labor broker is able to reach the preferred kind of workers—village women without previous overseas experiences—at low costs. Besides, the migrant family places more trust in a local sponsor than in some stranger from the city; they feel more comfortable sending their daughters with a fellow villager to explore the unknown outside world. In the same vein, labor brokers rely on the social network between migrants and sponsors to conduct surveillance. If a worker "runs away" from her contract employer in Taiwan, the labor broker, through the mediation of the sponsor, can hold the family responsible for the unpaid agency fee. Kinship ties and social networks are mobilized for the purpose of labor management—monitoring the worker's behavior and suppressing the tendency to seek "illegal" employment.

Mr. Chen emphasized to me that "ideal servants" could be found only in rural areas; "the poorer, the better" is his golden rule of recruitment. He usually targets impoverished villages and locates prospective workers via kin networks. This venue of recruitment creates an effect of "localistic control" similar to what Ching-kwan Lee (1998) describes about migrant factory workers in Shenzhen: inexperienced migrant women depend on local networks for getting job referrals and necessary permits during recruitment, and yet these networks become a mechanism of surveillance and discipline at work. Said a Taiwanese manager in a recruitment agency:

> I like to recruit people from the same village, the more the better, so they can tie each other up. Suppose that two sisters both come to Taiwan. If the younger sister does not behave well, the elder sister feels embarrassed. Perhaps the auntie comes here, too. Then one of the sisters is not good; the auntie will scold her. Coming from the same village, people keep an eye on each other.

Labor brokers also produce "docile" migrant workers through a careful screening process. They tend to exclude applicants who "have a strong character" or "look too smart." They do not prefer those who have worked in Taiwan before or even those of Chinese descent. A familiarity with local society and language is not considered an advantage for job performance but rather a barrier to labor control. Employers want the workers to learn some Chinese for the sake of communication, but they do not want the workers to master the local language. One recruiter explained this, saying, "If they speak good Chinese, they would ask people, to compare with others. If they have local connections, they run away."

In addition, regionally based stereotypes encourage labor brokers to make preferences based on the origins of Indonesian women. They like to recruit women from East and Central Java, who are considered to have "better quality"—obedient, hardworking, plain, and simple. By contrast, West Javanese are not preferred despite the geographical closeness to Jakarta, where most agencies are located. It is said that women from West Java are more militant, lazy, and pretty. Their fair skin may worry the female employer about the possible seduction of her husband.

It should also be noted that migrant workers are not passive recipients of these racialized images. Some consciously play out labor brokers' preferences to their own benefit. For example, some migrant workers I met in Taiwan told me that they hid their previous overseas experiences from the brokers; some West Javanese lied to their brokers about their hometowns, pretending that they came from East or Central Java. They selectively disclose or disguise the information about themselves to satisfy labor brokers' imagery of "docile servants."

Training

After being recruited by sponsors, prospective migrants are sent to agencies for a months-long training program. Most training centers are located in the suburbs of Jakarta and Surabaya. The center I visited was composed of four houses—three were dormitories and a larger one was a training center. As there were 450 prospective workers in residence, the living space was very crowded. Fifteen to twenty people shared a room. The staff had just purchased bunk beds and mattresses to meet the Indonesian government's regulations on the basic living conditions of the training centers. This policy has been enforced only since 2003, after NGOs reported many cases of abuse, malnutrition, and mysterious deaths at training centers.[46] Most migrant workers I met in Taiwan were placed in substandard living conditions during the training period: they slept on the floor; they ate only rice and vegetables; hundreds of people took showers together because water was supplied for only one hour a day. One worker humorously described the dreadful environment, "We were like cows, like sheep. You see how they wash cows? We were just like that."

In the center I visited, all the trainees have to wake up at 4 a.m. and go to bed at 10 p.m. They have classes from Monday to Saturday. Sunday is the only day off, but they cannot go out; only visitors are allowed. One worker characterized their days in the center as "staying in prison." At night they were locked in the building, often suffering from hunger because of insufficient portions provided for dinner. One vividly described how they used a rope to lower a basket down to street vendors in order to bring food upstairs. In general, a migrant worker stays in the center from two to three months before her departure to Taiwan, but I have heard of people who awaited a job order for as long as six months.[47] The content of the training courses is listed in Table 3.

The introductory part of each training program usually includes a few hours on moral education, work ethics, and other general preaching. When I asked the Taiwanese agent, Mr. Chen, what he considers the most important subject of training, he answered without hesitation: "*li-yi-lian-chi*" (sense of propriety, justice, honesty, and shame). He draws on the Confucian principles of morality to highlight what he perceives as the "moral inadequacy" of migrants. These lessons, according to Mr. Chen, fulfill a critical function of taming migrant women's beast-like sexual energy. They also keep migrant women away from prostitution, which, in his eyes, is a common survival strategy for Southeast Asian women to get out of poverty. More importantly, these moral lessons aim to discipline villagers into productive and obedient laborers by cultivating an attitude of subservience toward employers. In my observation, the instructor, an Indonesian woman of Chinese descent, preached to the trainees: "Work hard, appreciate the opportunity to make money, don't fight with your employers, and don't fall under bad influences."

A more substantive part of training involves knowledge and skills for housekeeping and caretaking. These courses instruct prospective workers not only how to get work done in the house but how to do it in an "efficient" and "proper" way. They learn how to use modern electronic appliances, such as washing machines and microwaves, which they do not

TABLE 3. *Content of training for prospective Indonesian migrant domestic workers*

Subject of Classes	Hours of Classes
Introduction (mentality, religion, sanitation, motivation, discipline, employment relations)	15
Housekeeping (bed making, bathroom cleaning, vacuum cleaning, mopping, car washing)	27
Babysitting (bathing, dressing, feeding, and interacting with preschool children)	27
Eldercare (bathing, feeding, medicine, nursing skills, massage, exercise)	27
Table serving (table manners, menus, arrangement of utensils, order of serving, napkin folding)	27
Cooking	24
Ironing	18
Laundry (hand washing, machine washing, drying)	9
Electronics (how to use a juicer, toaster, microwave, and refrigerator)	27
Basic English vocabulary and conversation	114
Basic Chinese vocabulary and conversation	138
Total	454

Source: data provided by a recruitment agency in Indonesia, August 2003.

own or need in a rural lifestyle. Such transmission of household skills aims to correct migrants' "technical backwardness" and re-orient them toward the lifestyles of modern households (A. Cheng 2003: 176). Migrant women's previous homemaking experiences, childcare in particular, are disregarded as backward customs without proper sanitation. They are instructed how to take care of babies and children in a doctor-approved, germ-free way, in parallel with the growing trend of "scientific motherhood" in Taiwan.

In the program, they also learn how to set a table, placing utensils, napkins, and water glasses in the "correct" positions. During my stay in Indonesia, I noticed that Westernized formal dining scenes were common

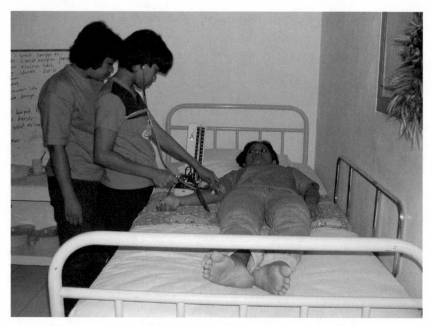

FIGURE I. *Prospective migrant workers practicing medical care*

in television soap operas despite the reality that most Muslim families eat with their hands while sitting on the carpet. The inclusion of Westernized table manners in the training program reflects a colonial imagination of the upper-class lifestyle. The villagers have to improve their "cultural civility" to play the servant role in the picture. Ironically, several migrant workers complained to me that this part of training is quite useless, because most Taiwanese households use casual table manners at home or do not even know how to set a formal Western table setting.

A large number of training hours are spent on language courses, especially Mandarin Chinese. As I noted above, such linguistic capability is the major advantage Indonesian workers have over their Filipina competitors. The transmission of language skills has its practical function—it facilitates communication between migrants and non-English-speaking Taiwanese employers. But it also has an underlying purpose of consolidating the authority of employers by subordinating migrant domestics to the master's language.

Daromir Rudnyckyi (2004) observed a training center in Jarkata for future domestic workers in Saudi Arabia. Drawing on Foucault, he coined the concept "technologies of servitude" to convey that these training programs not only aim to deliver certain skills and capacities to potential migrants but also intend to endow them with proper attitudes and disposition for domestic servitude. The technologies in his observation included score sheets for the evaluation of forms of speech and bodily discipline. The most striking example was that the trainees were instructed to only speak up to their superiors from a kneeling or stooping position.

These capacities and attitudes defined by trainers as essential in the conduct of domestic labor, on the one hand, are in contrast to the undesirable differences of migrant workers as perceived and imagined by both labor brokers and employers (Chen 2003). On the other hand, the design of training courses mirrors the desirable order of the modern home, which is nonetheless also a cultural construct that does not always match the reality of employment. In addition to the example of table manners, electronic appliances serve as essential props for the staging of the modern home scene. Yet in some households, only housewives have the privilege to use these labor-saving appliances. A few migrant domestic workers in Taiwan reported that they were requested to wash clothes by hands given the availability of washing machines in the households.

It would require more in-depth observation to discern whether the intended effects of these technologies are realized in the subject making of migrant women. Putting aside their actual effectiveness, the primary function of these programs is symbolical as they represent a rite of passage— a process of modernizing and civilizing the savage. Migrant applicants must go through the training program to prove to foreign recruiters that they are now capable of working in a modern household. And labor brokers utilize this ritual to assure Taiwanese employers that these "disdained others" have passed quality-control testing and become "professional servants."

Presentation

While visiting the training center in Indonesia, I was amazed that so many individuals could gather in such a limited space, yet in such an orderly manner. In separate rooms, some were ironing clothes, some were cleaning the carpet, some were cooking Chinese cuisine, and some were practicing massage on their classmates. Most amazingly, a line of women was practicing changing diapers and feeding bottles to dolls; they talked to

FIGURE 2. *Prospective migrant workers in the training center*

the dolls by reciting a Chinese script as instructed. In another classroom, a few dozen women sat still in neatly lined-up chairs, watching a video about CPR. I stood by the door trying to observe the class quietly, but most of the trainees diverted their attention from the screen and displayed much excitement and curiosity at my presence. An agency staffer then entered the room, introducing me as a guest from Taiwan. The crowd applauded and said in unison and in crisp Chinese: *"Xiao-jie, ni-hao* (Hello, Ma'am)."

I later realized that what I saw that day was not exactly how the courses were routinely conducted. It was, rather, a show carefully staged for overseas employers and recruiters. All the workers were instructed to wear a clean T-shirt and jeans (no standard dress codes on regular days); the colors of the T-shirts corresponded to the classification of workers by country of destination: yellow for Malaysia, orange for Singapore, white for Hong Kong, and red for Taiwan (because, said the agency staffer, Chinese people consider red a lucky color). Siti, a migrant worker I interviewed in Taiwan, recalled the situation when overseas recruiters came to the training center where she stayed for four months:

We are all dressed up, hair combed, and wearing the uniform. [They told us to] walk in a hurry. No crying face. Smile. They are coming soon. Smile. Say "hello sir," "hello ma'am." [*So this is different from the usual?*] Yes, it's difficult for us. They told us we must smile. But we have been there for a long time, very unhappy, but we still have to smile.

In spite of the weariness incurred by a long period of unemployment and family separation, trainees are asked to represent a spirited self. Just as they wear uniforms, they wear standard smiles and offer deferential greetings in order to pass the evaluations of recruiters. In some training centers, trainees are not called by their names but by assigned numbers. They wear a name tag with the number attached to the uniform. Their bodies are depersonalized as commodities coded by color and identified by number.

In contrast to the apparent feminization of domestic work and the latent potential of sexual exposure at such employment settings, the bodies of prospective migrant domestics are defeminized and desexualized during the presentation. Wearing make-up is not allowed and short hair is the required style. In Indonesia, long hair is generally considered an integral element of beauty and femininity. Several workers I talked to in Taiwan recalled the saddening moment when their long hair was cut off when they registered at the center. Some saved the cut hair and mailed it back to their family for remembrance or to make a wig for their mothers. Many felt embarrassed at showing me the photograph on their ARC (Alien Resident Certificate) taken when they first arrived in Taiwan: "I looked very ugly! Like a boy!" Such a hairstyle aims to repress the feminine look of migrant women, something usually not preferred by female employers; this mode of presentation also aims to accord with the classist image of a "maid"—plain and lacking style. In sum, through such management of dress code, hairstyle, and manner, labor brokers present a proper image of migrant women—defeminized, disciplined, and innately subservient—to mirror the expectation of employers.

REINFORCING GROUP DIVIDES

A Filipina describes the working conditions of her Indonesian neighbor with sympathy: "No sleep, no days off, and no complaints." When going out on Sundays, she bought food and phone cards for the quarantined neighbor. Despite some cases of solidarity building, the racialized boundaries marked by labor brokers and employers create a sense of rivalry among migrant workers of different nationalities. Oftentimes Filipina domestic workers feel hesitant about asserting their rights because their employers threaten to replace them with Indonesian workers. In such circumstances, some Filipina domestic workers reproduce racialized stereotypes to assert their superior capability and reliability over Indonesian competitors.[48] They talked about "those Indonesians" as uneducated, short on English skills, flirty with male bosses, stealing employers' belongings, and being too backward to handle housework in a modern household. In particular, they disapprove of Indonesian women's romantic involvements with men outside the ethnic group. One Filipina commented:

> Some employers think Filipinas have boyfriends. Wrong. Indonesians make boyfriends. Did you ever go to the park across the streets from the Mosque? Indonesians are with blacks, Niggers, or Thais. Filipinas are wise; they know making boyfriends is stupid. We are here to work, not to play.

Nicole Constable (1997a: 185–87) found many articles in *Tinig Filipino*, a magazine that targets overseas Filipino workers, in which migrant authors invoke national pride to remind their compatriots of the importance of self-discipline. They believe it is their moral responsibility to oppose Chinese stereotypes about Filipinos such as drinking, loitering, and loose sexual morals. I also found that when Filipina migrant workers view and treat their own bodies as an extension of national territories, they simultaneously project ethnic-national differences on the bodies of other groups of migrant women. Filipina workers find fault with the behavior of their Indonesian competitors while imposing discipline on themselves to establish evidence for their work ethic and moral credibility.

Among Indonesian workers, I sense similar hostility and criticism toward their Filipina counterparts. Several Indonesians complained to me about this situation: their employers grant to them only one or two days off each month, while the Filipina worker hired previously had every Sunday off. Or some Indonesian workers are assigned extra work without additional pay, while the previous Filipina workers had no such work or received a raise for the increased workload. Despite harboring a strong feeling of unfairness, few of them ever confront their employers about such

uneven treatment. When asked why, Indonesian women describe themselves as *"takut"* (afraid)" and Filipina workers as *"berani"* (brave)" in
terms of insisting on their rights to employers and brokers (Loveband
2004b).

Although some Indonesians envy the assertiveness of Filipina workers,
others consider avoidance of confrontation to be more appropriate, morally and religiously. One emphasized the impact of her upbringing: "I am
used to this [way of behaving]. The same way I was back home in Indonesia. My mother taught me that we have to be courteous no matter how
people treat us." Another pointed to the teaching of Islam: "My Ma'am
yelled at me. I never yell back. I only pray. I endure it."

In the eyes of many Indonesian migrants, Filipina workers are the
"high class" who are better-educated, English-speaking, and arrogant
(showing no interest in talking to Indonesians in Chinese). Migrant workers' perceptions of ethnic differences are framed by employers' racial discourses. For example, Utami, a twenty-five-year-old Indonesian, described
her employer's uneven attitude: "They treat Filipinas better. They think
we Indonesians are no good; we are stupid. They say Filipinas are smarter,
better, prettier, their skin lighter. Not like us, they said, dark skin, no
good-looking." When Utami first arrived, her employers even bluntly said,
"Your skin looks like [the color of] slippers." Utami masked her discontent
and simply answered, "Oh, thank you."

As well as education and skin color, English proficiency is another
marker often used by employers to denote the stratified differences between these two groups of migrants. Utami, however, developed a coun-
terdiscourse to the employer's perspective:

> They said Filipinas are smarter; they speak English. But they forgot that
> Filipinas don't speak Chinese. I told them that you hire me here to
> work, not to talk, right? If you want someone to talk, Filipinas know
> how to talk, to speak English. But I'm here to work, to take care of
> children, to cook, to wash, to clean. Do I need to speak English? Plus, do
> Grandpa and Grandma speak English?

Similar to Filipinas, Indonesians fortify the racialized boundaries in
moral terms. Some criticize Filipina migrants for their alleged engagement in drinking, smoking, and having sex out of wedlock. They establish
their moral credibility by appealing to the image of religious, conservative

Muslim women; by contrast, they perceive the Westernized Filipina as suspect of loose morals. Work ethic is a major theme that Indonesian workers use to characterize their moral superiority. During interviews, several Indonesian informants established their own merits of loyalty, diligence, and cooperation by portraying Filipinas as being militant, ruthless, selfish, and lacking the patience and perseverance required in domestic and care work: "I am not like the Filipina. She argued a lot, 'I want this, I want that.' I don't like to argue. I just do it. I don't talk." "My neighbor said I take care of the grandpa much better than the previous Filipina worker. She was careless and rude." "They don't work hard; they only care about themselves. We may be stupid but we are courteous."

The group-based antagonism among individual migrants is situated in broader contexts. A potential relationship of competition in the labor market induces a sense of opposition among migrant workers of different nationalities. Linguistic barriers also obstruct communication and interaction between English-speaking Filipinas and Chinese-speaking Indonesians. Chapter 5 will further discuss the spatial distribution of migrant communities that materializes such national divides. Under these circumstances, migrant workers may subscribe to the discourse of labor brokers and reinforce racialized boundaries to mark their differences from other groups of migrants. This can lead to a practice of "self-racialization": when a minority group reproduces the dominant stereotypes to marginalize other minority groups, it ends up subjugating itself to the same normative control of racialization.

THE MAKING OF FOREIGN MAIDS

This chapter has mapped the discursive terrain of stratified otherization in which the racialized images of migrant domestic workers are constructed in relation to Taiwanese citizens and other ethnic others. I have also emphasized that the recruitment of migrant women as foreign maids involves not only an organized process of locating and placing labor power but also a discursive and disciplinary process of subject making.

The discursive construction of Southeast Asian migrants has appropriated antecedent racist narratives placed on Taiwanese Aborigines. While the old ethnic other has been incorporated into the new Taiwanese national identity, foreign workers become the new ethnic other, subject to the twofold process of racialization. On the one hand, Southeast Asian migrants are constructed as a racialized collectivity, and on the other hand, they are divided by nationality and attached with fixed and essentialized characteristics. This indicates two parallel approaches to boundary making: social boundaries are fortified through playing down differences within groups (*lumping*) and widening the perceived gaps between groups (*splitting*) (Zerubavel 1991: 27).

Popular discourses represent *wailao* as the inferior other, associated with poor hygiene, cultural backwardness, and criminal orientation. These denigrated images greatly contrast with the privileged status of "foreign talents"—managers, professionals, and English instructors from wealthy economies and "superior" civilizations. Only in this context can we comprehend the anomalous subject position of "Filipina maids" in Taiwan, whose additional job assignment of English tutoring could simultaneously polish and damage the upgraded status of newly rich Taiwanese employers.

Labor brokers promote Indonesian women as a better model of "ideal servants" in opposition to Westernized Filipinas. The racialized stereotypes are materialized in the organized activities of recruitment and training. Through a careful selection of recruitment venues, brokers seek "docile" village women to meet the image of "the traditional other." And they attempt to "modernize" the primitive by imposing an extensive training program. With such symbolic rite of passage, they announce the production of "professional servants" ready to be shipped out to their overseas assignments.

3   JEALOUS MADAMS & ANXIOUS MOTHERS

A common scene at the end of the day at a Taipei elementary school: children run out of the gate with excitement while the bell is still ringing. Some yell at one boy in a teasing tone: "Wang Shiao-ming, your Filipina maid is waiting for you!" The boy looks embarrassed, eyes downcast, and plays with his palm pilot; then he strides forward, leaving the maid a few steps behind. A girl delightedly runs to another Filipina and gives her a big hug. They walk hand in hand on the way home, a picture not so different from a Taiwanese mother and her child except that they speak English to each other. The blurring of mother and nanny is not unusual. A Taiwanese mother described an episode to me: "My Filipina maid has fair skin. She brings my son to an after-school computer class twice a week. She just sits in the back and waits for the class to be over. After two or three months, one day the teacher went to talk to her, calling her 'Mrs. Chang. . . .' She didn't answer at all. Then the teacher finally realized that she's the maid, not the mother!"

The distinction between maid and madam, or mother and caregiver, is a thin line. Both women perform similar labor activities, whether unpaid or paid, in a home setting. In fact, while outsourcing a great chunk of domestic labor to market surrogates, most female employers continue to do some housework or caring labor themselves. This chapter investigates why Taiwanese women hire migrant domestic workers and how the employment impacts their family relations and gender identities. I probe the following questions: How do female employers draw boundaries between themselves and migrant workers to sustain their version of womanhood of "superior" class and ethnic characteristics? How do they redefine the meanings of domestic labor and interpret various components of domestic labor to pursue a socially appropriate division of labor between themselves and market surrogates? And how do they avoid confusion and even replacement given the presence of another woman at home who performs a similar domestic role?

This boundary work not only concerns the dyad of maid and madam but also involves multiple sets of triangular relationships mediated by the madam's husband, children, and mother-in-law. The intervention of migrant domestic workers leads to a rupture in the "regime of practices" (Foucault 1991), which provides a critical moment for us to examine the regime of Taiwanese families, including the social institutions and cultural values of marriage, motherhood, and filial piety.

BARGAINING WITH PATRIARCHIES

Deniz Kandiyoti (1991), in her famous article "Bargaining with Patriarchy," looks at women's survival strategies and coping mechanisms within a given set of patriarchal constraints. As noted in the introduction, we should pluralize "patriarchy" to localize the configurations of gender domination and women's agency. Here I describe the patriarchal bargaining of middle- and upper-class Taiwanese women through the purchase of migrant domestic service. Women seek helping hands for different matters related to their multiple gendered duties as mother, wife, and daughter-in-law. I categorize their purposes into three major types: seeking in-home childcare; transferring "work in the house"; and subcontracting the filial care duty.

Standby Subservient Nannies

A-sue, who is in her early thirties, works as a marketing researcher in an advertising company. She met her husband at work and they have a two-year-old daughter. Like most Taiwanese women in her generation, the idea of full-time mothering does not appeal to A-sue. She continues working to achieve her career aspirations and to pay off their heavy mortgage. Since the beginning of her pregnancy, A-sue deliberated about the arrangement for future childcare. Extended kin are not an option for her, because her husband's parents do not live in Taipei and A-sue's parents are not in good health. She finally decided to hire a Filipina worker despite her concern about the safety issue. Her worry remained: "I heard that some family had hired a Filipina maid for three years, and they left the baby with the maid when going abroad. After they came back, both were gone. They couldn't find the baby at all. So sometimes I wonder, maybe one day when I come home, the baby is gone."

A-sue thought of hiring someone who is "one of our own." But after making some visits to observe local women who offer childcare service in their own homes, she concluded that hiring a migrant caregiver was an unavoidable solution for her family: "I am nervous, but there's nothing I can do. I don't want a local nanny. You have to transport the baby every morning and evening. I'm not working nine to five—how can I accommodate this kind of schedule? It's too inflexible. Plus, a child is not a commodity. To set up such a rigid schedule, it doesn't sound like love to me."

Many Taiwanese dual-career couples like A-sue and her husband have turned to migrant women for the assistance in childcare. The prevalence of the nuclear household pattern in contemporary urban Taiwan has decreased the likelihood of sharing childcare labor with elder relatives, especially mothers-in-law. The proportion of Taiwanese parents arranging childcare through commercial agents and institutions has continued to grow. Compared to local caregivers, migrant domestic workers not only charge a lower rate[1] but also provide a broader variety of services for employers.

Live-in service is the primary advantage in the employment of migrant nannies. Parents can thus avoid the task of transporting children on the designated schedules of local caregivers. In A-sue's perspective, rigid timetables in day care are inconvenient for parents and not "loving" for children. In-home care, in contrast, is considered more comfortable, safe, and attentive to children's needs. Mothers also feel more in control of the condition of live-in care compared to placing children in an institution or someone else's house. Live-in childcare, which approximates the ideal of stay-at-home motherhood, is generally viewed as a better option for mothers at work.

In addition, some employers prefer migrant workers because they are more docile and controllable than Taiwanese nannies. Melissa, a thirty-six-year-old business manager, explained why she hired a Filipina maid to replace her previous local caregiver: "That nanny has a very strong personality. She didn't take any commands from parents. She thought she was a professional." The majority of local caregivers are middle-aged women with experience from raising their own children. They establish an authority claim based on experience and seniority. Young employers often have difficulty in challenging the caregivers' opinions given the Chinese tradition of deference to seniors. For example, Wen-jen, a thirty-three-year-old researcher with a shy, quiet demeanor, explained to me why migrant workers suit her needs better than local ones: "The local workers talked to me like talking to kids. It was very hard to make requests upon them and they didn't listen to you. They had too many opinions of their own."

Other employers hire migrant workers to replace childcare provided by extended kin, mostly on the husband's side. Traditionally, a Taiwanese grandmother plays a crucial role in the care of her son's children; she supervises her daughter-in-law and intervenes when the job is not being done in a way she deems proper (Wolf 1970). It remains a common practice that a mother-in-law takes care of her grandchildren if her daughter-in-law is working outside the home. This arrangement may happen in three-generation households or in situations where mothers-in-law live nearby. Catherine and her husband, in their early thirties, both received MBAS in the United States and work in Taipei as market consultants. When Catherine returned to work after three months of maternal leave, her mother-in-law took over caring for the couple's newborn baby. The couple sent the baby to the grandparents' house every morning and picked her up after work. Without being asked, Catherine paid her mother-in-law NT$15,000 per month, an amount equivalent to the lower-end wage of a local caregiver. Although saving herself the worry of leaving the child with a stranger, Catherine felt that this arrangement caused difficulty and tension in dealing with her mother-in-law:

> We argued almost every day. [*About what?*] Nothing major. She was just exhausted, unhappy, and then she gave me a poker face. Every time when we picked up our daughter, we didn't know if we should leave or stay. If we left, she would say, "You guys just want to get your child." If we stayed, she would say. "I have been working so hard, I take care of your child and now I also have to cook your dinner?" She was not saying these to her son, only to her daughter-in-law.

Not only was Catherine's mother-in-law exhausted by the job of caring for a newborn baby but she felt deprived. She felt that she had sacrificed the comfort of her old age to maintain her son's family, a duty that was supposed to fall to her daughter-in-law. Catherine later hired a migrant worker to care for her daughter. She spent the money in order to spare the emotional costs. Young mothers hire nannies also to safeguard their parental autonomy and to avoid confrontations with the older generation. An-ru, a thirty-two-year-old stockbroker, explained to me why she preferred a migrant caregiver to her mother-in-law: "When there are different opinions regarding childcare, you somehow have to listen to the elderly. Then you lose your autonomy. I cannot control my mother-in-law, but at least I can control my Filipina maid, right?"

Work in the House

By hiring a migrant domestic worker, employed women not only resolve the thorny problem of childcare but also unburden themselves from a substantial amount of housework. Sociologists have found that American middle-class dual-career households employ domestic workers to reach the goal of "spousal egalitarianism" (Hertz 1986). In this way, women employers are able to "[avoid] the tensions and conflicts that can arise when they push their husbands toward more equal participation" (Wrigley 1995: 142). A similar scenario exists in many dual-earner households in Taiwan as well.

Mr. Yu is a thirty-nine-year-old business manager who married a secretary; they have two children. He considers domestic employment a necessity in the maintenance of both their household order and conjugal harmony. He talked about the two months when they were waiting for a new maid: "When the maid was gone, our life is filled with tension and chaos. It was a really painful period for us. My wife and I argued a lot in terms of how to divide housework, who would pick up the children today, etc." He concluded, with a grin, "That's why I said to my friends that we got addicted to hiring a foreign maid!"

Some Taiwanese men, mostly in middle-class dual-career young couples, do perceive housework as a collective responsibility but still cannot bear the burden of double shifts. The employment of migrant domestic workers offers a convenient, economic way for them to "buy out" their responsibility. Catherine described the critical moment when her husband agreed to her suggestion of hiring a foreign domestic worker:

My husband objected in the beginning; he thought it was kind of weird to have a stranger in the house. I said, OK, then don't complain when I ask you to share the housework. Then one day he was doing the laundry, hanging up the clothes on the balcony . . . He came inside and said to me, "I don't want to live like this anymore. Let's hire a foreign maid!"

I interviewed seven female employers who were not gainfully working at the time. Five of them are from wealthy households headed by their husbands as business owners, lawyers, or doctors. For homemaker employers, the purpose of hiring a foreign worker is mainly for housework. In these households, housework is demanding because of their spacious residences and higher sanitary standards. With the employment of domestic workers, these homemakers are able to concentrate on childcare, a more "spiritual" kind of domestic labor, and can participate in charity, socializing, and community activities.

For instance, Mrs. Liu, in her early fifties, is a mother of four. She received a bachelor's degree in business from a top university in Taiwan. Yet she entered marriage right after college and never held any waged job, accommodating the objections of her husband, a successful attorney who believes in the conventional ideal of the male-breadwinner family. Mrs. Liu has been hiring domestic workers for more than twenty-five years, first local day workers and subsequently foreign maids. She explained the reasons for hiring paid domestic help in her family:

> I don't think it is absolutely necessary to hire someone, but my husband likes to have a maid. He likes to enjoy a clean house . . . But it's still better to take care of children yourself. I hire a maid only for housework. This is important for housewives, so they won't be tied up by housework and can save some time to do things outside the house.

Another homemaker employer, Shin-yi, is a college graduate in her early thirties. She left her profession as a nutritionist after giving birth to her first child. She strongly believes that full-time motherhood benefits children, but she feels worn out by the heavy workloads and the monotonous life at home. When she was pregnant with her second child, she hired a Filipina worker. With helping hands at home, she is able to enjoy some personal time and take up craftwork and painting, her hobbies in college. She evaluated the costs and gains in the employment: "Some people think of this as a luxury. Well, not us. We are actually tightening our budget to afford it. But I think it is worthwhile, because now I have more time in my life. So I won't feel sorry for my children but I won't feel sorry for myself, either."

Depending solely on the salary of her husband, a resident physician in a public hospital, Shin-yi's family faces a moderate budget given expenses of all kinds. Hired domestic help enables her to escape the domestic shackles but increases financial pressure and social blame—it seems less legitimate for middle-class homemakers to hire someone while they are not contributing to the family income. Shin-yi told me: "My mother-in-law always said that it was kind of strange that I don't work but still hire a maid. 'Strange' is the word she used. Of course, I know what she meant by that." She sighed and continued: "She thinks I'm just lazy and I shouldn't have hired a maid."

At the time of the interview, Shin-yi was debating whether she should start searching for a waged job. Her situation indicates that women often transit from domesticity to part-time or full-time employment and vice versa (Hochschild 1989; Hondagneu-Sotelo 2001). They constantly negotiate their work trajectories in the balance of economic costs, family welfare, and personal gains. Man-jun, a forty-year-old freelance travel agent, recalled how she considered shifting between the roles of homemaker and waged worker:

> I thought of quitting my job and letting the maid go, because my income was not very stable. But my husband objected. He said I am such an outgoing person that I could not bear staying home. And he has a high standard [on cleaning]. He cannot make demands on me, but he can make demands on the maid. So he'd rather spend money. We call this *huan-gong* [work transfer] [*laughs*]. All my income goes to her wage, but I won't be disconnected from the society in this way.

The life of a full-time housewife in the perception of Shi-yi or Man-jun is not that different from what Ann Oakley (1974) described about British housewives three decades ago—monotonous, exhausting, isolating, and alienating. In contrast to unpaid domestic labor, white-collar waged employment is considered less burdensome and more organized and rewarding. More than one employer made similar remarks: "Sitting in the office the whole day is an easy job; housework and childcare are much more tiring." "Taking care of children is a pain; going to work is like my escape." For the homemakers or employed women who can afford the "work transfer," migrant domestic workers help them flee the shackles at home.

Work in the house has broader components for *taugaynewn*. This Hoklo term literally means "the boss's wife" and usually refers to female owners of family business. Small-business owners in Taiwan work extensive hours, often as long as twelve hours a day. Their stores and residences are usually geographically close to each other. Three employers I interviewed have stores or offices on the ground floor of their residential buildings. Consequently, they can integrate family life and work more easily by watching children do homework in the store or by taking a lunch break at home.

Shu-wen, a mother of three in her late thirties, runs a small electronics store on her own, while her husband manages a security guard agency. When I called to set up an interview, she kindly said, "Just come to my store. We are open every day from 10 a.m. to 9 p.m." The store includes a five-hundred-square-feet sales floor, a tiny bathroom, and a stock room in the back. Shu-wen applied for a foreign helper while she was pregnant with her third child; her first two children were under the care of local caregivers. The recruitment process took longer than she expected. She described what happened during the first three months after her baby's birth yet before the arrival of the Filipina worker: "That was a nightmare. I still shiver when I think about those days now. I don't know how I made it. I was even sent to the hospital for a few days." She pointed at a small table in this cramped space: "At that time, I came to the store every day, too. And the baby was sleeping right on that table."

Since there is no clear boundary between work and family in the daily schedule of *taugaynewns*, they make no such distinction in assigning tasks to their domestic employees either. Migrant workers hired by family business owners usually have double shifts, despite a government ban on such practices. During the day, they accompany their employers to work, cleaning stores and offering other assistance. In the evening they continue working in the house and taking care of children as the surrogate of the mother, who is still occupied by business. These workers usually receive no extra pay or only a small bonus for the second shift. Indeed, the fusion of the public and private spheres characterizes the lifestyle of *taugaynewns*, who require assistance across the domestic and nondomestic spheres. However, such a work arrangement violates legal regulations and exacerbates labor exploitation.

SUBCONTRACTING FILIAL PIETY

Mrs. Chang is a retired high school teacher in her late fifties. She and her husband, also a teacher, own a modest three-bedroom apartment in Taipei. Mr. Chang's mother moved from the province to reside with him, her eldest son, after her husband's death. Mrs. and Mr. Chang later rented the apartment across the hallway to accommodate the mother-in-law so they could remain the ideal of three-generation cohabitation yet have enough rooms and privacy for their two grown-up daughters and themselves.

According to Han-Chinese cultural norms, the main axis of father and son defines family membership, inheritance of property, and distribution of authority. A daughter is considered "spilled water," given away after marriage to another family headed by her husband's father. In contrast, giving birth to sons assures parents more security for their future welfare. As a Chinese proverb says: "To protect yourself at old ages, raise a son." The eldest married son is obligated to reside with and care for his aging parents; placing parents in a nursing home is stigmatized as immoral and irresponsible. Despite the increasing tendency of parents to live alone, the filial norm continues to pressure sons to take care of elderly parents (see chapter 1 for statistical details).

The actual work of serving a man's aging parents is, however, performed mostly by his wife. Mr. Chang provides economic support for his eighty-year-old mother while his wife serves as his filial surrogate, offering care and service on a daily basis. Two years ago Mrs. Chang convinced her husband to hire an Indonesian worker to take care of his mother, who had grown frail and needed daily assistance and personal care. Mrs. Chang then transferred most of her previous duties like preparing meals, bathing, and changing diapers to the Indonesian worker. More than once during our interview, Mrs. Chang felt compelled to legitimize her decision of hiring someone to take care of her mother-in-law:

> I may sound like I have no sense of filial piety to you, but I have been serving her for twenty years! If you want to be a good daughter-in-law, you can no longer be yourself. Fortunately, it doesn't cost that much to hire a foreign caretaker these days . . . After I retired from school, I'm still doing some part-time work. I don't want to stay home, not a single day. And I can make some money. But all the money goes to the Indonesian maid [*smiles bitterly*].

Mrs. Chang points out the conflict between performing the traditional role of the servile daughter-in-law in subordination to family authority and seeking individual autonomy and self-achievement. Liu Zhong-dong

(1998) has argued that the traditional idea of care giving in Chinese societies is associated with the hierarchical concept of "serving" rather than the more egalitarian notion of "caring." The typical image of caregivers in Chinese families is female kin in subordinate positions, such as a wife serving her husband and a daughter-in-law serving her parents-in-law. The act of care giving is strongly tied to the ideal of womanhood, and the failure of these gendered obligations incurs social stigma. Mrs. Chang continued working even after retirement in order to avoid the full-time duty of "serving" her mother-in-law. She exhausted the wage of her part-time job to hire another woman to be her filial agent, but the employment was still opposed by both her mother-in-law and husband:

> She [the mother-in-law] always says bad things about the Indonesian maid because she wishes we would stop the employment so she could live with us.
>
> *How about your husband? He objected, too?*
>
> Of course. First, it costs money. Second, in this way, it doesn't seem that we are a family, and he won't be able to make the ideal of a filial son.

The mother-in-law considered a nonfamily worker to be an obstruction to her tie to the son's family. The son was also concerned that the employment would ruin the image of family union and his filial reputation. Both perceptions reflect the deeply rooted ideology of *san-dai-tone-tang* (three-generation cohabitation) (Hu 1995). The romanticized myth of a "big happy family" is, however, sustained mostly by the daughter-in-law's unpaid kin labor. Mrs. Chang expressed anguish about the unequal division of filial labor between her and her husband:

> I worked as hard as he did, but he said taking care of children is women's business; serving the mother-in-law is women's business. This is really unfair. I am also educated; I cannot accept this. If you want to be a dutiful son, then you should be the one who serves your mother, not me! My mother brought me up. I should take care of my mother, not yours. She's the mother of you and your six siblings, not mine. You cannot just leave her to the daughter-in-law.

To bargain with the "unfair" gendered assignment of serving her mother-in-law, Mrs. Chang seeks a market surrogate to perform the filial duty for her. There is a "transfer chain of filial care" consisting of two components: first, gender transfer of the filial duty from the son to the daughter-in-law, and second, market transfer of elder care from the daughter-in-law to nonfamily care workers (mostly women). As another female employer put it, "Many husbands say women today are luckier than ever because they have foreign maids to help. But actually, who's your wife taking care of? She's taking care of your mother!"

Some Taiwanese husbands, mostly from younger generations, are willing to share some housework, but their mothers object. When I asked Li-yun, a forty-three-year-old real estate agent, if her husband helped out with housework, she answered:

> More or less. He's a neat person. Once he saw some dirt on the floor and couldn't help but mop it. The maid was on vacation or something. My mother-in-law was visiting us and she was shocked when she saw this. She must be thinking, "My son never did anything like this in *my* house! Now he is mopping the floor!" So I rushed to ask my husband to stop and told him I would do that later.

This scenario demonstrates not only a generational gap in viewing the division of housework between a couple but also an implicit competition between the mother-in-law and daughter-in-law over the son. The extended family and conjugal family are marked as separate territories dominated by the two women across generations ("my house" versus "your floor"). The mother-in-law viewed the son's participation in housework as an indicator of his subordination to his wife, and concomitantly, of the weakening of his ties to his mother and extended family.[2] Some daughters-in-law, such as Emily, a twenty-nine-year-old financial consultant, hire a domestic worker to avoid potential disputes with a live-in mother-in-law around the division of housework:

> I'm thinking that when my daughter gets married in the future, I'll also hire a foreign maid for her. That way she can avoid a lot of problems with her mother-in-law. You can't let your mother-in-law do housework like cleaning and cooking, but you also feel reluctant to do it alone—there's no way she'll let her son do it, right?

Some female employers more assertively use the hiring of domestic workers as a strategy to resist three-generation cohabitation. Shiao-li, thirty-six years old, has a junior college degree and worked as a nurse before giving birth to her son. Her mother-in-law volunteered to move to Taipei to be their live-in caretaker, but Shiao-li rejected this proposal, saying she would seek a migrant caretaker. Shiao-li described what happened then:

> My mother-in-law is a very sharp woman. She said to me, "Your father-in-law thinks hiring a foreign maid is a bad idea."—She wouldn't say it was her who thinks it's a bad idea. Whoever she ran into—my friends, relatives—she told them, "You talk to Hsiao-li, tell her to let me watch the child." Anyway, the main point is that she wants to live with her son. She doesn't really love the grandson. She loves her son!
>
> *And what does your husband think?*
>
> He?! Of course he likes to live with both his wife and his mother! Then he can be a baby forever. Everything is taken care of by others.

The mother-in-law exerted her social pressures by proxy, framing her objection as though it were that of her husband, the patriarchal authority in the extended family. In another interview, I heard a story about a mother-in-law who, when visiting her son's family, expressed her anger by throwing out the migrant worker's baggage. She thought that if there were no migrant nanny, the couple would have invited her to live with them and take care of the grandchildren. These mothers-in-law feel anguished not because their grandchildren are "taken away" by the domestic workers but because they have been denied the link they would have enjoyed with their sons' families. Later in this chapter I discuss how daughters-in-law manage to smooth over the anxieties of their mothers-in-law.

WHY ARE MADAMS PICKY?

Many migrant domestic workers complained to me that their madams are more "picky" or "harsh" to them compared to their male employers. "Why are madams picky?" When I put this question to female employers during interviews, many admitted to being the major agents of labor management at home while their husbands tend to be indifferent or uninvolved in relevant maters. Bi-lan, an employer and a mother in her early forties, explained such a gender difference: "Men don't care, because there's always some sort of help for them. They didn't do the housework before, so whether the foreign maid is good or bad makes no difference to them."

As Bi-lan points out, women employers tend to hold stronger opinions regarding the performance of domestic workers because they, rather than their husbands, were responsible for the duties now done by the workers. Some husbands even perceive hiring a domestic worker as a "gift" for their wives—something to prove the "sweetness" of the husband who buys out his wife's second shift. When I asked Shin-yi, the doctor's wife, if her husband shared any housework, she answered with a sense of bitterness: "My husband? Not at all! The only work he does is to hire a foreign maid for me. Sometimes I would complain and he would say, 'Why do I bother to hire a maid, then? She costs me almost NT$20,000 a month!' "

Although women employers are now elevated to the status of "mother-manager" (Rothman 1989), they remain accountable for the performance of domestic workers they hire. Pressured by the hegemonic ideologies of domesticity and motherhood, women employers still perceive housework and childcare as their primary social responsibilities. Li-yun, the forty-something real estate agent, described herself as "one of those mothers who love their children too much." Her strong "maternal nature" often stirs feelings of guilt when she has business meetings in the evening. And yet it was her idea to hire a Filipina worker and her money that pays for it. When I asked how the husband responded to her proposal, Li-yun considered it an unnecessary question:

> He? It's my money, so he is OK, no problem at all. It has always been me who pays the maid's salary. You may think I look like a liberated woman, but I grew up in a very traditional family. I still feel like this [childcare] should have been my job. Since I'd like to work outside, then I should pay for the maid.

Many Taiwanese women pay the wage of domestic workers out of their own pocket because they feel "this should have been their job." The "mother guilt" is an internalization of social blame. Many employers feel urged to defend themselves against accusations of being "bad mothers" who leave their children with migrant caregivers who are often stigmatized as "filthy" and "uncivilized." For instance, A-sue recalled:

> When I hired my first Filipina maid, people told me a lot of horrifying stories about bad Filipinas. For example, they had the AIDS virus, or they threw children off the balcony . . . I was terrified for a while, but I think those people are just pathetic. They actually want to hire Filipina maids but don't have the guts, so they say these bad things instead.

Women employers may experience more direct pressure from their husbands and fathers. In Shin-yi's case, when the first migrant worker they hired "ran away," her husband blamed her for being an ineffective "manager"—not even capable of watching a maid. Another employer, Yu-mei, often brings her Filipina worker along when visiting her parents. Sometimes she and her mother teach the maid how to cook, but other times they just chat in the living room and leave the worker alone in the kitchen. And her father would complain, "She [the maid] wouldn't be able to cook a good meal! Why weren't you women staying in the kitchen?"

Yu-mei's father pointed at the domestic terrain (kitchen) and activity (cooking) that are deemed socially appropriate to be in the charge of women, maid and madam alike. Although younger generations of Taiwanese women embrace a modern version of career womanhood, they are still burdened by the traditional ideals of womanhood characterized by the Chinese expression *xien-chi-liang-mu* (the virtuous wife and good mother). The social responsibility for domestic labor has never been removed from the shoulders of women, whether they actually do the work or not.

All of this demonstrates a critical feature of domestic employment: migrant domestic workers serve as a surrogate or an extension for their female employers, but they are "shadow laborers" whose importance in the family life of employers is rendered invisible.[3] The "shadow work" of domestic workers is actually an essential complement to the achievement of domesticity and motherhood by female employers. Employed mothers seek substitutes for their in-home motherhood, modern daughters-in-law hire agents for their pious duty, and homemakers need someone else to make their homes clean and orderly. For female employers, domestic employment is not simply a purchase of labor service but involves moral meanings rooted in the social construction of womanhood. Therefore, rigid timetables or specific assignments cannot fully describe the expected labor output. Employers expect that domestic workers can help them achieve their wifely, motherly, and filial duties.

Women who hire domestic help want a competent surrogate but they want her to hover around the margins, where she will not overshadow their wifely and motherly status. I turn next to a discussion of the consequences of recruiting another woman into a family's life. Female employers feel anxious about how domestic employment impacts their marriages and bonds with children, so they manage to confirm the hierarchical distinctions between wife and maid, between mother and nanny. Not only young mothers but also their mothers-in-law feel threatened by the presence of migrant domestic workers. The older generations of mothers used to be full-time housewives and they now worry that migrant women might undermine their authority and security in the domestic castle.

STILL THE LADY OF THE HOUSE

A Taiwanese newspaper article titled "Everybody detests women who do no housework" gives an explicit warning to women who hire foreign domestic workers. It argues that women should not give up housework, the fundamental "women's work," no matter how successful they are as career women.[4] Facing social condemnations for their violation of the traditional ideal of domesticity, female employers redefine and negotiate the social meanings attached to the division of housework: they deliberate about which labor is socially acceptable to transfer to market agents without diminishing their image as the "lady of the house" (Kaplan 1987: 92).

Female employers usually turn over cleaning chores to their domestic workers but retain duties associated with the maintenance of affective ties in the family. On of these is the preparation of family meals, a task involving not only buying food and cooking but also the affective work of "constructing the family" based on tacit knowledge about family members' tastes and nutritional needs (DeVault 1991). Cooking also involves cultural knowledge of cuisine that is comparably difficult for foreign workers to master. The social significance of preparing family meals becomes critical when the wife has transferred the rest of the housework to the maid but takes charge of meal preparation as a chance to display affection for her husband and children.

Some female employers cook on a regular basis; some others do so at the request of their husbands or children. Shu-wen, the electronics store owner mentioned earlier, described an event in which she felt compelled to cook for her husband even after hiring a migrant domestic worker: "Last night when I got home late, he said to me, 'I am hungry! Did you bring any food home?' I said, 'No. How about some dumplings?' 'Okay, I want thirty pieces!' He just sat here and said so! See? Although I was exhausted, I still cooked dumplings for him." I pressed her to explain why she did not ask the maid to do it, and Shu-wen answered: "She was busy with other things at that time. Plus, I was thinking, now I hardly cook for my husband. Since he asked, I would make something for him."

Some female employers feel compelled to perform cooking duties even without requests from their husbands. A Filipina domestic worker vividly described a scenario in which her female employer competed with her to prepare breakfast for the male employer:

Two days ago, in the morning, he [the male employer] woke up. I asked him: "Sir, would you like some coffee?" [*in a sweet and respectful voice*]. He said, OK [*imitates the boss combing his hair without looking at her*]. So I made coffee, sliced a piece of cake. Then the wife followed me to the kitchen. She said: "Don't make coffee for my husband! Let him do it himself!" I said, "OK, Ma'am." Next morning, I said good morning, sir, and I went to the kitchen, pretending nothing. The husband again [*combing his hair without looking at her*]: "Lorna, make coffee for me!" The wife heard this—She woke up! Her hair was still messy, her eyes were still swollen . . . She ran to the kitchen to make coffee, slice cake and put them on the table!

Driven by feelings of insecurity, some female employers turn their relationship with domestic workers into a tacit competition of cooking skills, beauty, and other wifely qualifications. The husband, with or without acknowledgment, becomes the judge in this competition. Two other Filipina workers sense an attitude of rivalry and hostility from their female employers:

My employer doesn't like me to wear make-up. Once, we were going out somewhere, and she saw me wearing some lipstick. We were already in the car, you know? But then she went back into the house and she put on lipstick!

The wife always told me her husband didn't like my cooking and that my food didn't taste very good . . . But the husband would come into the kitchen and say he liked it! She's just jealous. [*Why?*] She feels insecure, I think.

"The wife's jealousy" is a narrative widely heard in the gossips of migrant workers. They also allege that the wife's revenge is a common cause for the dismissal of domestic workers. Maya, a twenty-something Filipina Chinese with fair complexion, told me a story in which tensions occurred between the employer couple because of the boss's friendly gestures toward Maya:

> One day the husband asked me when my birthday was, and he said, "Oh, that's next week, we should celebrate." The wife said, "I will buy a cake." But the next week the husband bought one, and she got angry. She said, "Why did you buy this? I said I'd buy one." They had a big fight and I didn't even get to eat the cake [*laughs*] . . . Another time, the wife was abroad for business. The husband, the children, and I went on a picnic. When the wife came back and found out about this, she got angry! So I don't talk to the husband anymore. I only talk to him when the wife is not at home.

In contrast to the frequent reference to "the wife's jealousy" among migrant women, only a few Taiwanese employers revealed personal details on this matter. Most of them described hypothetical situations or preferred to talk about secondhand stories of others. For example, Mrs. Chang, a homemaker in her early forties, explained how live-in domestic workers constitute a potential threat to marriages:

> A major problem with live-in maids is their relationship with men in the house. You have to be very careful about this. It's like planting a seed in your family. It's a challenge to your marriage. No matter if you hire Taiwanese or foreign maids, it's the same thing. There are tons of stories like that—the husband "picks up" the maid to be his concubine! A friend of mine hired a [Taiwanese] babysitter. She then hooked up with my friend's father! The father even wanted to give her a share of the family property! He's one of those chauvinist men. I still vividly remember what he said: "Even if a woman has a high education, the most basic thing is to know how to dress up and wear makeup. If you don't even know how to please men, I don't know how you are going to survive."

The scenario of "the husband picking up the maid to be his concubine" indicates a class-based polarization of femininity: the educated wife who is virtuous yet desexualized in contrast to the flirty maid who knows how to use her body to win the favor of men. The image of "flirty maid" is even more sexualized in the case of migrant women. Another employer, Honyin, a nurse in her early forties, talked about another story:

I have a relative. We were wondering why they don't hire a Filipina maid at home. They hire a Taiwanese *obasan* to clean the house and put the child in a babysitter's house. They have to go abroad for business from time to time. So you would think hiring a Filipina maid would be a lot more convenient for them, right? But the wife just doesn't want to. We later found out that her husband had an affair before. She's worried her husband may have something with the maid! My husband heard about this and said, "Then his taste is too low!"

"My taste is not that low" is an expression commonly used by Taiwanese husbands to mitigate their wives' worry in this matter. On the one hand, migrant women are viewed as "uncultivated" and "backward" so they are not socially capable of competing with Taiwanese wives. On the other hand, female employers are haunted by the racialized images of "tropical women": their plump bodies seem irresistible to male employers, and their intractable nature could make them active boss-seducers. Filipina maids, compared to other migrant groups, are particularly vulnerable to sexualized images because of their association with the West.[5] Ideas about the sex trade and "mail-order brides" from the Philippines fuel stereotypes about Filipinas as cunning, promiscuous women with low morals who may exchange sexual favors for money or the possibility of immigration (Constable 1997b).

Media stories with sensational titles like "Foreign maids ruined my family" further stimulate the anxieties of Taiwanese wives.[6] Wan-ru is a forty-year-old government worker whose husband runs a convenience store. She is concerned about her body shape after giving birth to two children, especially in comparison to the younger Filipina she hires. When I asked her if she harbors any worries about the dynamic between the worker and her husband, she answered:

Of course I do. Actually this is not a big deal, but sometimes, um, we women just can't help think about those things. Because I read all those reports on the newspaper, I was really much worried for a while . . .
What kinds of reports?
Usually, the female employer was not home, and the Filipina maid and the husband were alone at home, then something happened. Or, the husband harassed the maid, stuff like that. This was before. I was worried before.

So what did you do when you were worried before?

Nothing really. Just . . . this is nothing special . . . just be careful not to let the two of them alone at home, at least children have to be home. Well, situations like this rarely happen, very rarely. One evening I brought kids for shopping and my husband didn't want to go along. Then I was a bit concerned.

Then what did you do? Did you say anything to your husband?

NO. I tried to get him to go but he still didn't want to. Then I called him from outside and asked, "Is everything all right?" [*laughs embarrassedly*]. It's really nothing, but it's still better to have some caution, right?

Wan-ru repeated phrases like "It's really nothing," "no big deal," and "I was worried before" throughout the interview. Her tone demonstrated a deep worry, whether past or present. She nevertheless tried to downplay her concern to avoid the embarrassment of sounding like a "silly" woman who lacks sufficient confidence vis-à-vis a maid. Meanwhile, she and many other female employers cautiously keep an eye on the interactions between domestic workers and their husbands to safeguard their wifely status.

Male employers tend to keep some distance from migrant workers, especially in the presence of their wives. Some interviewees explained that, as *da-nan-ren* (big men),[7] they feel embarrassed in initiating conversations with a maid—not only because they want to avoid their wives' misunderstanding but also because they downgrade domestic service as a trivial matter and a feminized sphere. Migrant women also consciously minimize contacts with male employers to ease the wife's anxiety and to lower the risk of sexual harassment. As part of the deferential performance, domestic workers act to validate the distinction between maid and madam. At work, they dress down to mark themselves different form "the lady of the house" and they "desexualize" their bodies by wearing loose-hanging clothes that reveal no body shape. They avert eye contact and smiles while talking to male employers. And they artfully flatter female employers for their looks and fashion sense.

Another similar triangulated relationship occurs between the female employer, the migrant nanny, and the employer's children. Unlike male employers who can intentionally minimize interactions with the domestic workers, children develop emotional attachments to caregivers who play the role of substitute mothers. Female employers may confront stronger anxieties and take more active measures to maintain the boundary between mother and caregiver.

STRATIFYING MOTHERING LABOR

Taking care of children involves not only physical labor but also "labor of love." In addition to custodial childcare, such as bathing, feeding, and attending children, employers expect investment of emotional labor by their workers that includes affection, commitment, and love for the children. Some Taiwanese mothers complained to me about the quality of childcare provided by migrant nannies. For instance, Melissa described her Filipina worker: "The way she takes care of the baby is just feeding her, watching her, getting her to sleep . . . really just basic needs. Not like us, we want the children to learn; we want to play together with her; we want to be part of their lives. She doesn't enjoy this or understand this. She doesn't give more, you know, LOVE."

Melissa was discontent with the limited affection offered by the Filipina caregiver. However, if this Filipina did invest much love on Melissa's children, Melissa might have experienced other emotions like jealousy and deprivation. Mothers who hire childcare workers face an emotional dilemma: they want nannies to love their children so they can mitigate their anxieties about leaving their children with others; yet they feel uneasy if the children develop strong attachments to nannies or even confuse nannies for mothers. Mothers' solution is to stratify the division of mothering labor: how can they recruit childcare workers to be their *partners* in motherhood yet only *part* of it?

Full-time homemakers, mostly from wealthy households with ample time to spend with children, usually delegate household chores to domestic workers and perform most childcare labor themselves. In this way, the mother is able to restrict the role of the domestic worker to the "maid" and maintain a status distinction between herself and the worker. The status distinction is required by other family members as well. A Filipina employed by an affluent Taiwanese family reported: "My Ma'am told me this: Once I was playing with the children, and her sister-in-law said to her, 'Why do you let Theresa get close to your children? She's just a maid. I wouldn't let my maid get close to my children.'"

Unlike homemakers, working mothers hire caregivers for the purpose of childcare; they nevertheless maintain a hierarchical division of labor by distinguishing the "menial" and "spiritual" aspects of mothering work. Dorothy Roberts (1997) has argued that the split between spiritual housework and menial housework enables middle-class white women to transfer part of reproductive labor to colored or working-class women without disturbing the norm of female domesticity or the moral meaning of home. Cameron Macdonald (1998: 33) coins the term "manufacturing motherhood" to describe how mothers and caregivers create a symbolic order that redefines the menial/spiritual split of mothering work to magnify the significance of mothers at home and to minimize the presence of nannies.

"Spiritual motherhood" involves those mothering tasks considered by mothers to affirm their primary status and enhance their affective bonds with children; the nature of those tasks can vary by history, society, and household.[8] The jobs associated with dirt and disorder—such as changing babies' diapers and cleaning up messes in the playroom—are usually avoided by mothers and assigned to domestic workers. Mothers tend to take over the duties related to acculturating and socializing, such as reading books to children and assisting children with schoolwork. These jobs are rarely designated to migrant caregivers, who are considered culturally "unfit" or "disqualified" to fulfill them.

Bathing children and sleeping in the same room with them are two other examples of "mother-only" tasks that were cited regularly in my interviews. These tasks involve intimate contact and are considered the foundation of the mother-child bond. For parents of school-age children, picking them up after school is another daily ritual that is considered to hold much emotional value or symbolic significance. Chao-ju, a lawyer in her late thirties, manages to pick up her two children every afternoon despite her heavy workload. She would rather bring work home than lose this precious experience shared with her children:

> I pick them up after school every day. In my view, it takes only twenty minutes but the kids feel very different. Yeah, twenty minutes, after going home I just leave them to the maid . . . Before, it was the Filipina maid who picked them up, but once my daughter told me, "Mom, you only picked me up twice." I thought, wow, I have to do this myself. I have to find time to be with them.

The stratified division of mothering labor consists of a division of child-care duties and also a division of mothering styles. Margery Wolf (1972: 65–73) observed parenthood in Taiwan in the 1960s: parents believed that if they were "friends" to their children they would not be able to "teach" them. Therefore, parents, especially fathers, became physically and emotionally withdrawn from their children as they grew older. The primary principle of parenting at that time was *guan-jiao* (disciplining and teaching) because Taiwanese parents believed that the only way to encourage desired behavior was to severely punish undesired behaviors.

Younger generations of Taiwanese parents have developed new parenting practices that deviate from how they were brought up. As a result of the declining fertility rate, children, usually one or two in a household, receive focused attention from their parents.[9] The rise in household incomes also allows middle-class parents to afford expensive toys, overseas travel, and a variety of after-school classes for their children. Severe physical punishments have become legally and socially unacceptable. Neophyte parents seek guidance not only from their parents but also from books written by childcare experts, many translated from the English-speaking world. The parenting style of contemporary Taiwanese parents is gradually moving toward what Sharon Hays calls "intensive mothering," which views child rearing as "child centered, expert guided, emotionally absorbing, labor intensive and financially expensive" (1996: 69). However, the traditional idea of parenthood based on the disciplinary principle remains an important legacy in the current practices of parenthood.

As discussed in chapter 2, most Taiwanese employers favor Filipinas over Indonesians as childcare workers. In addition to their adequate education, Filipina caregivers are described by employers as being "affectionate" and "loving" to children. This image essentializes Filipina women as "naturally oriented" or "culturally suited" to care work. In contrast to "nurturing nannies," Taiwanese employers become "moralizing mothers" who are authority figures responsible for the moral education of children. Again, the rationale behind this division is related to the downgrading of ethnic others—migrant nannies are not sufficiently civilized to safeguard the moral development of Taiwanese children.

A Taiwanese mother described such stratified division of mothering labor in her household: "They [her children] know they can go to *yaya* (babysitter in Tagalog). Mama is harsh; may scold them and punish them."

For some Taiwanese mothers, such a division does not challenge their motherly status but helps transfer the mothering labor associated with physical or emotional intimacy to the caregivers, so they can maintain a distant image to enforce effective moral discipline on children. One such mother is Fang-ping, a store owner and a mother of two in her late thirties:

> My sister often makes fun of me: "When I see you go out, she is much more like a mother than you are. Your children hug her much tighter than they hug you." I said, "I don't mind. I don't like my children to hug me or even hold my hands. I don't feel jealous at all. It's better that your children don't stick to you all the time, so they can have some discipline."

The other reason why employed mothers are satisfied with their loving nannies is that they are too exhausted after work to perform emotional labor toward their children. Emily, a financial consultant in her late twenties, is grateful to her Filipina worker, who offers twenty-four-hour attentive care for Emily's one-year-old daughter. During our interview, Emily mentioned that the previous day she had moved her daughter to a new bed. Unfamiliar with the new environment, the baby cried a lot upon waking up. Emily went to tap her but she wanted only the nanny. I asked Emily if she felt upset about this, and she answered at ease:

> Not really. It has always been like this. It's good she likes to go to her. Because Filipinas are very loving. Perhaps because of transference, they treat the employers' children very well. Children are like an object for them. They really concentrate on them. It's impossible for us to do that. I don't feel jealous. I am exhausted and I need to work the next day.

Since full-time motherhood is unattainable for her, Emily views the transference of migrant workers' affection—from their own children left at home to the employers' children at work—as a validation of their quality childcare. Another Taiwanese mother gladly told me an episode in which the Filipina nanny misnamed her own child: "The Filipina maid is like my son's half-mother. Last year when she went home for vacation, she even called her son my son's name by accident!" It was an unfortunate accident resulting from the long-term separation between migrant mothers and their children, but it became a proof presented by the employer to evidence the provision of affective care by the Filipina nanny.

Nevertheless, some Taiwanese parents consider the kind of love offered by Filipina caretakers to be "excessive" and an interference with the appropriate discipline imposed on children. Wan-ru appreciates the affective care provided by the migrant nanny, but she is also concerned that the nanny may spoil her children rotten:

> Sometimes our kids ask for some snack, and we don't want to buy for her, because she is a bit overweight. But the Filipina maid would say to her, "Don't cry, Felix will buy that for you later." Sometimes she actually bought things out of her pocket. I said, "We don't want you to do this. We are trying to discipline her." She said, "It's OK. I love her." She really loves our kids a lot, but in this way they would grow up without discipline.

Taiwanese mothers also feel troubled when children favor the "nurturing nanny" over the "moralizing mother." As an employer described: "the maid lets her [the daughter] do whatever, so she is spoiled and she thinks we treat her bad." To enhance their symbolic maternal status, some Taiwanese mothers feel compelled to display affection to their children in excess of that offered by caregivers. For instance, Wan-ru expresses her love to her nine-year-old son and five-year-old daughter in a candid manner and seeks transparent emotional feedback to assure herself that the children still prefer her as mother to the Filipina caregiver:

> Honestly, I spend a lot of time at work, so when I talk to my children, I would say to them, "I love you a lot. I really love you." I want them to feel my love and they would answer, "Mommy, we love you, too." But my son, the older one, once told me, "Mommy, sister said she loves Felix more, she said she loves the Filipina maid more."
>
> *Your son told you your daughter said that?*
>
> Yeah, he said, "When you are not home, sister always said that. What she told you was a lie. She doesn't love you. She only loves Felix."
>
> *How did you feel when you heard that?*
>
> Of course I felt kind of bad. How come she loves Felix more? But I didn't believe it. So I asked my daughter again. She's such a smarty. When I asked her, she didn't admit it. She said there was never anything like what her brother told me. So I on purpose asked her in front of the Filipina maid: "Whom do you love more?" Then my daughter said, "Oh, I love you both, both I love."

The division of mothering labor between harsh mothers and loving nannies may turn the other way around in some households. Some prefer to be warm and loving mother figures, delegating the harsh, disciplinary role to migrant caregivers. Two employers mentioned instances in which mothers requested migrant workers to enforce discipline on children yet reserved the role of "loving mommy" for themselves:

> I spoil my children too much. I cannot enforce discipline on them . . . For example, every night, the children cry and don't want to go to bed. How do I deal with them? I just stand aside and I let the auntie [the Filipina worker] get them to bed. And guess what? They go to bed obediently! She can play the poker face, the harsh person. When the children are naughty, I just said to them, "I don't mind you at all. The auntie is coming." Then they got scared.

> Mothers usually have their maids do more difficult jobs. By "difficult" I mean being the bad guy. You know, children can be very annoying sometimes. They don't listen to you and don't take anything you give them. I saw some mothers choose not to get involved during these situations and let their Filipina maids take over. So the Filipina maid becomes the bad person and the mother can maintain a better relationship with her children.

Employers also maintain a stratified division of motherhood with their caregivers by distinguishing their different time spans of mothering labor. Mothers who hire live-out caregivers can mark the beginning of family time with the physical departure of the caregivers (Macdonald 1998: 35). Taiwanese employers who hire live-in migrant workers cannot draw a clear-cut boundary for the caregiver's "time out." Some employers specify to their caregivers when they will "take over" the duty of childcare when they return home after work. Employers also try to make good use of Sundays, the rest day for migrant workers, as their family "quality time" to build attachments with their children.

In addition, Taiwanese mothers distinguish their permanent motherhood from the substitute motherhood by emphasizing migrant caregivers' temporary presence. The government stipulates that a migrant worker's contract cannot be renewed past three years; a subsequent reentry into Taiwan was not allowed until 2002. Although this policy burdens employers with additional costs in training and recruiting new workers, some mothers nevertheless see it as a positive measure. Constant turnover severs a child's attachment to a particular nanny, thus consolidating the primary tie between parent and child. For instance, Hon-yin was confident that the intervention of migrant caregivers would not challenge her maternal bonds with her child, since the worker's stay is inevitably temporary in Taiwan and in her family:

> Once we went to a class about improving the relationship between children and parents. The Filipina maid went together with us, too. Then my son went to sit on her lap, not mine. Other mothers saw this and said to me, "Aren't you worried that the child likes to be with her rather than you?" I said, "It's all right. She's only temporary in our lives. She's here at most three years, but I will be his mother forever."

Several interviewed mothers quoted the expression "Blood is thicker than water" to assure me, and themselves, that their motherly status is secure from encroachment from migrant caregivers. They view the parent-child bond as biologically given and sealed by common culture and language. For instance, Jessica's four-year-old son sometimes calls the Filipina caregiver "mama." Unlike some mothers who are troubled by this, Jessica showed total confidence in the mother-child bond, given her son's attachment to the caregiver: "I am confident that my status won't be shaken. Nobody can replace me. When children are small, they call everyone mama. When they grow up, they will change their definition of mothers. And the gap in language between [the child and the maid] will grow bigger in the future."

Mothers like Jessica apply the narrative of ethnic differences to mark the mother-caregiver boundary. To enact such "ethnicized motherhood," they highlight some components of mothering labor that are based on common culture and language and therefore reserved for mothers only. Reading books and telling stories to children are significant examples. Chao-ju maintains a bedtime routine of story telling—something "the auntie is unable to do"—to win the favor of her children. She also argues, "Only I could be their friend. I can *communicate* with them. This is something other women cannot do." In some extreme cases, mothers go as far as to "racialize" motherhood. One Indonesian worker, Rocha, told me that her employer's three-year-old child was quite attached to her. The mother was upset, saying to the child: "You cannot like Auntie Rocha. She's different.

She's a black person. Her skin color is different from ours." By using such racialized rhetorical devices, the mother marks her "fundamental" motherly status in distinction from the temporary passage of foreign substitutes.

ANXIETIES OF MOTHERS-IN-LAW

Several Taiwanese women went through a "revolution" to win the consent of mothers-in-law for hiring domestic help. They have to convince their mothers-in-law that they are not irresponsible mothers or lazy wives. After all, most elder Taiwanese women were full-time homemakers and mothers at the age of their daughters-in-law. Wan-ru and her husband and children share a two-flat apartment with the husband's parents and unmarried siblings. The first time she hired a migrant domestic, she brought the worker to meet her mother-in-law right after the worker's arrival. When I asked Wan-ru why she did so, she replied:

> Well, you have to keep her [the mother-in-law] informed. You have to let her understand that you hire a maid to help, not because you want to be a *shao-nai-nai* [young mistress of the house]. My mother-in-law had a misunderstanding like this in the beginning. She would say, wow, someone else has done everything for you; you have no work to do; how lucky you are.

Some women employers continue doing some portion of housework to affirm the ideal of domesticity and to avoid negative judgments imposed by their mothers-in-law. Rowena, a Filipina domestic worker, observed the struggle of her employer, a successful coffee shop owner who nonetheless remained a powerless daughter-in-law in her patriarchal extended family. With great sympathy, Rowena described her employer:

> My employer works hard during the day, but she still works very hard after she gets home! I don't understand. I wouldn't if I were her! If you've worked hard all day, you should rest when you get home . . . When I complained to her I had too much work to do, she told me there was nothing she could do about it. She belongs to another family. She always needed to ask for [the mother-in-law's] permission to do anything.

Behind the objections of mothers-in-law resides their fear of being "replaced" by migrant domestic workers. Pei-chi and her husband, both in their forties, own and manage a small company that produces and exports computer chips. The husband's mother moved from the province to live with them in Taipei and helped raise her three grandchildren. Five years ago Pei-chi and her husband decided to hire a Filipina worker to do household chores so the mother-in-law could reduce her workload and focus on childcare. Pei-chi's mother-in-law, however, expressed no relief but anxiety, as Pei-chi recounted:

> The first time the Filipina maid moved in, my mother-in-law was really, really upset. She felt that we had deprived her rights of working . . .
> *Why does she think housework is her "right"?*
> Because she gave birth to seven children. Raising children and doing housework are not only her responsibilities but also her only achievement. She values herself solely based on that. So in the beginning, she was wondering if we didn't want her anymore, if we wanted to kick her out, if she still had any "surplus value." We had to communicate with her again and again, and finally we decided to save one job for her—cooking [*laughs*]!

Because Pei-chi's mother-in-law has been a full-time homemaker throughout her life, domestic labor is her domain of mastery and the foundation of her identity. She interpreted the hiring of a migrant domestic worker as an expression of doubt about her professional skills and a diminishment of her contribution to the family. She was also worried that she would become "useless" and abandoned by her son after her work was transferred to the migrant worker. Such anxiety is not a personal matter but a structural problem faced by a generation of mothers-in-law. The social norm of three-generation cohabitation has attenuated, and the moral ideal of filial piety can no longer guarantee paybacks from children. Under these circumstances parents "strive to make themselves dependable sources in order to ensure a measure of security" (Gallin 1994: 138).[10]

Frequently, a mother-in-law feels threatened by the arrival of a "professional" domestic worker on her territory. Because older Taiwanese in general speak little English, the language barrier further exacerbates a feeling of "losing control" among mothers-in-law vis-à-vis Filipina workers. Said Jessica of her mother-in-law: "She feels lost in her life. Her life has no more goals. All her jobs have been taken away by the Filipina maid, and the maid does even a better job than she did . . . To her, everything is out of her control now. And she cannot even control the Filipina maid because she doesn't speak English!"

A daughter-in-law who hires a migrant worker may have lightened her physical workload, but she has often taken on the additional emotional labor of soothing her mother-in-law's tensions and anxieties. One common strategy among female employers is to confirm the mother-in-law's authority. For example, they intentionally have their mothers-in-law release wages to migrant workers even though the money is actually from young couples. They also manipulate translations to minimize tensions between mothers-in-law and migrant workers. Jessica's mother-in-law felt so anxious about the worker's presence that she tried to outperform the worker around the house, especially in cooking, a domestic duty with considerable cultural and affective significances. One day, the mother-in-law made an unusual and complicated dish for the family. Jessica deciphered the message behind this dish making:

> I have been married into this family for years, and I never saw her cook that dish! She did this on purpose. It's a performance. [*Performance for whom?*] For the Filipina maid! She was trying to tell the maid: See, it's not that easy to take over my job. This is my territory. I can do a lot of things you cannot. So don't think that you can replace me.

Jessica took the opportunity to translate the worker's comments on that dish in a way that she knew would mitigate her mother-in-law's anxieties. By exaggerating the worker's compliments on the mother-in-law's cooking skills, she elevated the status of the mother-in-law beyond the roles of maid and cook: "I tried to sugarcoat the words of the Filipina maid when I translated them. I said, 'Mama, the maid said it's delicious. Chinese food becomes like magic at your hands. You can compete with those chefs in five star restaurants!' Then my mother-in-law was happy, and she put more food on the plate of the maid!"

The loss of status these mothers-in-law fear is no small thing. Indeed, the subordination of daughters-in-law and the authority of mothers-in-law have affected the quality of life for generations of Taiwanese women. In 1905, young adult women in Taiwan had a high rate of suicide compared to senior women, who had a relatively low suicide rate, coinciding with the empowered status (Wolf 1975). However, in 1984 the suicide rate for young women significantly dropped while the tendency for a woman to commit a suicide increased with age (Hu 1995). The suicidal tendency among elder women is partly explained by the decline in family status and economic security. Women of this generation have been adversely affected by the transformation of gender relations and intergenerational dynamics. As young adults, they sacrificed career achievement for the welfare of family. All the while, they looked forward to enjoying a secure and easy old age, as a Chinese proverb says: "A daughter-in-law must suffer to become a mother-in-law" (*xi-fu-ao-cheng-po*). But after surviving their own hardships as daughters-in-law, they are not accorded the authority their mothers-in-law received in the past.

Facing modern daughters-in-law who seek self-realization and autonomy as wage earners, mothers-in-law struggle to enhance their status in the family, even by contributing their kin labor (housework and childcare) in exchange for economic security and social support. In this cultural and social context, they perceive the employment of live-in migrant domestic workers as not only usurping their role in the domestic domain but also threatening their well-being, which is dependent on the support of their sons.[11] Their anxieties indicate the transforming position and identity related to (grand) motherhood, which once glorified their sacrifices to their families but no longer secures their welfare in old age.

MAKING BOUNDARIES RIGID

Taiwanese women hire migrant women to negotiate their gendered duties as mother, wife, and daughter-in-law. By transferring a great chunk of domestic labor to migrant surrogates, they are able to loosen the time bind between work and family, to avoid the gender battle with their husbands over housework, and to minimize the duty of serving their mothers-in-law. To some degree, domestic employment has "[turned] gender inequality into class inequality" (Wrigley 1995: 142), but gender inequality never disappears by being replaced with class inequality. Women employers remain burdened by the gendered norms of domesticity, motherhood, and filial piety.

The social meanings of domestic labor are strongly related to the cultural construction of womanhood. Previous scholarship has demonstrated that domestic employment is a critical terrain for the construction of polarized versions of womanhood in light of class divisions (Ozyegin 2000; Palmer 1989). I further emphasize that such distinction is not given but requires physical enactment and constant confirmation in everyday family life. Female employers deliberate as to what duties are socially appropriate to transfer to market surrogates without harming their status in the family. They divide childcare duties with their caregivers in a hierarchical order (spiritual versus menial), they attach different mothering styles to their caregivers (loving versus disciplining), and they privilege their permanent motherhood over the temporary substitute motherhood (blood- and culture-based versus contract-based).

When female employers attempt to carve out a rigid boundary between maid and madam, they are simultaneously participating in the construction of stratified womanhood and the imagining of class and ethnic differences. Taiwanese wives, who are worried about the potential affairs between husbands and maids, attach the threat of "primitive seduction" to migrant women, who are considered sexually aggressive and morally degraded. Also, they portray migrant caregivers as "naturally affectionate but culturally backward," therefore unqualified to compete with the "elegant madam" and "disciplinary mother."

When the society continues to define domestic labor as women's duties, a female employer tends to treat the worker as "an extension of the more menial part of herself rather than an autonomous employee" (Rollins 1985: 183). She transfers to the surrogate not only the work but also the social expectations placed on women associated with domestic labor. In other words, female employers expect market surrogates to facilitate their achievement of wifely, motherly, and pious duties. As it is, they often make requests that are unreasonable by the standards stipulated in employment contracts and ignore the reality that the worker's labor performance is not bound by moral norms tied to emotional commitment or family responsibility. These women-managers, whether consciously or not, are reproducing a relationship of domination and exploitation over other women, one that is ironically similar to the oppressive link between mother-in-law and daughter-in-law—the very dynamic that employers are themselves seeking to avoid.

Suna and I were sitting on the floor of her bedroom, each wearing a pair of the pajamas she bought in a night market in Taipei. She had just returned home, to a small village in East Java, for one week. I asked her how she had found village life after living in Taiwan for three years. She shook her head and started delivering her complaints: "The road is muddy, hard to walk on. The house is dark, not much light." She pointed at the dim light bulb hung on the beams of the old, ceiling-free roof and continued: "I cannot go out in the evening. I have to come home before 8 p.m., or my dad would get angry. My neighbors would say, 'This girl is no good.' My dad doesn't allow me to wear some clothes I bought in Taiwan [sleeveless shirts and tight jeans]. The life in Taiwan is different. I could hang out with friends until 10 p.m. on Sundays." The last thing she mentioned struck me in particular: "Things are expensive here." "How come?" I couldn't believe how bad her math was. Suna smiled at my confusion and said in a crisp voice: "Because I made more money in Taiwan. Here, I earn nothing."

While chatting with me, Suna was charging the battery for her cell phone, an updated Nokia model she bought in Taipei with more than half of her monthly wage. From time to time, her friends in Taiwan sent messages to complain about the hardship or boredom at work, and her boyfriend, also a migrant worker employed in a factory in Malaysia, called her daily. Suna spotted his picture among dozens of "seeking-friends" advertisements in a magazine that targets Indonesian overseas workers. She called him on his cell phone and a long-distance romance ensued. After one year of courting, they are discussing the prospect of marriage upon his return despite that they have never met each other.

Electricity, paved roads, unveiled clothing, mobile phones—these are markers of an urban and modern lifestyle. They lighten the overseas tour of migrant workers, which is simultaneously a dark course of hardship and isolation. This chapter investigates why migrant women work abroad, a decision that most Filipina and Indonesian migrants made on their own. Some even persisted against the objection of their husbands or parents. Their moves are not an unavoidable consequence between the "push" of domestic poverty and the "pull" of overseas wealth. Their migration decisions are rather propelled by "intersecting circumstances of vulnerability" (Yea 2005) that may include financial distress, family dissolution, and lack of direction and choice in the homeland. However, migrant women should not be viewed as merely victims or commodities in international labor trafficking. They assert meanings and exercise agency against the imposed structural constraints. Their overseas journey is a form of "cross-border gambling" (Aguilar 1999) that involves as many risks as opportunities to satisfy personal desires and achieve self-transformation. In addition to financial gains, migrant women go abroad to search for autonomy and to escape domestic constraints, and they look for a ticket to an adventure in global modernity.

This chapter also examines the patriarchal bargaining of migrant domestic workers with regard to marriage and motherhood, two major institutions that characterize the gendered division of reproductive labor (Tung 1999). To enter the debates about the extent and duration of women's empowerment resulting from migration (Pessar 1999), I argue that the feminization of domestic labor enables women's emancipation and concomitantly sustains gender subordination in the context of global migration. While maintaining others' families overseas, migrant women face difficulties in their own fulfillment of domesticity and motherhood. Migrant mothers become household breadwinners at the cost of detaching from their husbands and children back home. Single migrant women serve as dutiful daughters to their original families while having troubles in building their own families. I will demonstrate how these women reconstitute the meanings and practices of domesticity and motherhood to reconcile these predicaments in the sojourn of migration.

MONEY AND MODERNITY

When I asked, "Why did you decide to work overseas?" nine out of ten migrant workers would give me the same answer without a second's hesitation: "Earning money! There are no jobs back home!" Economic incentives are undoubtedly the major driving force behind the cross-country moves of most workers. Both Indonesia and the Philippines suffer from a shortage of job opportunities and rising unemployment rates. The ranks of the unemployed in the Philippines have risen since the early 1980s (Abella 1993), and the number in April 2004 was as high as 13.7 percent.[1] The unemployment rate in Indonesia was 4.7 percent before the financial crisis in 1997, and it quickly rose to 8.1 percent in 2001.[2] And the unemployment rate among women is significantly higher (Nayyar 1997: 18).

Trina moved to Manila after finishing high school in her hometown in Negros; she had worked in various factories since then. The unstable economy in the Philippines and frequent shutdowns of local industries pushed her to move farther for more stable and lucrative jobs overseas: "Every two or three years, the factory shut down. I had no work for a few months before the next one started. How could I live like this? So I applied to work in Singapore when I was twenty-eight years old."

Layoffs and unemployment have also changed the fate of many middle-class professionals in the Philippines. When I asked Rosario, a college graduate and a mother of two in her forties, about her previous occupation in the Philippines, she looked embarrassed and answered softly: "It's a shame to say. I worked in a bank. I worked there for twelve years. The salary was only three thousand pesos a month, but it was OK for living in the province. The bank was closed seven years ago. It's very difficult to find a job if you are from a bankrupt company. So I didn't have a choice. I had to work abroad."

The statement "there are no jobs" refers to the rising unemployment rate in home countries; it also implies that there are no "good" jobs that provide a sufficient and stable salary. In the Philippines, real wages have deteriorated since the mid-1980s with the further devaluation of the peso after the implementation of economic liberalization (Basch et al. 1994). Declining household incomes, compared with rising living expenses in urban areas, creates difficulties in making ends meet. Even middle-class status no longer guarantees a secure and comfortable life. The steady depreciation in the exchange rates of local currency has made overseas wages even more attractive.

Many migrants decide to work overseas not for urgent economic needs but to prepare for their children's future welfare. This is a significant factor for Indonesian mothers who were farmers or fishers in rural areas. For example, Naya is a thirty-one-year-old mother of two young children who used to help her husband with fishing in a Javanese village. She told me why she decided to work abroad: "I was afraid of going abroad. [I heard] some people have bad employers; they got beaten up. But I think, I am still young; I would be too old to work in a few years. So I have to make more money now. I want to save it so my children could study in college. I want them to study high, so I am not afraid anymore."

Despite the primacy of economic incentives in most narratives of migrants, wage disparity between the sending and receiving countries is a necessary rather than a sufficient condition for their decisions of migration (Massey et al. 1998: 175). Neither Indonesia nor the Philippines is the poorest country in Asia, but each supplies a great number of migrants in this region. Statistics also demonstrate that migratory flows in the Philippines do not come from the poorest areas but from more developed regions.[3] These facts indicate that financial pressure and economic deprivation are mediated by other factors, including the social construction of achievement and adventure, and the postcolonial, global imagination of modernity.

When I was visiting an Indonesian migrant in her hometown, she was happy to see me, yet commented, "You Taiwanese go abroad to play. We Indonesians go abroad to work." The opportunity of working abroad, however, contains some attractions in the senses of adventure and exploration for those who might never otherwise be able to travel overseas. I met Eka, a single Indonesian woman in her early thirties, when she worked in Taiwan as a domestic worker. Before this journey, she had traveled to South Korea for factory work when she was in her early twenties. At that time, she was thrilled at going abroad for the first time in her life: "I wanted to experience! I wanted to take the plane, not to make money. I'd like to see snow, so I chose Korea." When talking about her first travel by plane a decade ago, she still remembered the excitement vividly—her voiced raised and her eyes brightened—"I was very very happy—I could fly!"

Many migrant women perceive the overseas journey as an odyssey to the material affluence and sexual liberation in advanced economies and modern societies. Claudia, a single Filipina in her early thirties who has a college degree in pharmacy, described, in a group discussion, her motives for working overseas beyond economic:

> I think there is also other . . . how to say . . . compensations people receive when they are in Taiwan. If you are in the Philippines, you are a

mother, a plain housewife only. This will not happen—going to the disco every Sunday and having your cellular phone! [*Everybody laughs*]. Yes! That's true! Joking, eating in McDonald every Sunday—can you do that in the Philippines? [*Others shake their heads*]. Yes, this is the difference. We are wearing jewelry, short skirts—you cannot wear that in the Philippines! In my hometown, people are very conservative. If I wear [clothes] like that, people will stare at me! That's why we want to stay abroad because of these compensations!

The decision to migrate often starts as curiosity or envy toward others' experiences of working abroad: "There are already many people abroad. I want to experience that too." The adventurous experiences of working abroad, whether they conform to their previous expectations or not, validate the distinctive status of migrant workers from fellow villagers. One Sunday in the church, Johna mentioned that her employers were going to the United States for two months for a training program. They were considering whether to bring her along or to let her take a vacation in the Philippines. Another Filipina, Adora, gave her the following advice:

Adora: Don't go to the Philippines! You should go to America with them!

PCL: But even if she goes to the U.S., she will probably just stay home all the time . . .

Adora: It doesn't matter! Even if you only go to the airport, you still go to America! Then when you go home, you can tell people you've been to America! [*Turned to explain to me*] Because people in the Philippines have few chances to go abroad, so you are proud you have been abroad!

PCL: How about coming to Taiwan? You also feel proud about it?

Adora: Yes, the same. That is why we like to take pictures here. Then you can tell people you go abroad, not by mouth [but] by pictures! So Johna, remember to take pictures in the airport of Los Angeles!

Every Sunday, in tourist spots such as Chiang Kai-shek's memorial park or even simply in the corridor of a shopping mall, migrant workers, women in particular, are found posing for photographs. My informants laughed at my curiosity when I asked them why they were taking so many pictures in Taiwan: "For the memory!" "To let my sweetheart see my fair skin!" These photos selectively record their life experiences abroad, frozen into snapshots of happy tourists wearing fashionable outfits in metropolitan scenes. Their aspiration for light skin signifies a longing for an urban, middle-class notion of femininity. A Filipina migrant worker interviewed by Lin Hsiu-li (2000: 43–44) reported that her cousin convinced her to work in Taiwan for the extra benefit that her skin would become lighter and she would look younger. For Southeast Asian migrant women, fair skin, as well as the life overseas, symbolizes a desired identity associated with affluence, femininity, and modernity.

I met Rocita in a province that is a three-hour bus ride from Manila. She worked in Taiwan for one year but failed to renew her contract, getting almost nothing after paying placement fees and loan interest. Her husband used to work in Palau as an undocumented construction worker but returned after being injured at work. Her daughter, who is currently working in Taiwan as a factory worker, earns the family's entire income. At the end of our interview, I asked Rocita if I could take a picture of her. She went straight to her cousin's house, a cement house that had been renovated with the money earned by her cousin working abroad. I asked her, "Why not in front of your house?" She was embarrassed, saying, "My house? It's crappy! I will let you take the picture next time after my daughter sends money home and we build a new one!"

The dream of overseas exploration has figured in Rocita's family for a long time and has traveled farther than Taiwan. Rocita's father, who gained U.S. citizenship while serving in the U.S. Navy, lives in California now.[4] The dream of becoming U.S. citizens through family reunification is something Rocita expects to achieve with resources from her daughter's employment in Taiwan. She smilingly told me, "We have no money for the air tickets to America. So we have to work abroad to earn money for air tickets first!"

Rocita's family members have been seeking a better life by taking multiple routes to different destinations. Some stories had a happy ending and some failed. But they all share a similar dream of going abroad that is rooted in the cultural and historical context of the Philippines. Raul Pertierra (1992) studied the cultural construct of "the good life" (naragsak a panagbiag) in the Ilocano provinces of northern Luzon, a major source of out-migration in the Philippines since the beginning of this century. He argues that the main incentive for migration is not immediate economic gains but a general interest in maintaining a quality of life, including

FIGURE 3. *A renovated house owned by a migrant worker (on the right)*
in great contrast to the neighbor's old house, East Java

benefits that are difficult to quantify such as prestige, adventure, and
fulfillment. Locals romanticize foreign countries as "promised lands,"
while viewing the local community as backward and undesirable.

Such a cultural construct is also cultivated by schooling in the Philippines. According to James Young (1980), the general content of local
curricula under the influence of the American colonizer does not place a
high value on agricultural work in a subsistence economy and instead favors administrative and technical skills more appropriate to an industrial-
urban economy. Education cultivates in students a preference for fleeing
from the local community by imagining a life of plenty in foreign countries, especially in the colonial motherland, the United States.

Global popular culture, made possible by electronic mass media, is
another mechanism that shapes the imagining of global modernity among
migrant workers. The pop music industry in Taiwan has gained increasing
influence in the Asian market. For example, F4, a Mandarin pop-singing
band composed of four handsome young men, has attracted a pan-Asian
audience. They sold 3.5 million albums—an impressive record in a region

where pirated CDS are the norm (Seno 2003). In 2003, fans in Manila paid up to US$200 to see F4's live concert; even the Philippine president Gloria Arroyo received this boy band in person. When I was traveling in Indonesia, I saw F4 posters, T-shirts, and pirated DVDS of their TV drama sold everywhere, from department stores in Jakarta to local markets in small villages.

Indonesian migrants I met in Taiwan joked that they came here to see their idols. Their prior images of Taiwan were based on televised representation: "I saw Taiwan on TV and it looked very beautiful." Friends and neighbors asked them upon their return: "Did you see F4 in Taiwan?" The singing band and TV drama symbolize the influence of globalized mediascapes (Appadurai 1996) that shape an aspiration for particular looks and lifestyles associated with the cultural constructs of beauty and comfort among the Indonesian audience.[5] In such cultural context, the route of migration not only leads to income upgrading but also becomes a pilgrimage to global modernity.

In sum, colonial history and global mass media constitute the cultural imagery of "the good life" underpinning the decisions to work overseas among Filipino and Indonesian migrants. The forces of media and market have fueled consumerism throughout the world and increased the craving for new commodities and spectacles (Appadurai 1996: 40). In contrast to the impoverished economy, agricultural lifestyle, and tradition-bound villages, migrant women go overseas in the hope of experiencing the "modern" and "desirable"—the consumption of material goods, the maintenance of fair skin, and the enjoyment of a metropolitan lifestyle.

FROM HOUSEWIVES TO MAID BREADWINNERS

Naomi is in her mid-thirties but looks much younger with her Levis jeans and white T-shirt. I would not have guessed that she has a two-year-old son without her telling. Naomi and her husband have a chicken farm in the province of Batangas, three hours by bus from Manila. The business is okay but the household income seems modest when one considers the son's future education. Hence, Naomi decided to apply for jobs overseas, a decision she made on her own: "I decided [to go abroad]. My husband said okay. He will take care of our son with his parents. I have always wanted to work abroad when I was younger anyway." Naomi quit college and got married at the age of eighteen, and now she perceived working abroad as a belated chance to explore the world: "I want to see a different world, because before I never had a chance to see different things. You know, I got married too early. Now I can do many things I cannot do in the Philippines."

Forty percent of Filipinas in this study, including Naomi, are married women with husbands and children (twenty-two out of fifty-eight). Many of them were full-time homemakers in the Philippines (fourteen out of thirty-three, including married and recently separated ones). They personified the ideal Filipino family, which consists of a male breadwinner and a female housekeeper. Housework and childcare are predominantly considered women's duties (Go 1993). The male-centered family relations, inscribed by the cultural heritages of the Spanish and American colonial regimes, remain influential today (Illo 1995).

Paradoxically, the patriarchal logic that governs an unequal division of household labor creates a niche for Filipina women in the global labor market. Women even hold more advantages over their husbands in seeking jobs overseas. Most Filipino families in my study went through a similar migration pattern: during the 1980s the husband left the wife and children at home to work in the Middle East. In the 1990s it became the wife's turn to work abroad and the husband stayed in the Philippines with the children. This transition followed the decline of male-oriented construction and manufacturing jobs in the Middle East during and after the Gulf War, in contrast to the growing demands for domestic workers in other host countries (Tarcoll 1996).

Roland Tolentino (1996: 58) describes this transition for Filipina domestic workers: "unpaid home labor in the domestic sphere becomes paid labor in international spaces." When these women shift their status from housewives to domestic workers, they perform similar duties but in distinct settings. Their domestic labor, which was compensated by nothing but emotional value, is now paid for in cash when performed overseas. Anamaria, a homemaker in the Philippines, has a husband who worked in Taiwan before. Upon his return she decisively told him: "It's my turn now. I want to go to Taiwan. I want to experience Taiwan." She points out the similarities and differences between her former work and her new job of cleaning and cooking for a Taiwanese family: "Working here is the same as working in my house in the Philippines," followed by a naughty smile, "but I get paid here!"

It is true that many migrant domestic workers suffer from endless requests from employers and long working hours in a live-in employment situation. But for women who were full-time employees in the Philippines, the workload in a waged domestic job may be less intense than their double shifts at home. Said Vanessa, a former bookstore supervisor:

> In the Philippines, I am exhausted. I wake up early. I cook. I wash. When my children come home after school, I am still working. They heat the food I cook in the morning. Here, [the work is] easy. In the afternoon, I finish my work, I can just rest, watch HBO like this [*crosses her legs and puts her feet on the table*]. So look at me [*points at her body*], I have gained ten pounds in the last six months!

Vanessa and many other migrant women came to Taiwan on their own, separated from their husbands and children at home. Their migration pattern is different from the prevalent male-headed migration pattern, in which men's family authority and access to migrant networks favor husbands' initial departure. Women workers in Taiwan and other Asian countries emigrate alone because contract-based employment excludes the options of permanent settlement and family reunification. Such a feminized migration pattern channels migrant homemakers to transit from the position of unpaid homemaker to that of waged domestic worker, making them the primary breadwinners in their transnational families.

The feminization of overseas domestic employment offers migrant women an opportunity to seek financial gains as well as social emancipation. Many married women made their migration decisions independently from their husbands. They seize migration as an opportunity to expand their life horizons and achieve economic independence, challenging traditional domestic roles assigned to women. During a focus-group discussion, when I asked the participants why they decided to work abroad, a Filipina exclaimed: "To divorce my husband for a while!" Laughter and nodding followed throughout the room.

According to Rhacel Parreñas (2001: 64), migration for some women is not just a "strategy of family maintenance" but a "covert strategy to relieve women of burdens in the family." Married women seek overseas employment to avoid unpaid household burdens at home and to achieve independence through market wages. This rationale is especially applied to those who were homemakers in their home countries. Jenny, a former Filipina homemaker in her late forties, emphasized the feeling of empowerment based on financial autonomy from her husband: "I want to make my own money. I only got money from my husband. I want to have my own money and then I can buy whatever I want. I can give my children allowances. I can go eat outside. That is my hobby."

Some Indonesian migrants go abroad to escape unhappy arranged marriages. Working overseas provides them with some liberation and freedom in lieu of the constraints at home. Utami, an Indonesian migrant in her mid-twenties, got married to a village fellow after she returned home from a four-year employment in Singapore. Her mother pushed her to enter this marriage, worrying that she would become too old to marry (she was then twenty years old). After one year of married life filled with disputes, Utami applied for a job in Taiwan. During her three years of working in Taiwan, she did not make any phone calls or write any letters to her husband. Utami stated, "I don't like him at all. I got married only because of my mother." In Taiwan, she developed a romantic relationship with a Thai male worker. Upon her return home, her primary concern was how to file a divorce without the objection of her husband, who seemed to prey on the savings she had accumulated by working overseas.

When migrant women cross borders to work, they simultaneously transcend the traditional gender boundary. Only a few Indonesians in this study were full-time homemakers before going abroad. After their children grew older, many married women helped their husbands with farming or took a casual job such as market vendor or sales clerk. However, the norm of masculine breadwinning remains rooted in Indonesia. A husband disapproves of his wife's emigration not only for reasons of her deviation from the assumed domestic role but also to object the implication that he fails in the breadwinning duty. Tiwi, a thirty-four-year-old Indonesian mother, left her family for a caregiver job in Taiwan. She described the reaction of her farmer husband toward her working overseas:

When people ask my husband where I am, he simply says, "My wife is gone." He's not happy with me working outside. He wants me to stay home, taking care of children and the family. He said to me, "You go, whatever." But in his heart, he thinks not. He said, "If I told you not to go, you would ask me for a lot of money. But I don't have money." If people ask him where his wife is and he answers "making money," he would lose face. [People would wonder] "How come is your wife making money? Can't you make money?"

People in the Philippines use the terms "houseband" and "huswife" to mock migrant workers' husbands who stay home and take over domestic tasks. They become targets of ridicule when doing "feminine" chores in public: in Alicia Pignol's study (2001: 41), a Filipino househusband was sweeping the yard and some female students passing by shouted at him, "You will grow breasts!" Nevertheless, the structural shift of gender roles offers no guarantee that the "domesticated" husbands will take over household duties. To preserve a masculine image, some husbands seek employment elsewhere to avoid the domestic burdens passed over from migrant wives (Parreñas 2005).[6] Migrant women frequently complain that their husbands have taken over a bare minimum of housework and performed it poorly, especially in the matter of household budgeting. Some of their husbands drink or gamble to excess when they are no longer in charge of the daily duty of breadwinning. In addition, another major concern troubles the mind of many migrant women, as shown in this conversation I had with three Filipinas:

> *Helen:* You remember Lisa? She went home for a vacation and came back again. She caught her husband with another wife [*everybody sighs*].
>
> *Claudia:* Many families are into troubles when one of them works abroad. Because the wife works abroad, she sends a lot of money to the husband. Everyday is like his birthday. Then the man has a concubine and the woman has a relationship abroad. Because they feel lonely!
>
> *Olivia:* When the wife is not there, the husband finds himself so miserable, and he thinks I earn less than my wife, so he finds another woman!

The Philippine media coined the term "Saudi Syndrome" to describe the "haunting" fear of Filipino workers employed in the Middle East about their wives' infidelity at home (Arcinas et al. 1986, cited in Margold 1995). Male absence not only endangers the worker's control over his wife's sexuality but also impedes the reproduction of children. Overseas workers therefore pressure their wives into pregnancy when they return for vacation (Margold 1995: 282). Migrant women harbor similar worries about their husbands left at home. The likelihood that a migrant's husband will have an affair is considered greater than the likelihood that a migrant's

FIGURE 4. *The husband of an overseas domestic worker taking care of their child in an East Java village*

wife will. In the words of Claudia and Olivia, a "domesticated" husband feels "inferior" and "miserable" because his masculinity is "endangered" by a wife who makes more money than he does. Worst of all, the husband's infidelity often leads to offspring out of wedlock who will compete for the already limited financial resources in the household.

I interviewed Linda and her husband in a Philippine province where they lived. The husband used to work in Hong Kong as a construction worker but had been unemployed since his return. Linda then went to Taiwan as a domestic worker for two years. At the time of interview, the family income was earned exclusively by Linda, who sold snacks at street corners. As Linda's savings were being rapidly dissipated by supporting three children enrolled in expensive private schools, one of the parents would soon have to work abroad again. When I asked Linda about their future plans, she answered with uncertainty and hesitation:

> I don't know. He [her husband] said just stay home and sell *halo-halo* [a street dessert] again. He said he will go, because Filipino men want to

show they're macho macho [*laughs*]. I like life in Taiwan, because so much money. My employer said to me, your husband is very lucky, because you are doing everything. I sent all my money to the family. I fed four mouths, including my husband! [I was doing] the same job in Taiwan, ironing, cooking, [but] with a lot of money! Here? No! But here I can be with my children. This is the best.

Who was taking care of your children?

My husband. He said, [it is] very hard to be a father and a mother at the same time. That's why he doesn't want to stay behind again. I asked my children, "Do you want me to work abroad again?" They said, "No, not you, papa." My husband didn't like me to go to Taiwan. He said it's not yours, it's my responsibility to support the family. He feels ashamed.

So you will not work abroad again?

If my husband cannot find a job, I will be forced to leave again.

Studies of migrant families have found that inversion of gender status and male privilege resulting from women's migration is often transient or partial (Espiritu 2002; George 2000). And the "gains" of migrant women frequently come with stress and contradictions. Linda's husband seeks a job overseas not only to regain the masculine ideal of breadwinner but also to avert the feminized nurturing duty. He complained that "it is very hard to be a father and a mother at the same time," but migrant women like Linda have no choice but to fulfill the double obligations. They are torn by the emotional strain of leaving children behind and the financial pressure of being "forced to leave again." The crossing of national borders and gender boundaries enables migrant women to achieve independence and emancipation, but they remain burdened with stigmas and feelings of guilt in the moral terrains of domesticity and motherhood.

MOTHERING ALONE AND AWAY

Olivia is a mother of three in her early thirties. She went to college for two years but dropped out for lack of finances. At the age of eighteen she went to Saudi Arabia to work as a domestic worker along with her sister and sister-in-law. She met her husband while she was taking a vacation in the Philippines. She returned to Saudi Arabia and found herself pregnant (access to contraceptives was limited in the Philippines during the Marcos period). She quit her job and got married at the age of twenty-one. She looked back at this decision with huge regrets: "I wanted to keep my child but I didn't want to marry him. I wanted to raise the child on my own, but my mother cried and said if I don't get married, this will ruin my reputation. But look at me—what ruined my reputation?"

After Olivia stayed home as a full-time housewife for eight years, her husband, a salesman, left her for another woman. Olivia processed a legal separation because divorce is not legal in the Philippines. Legal separation may be granted on limited grounds such as physical violence and incest, but neither party is entitled to remarry afterward.[7] Given the bureaucratic and financial difficulties associated with the application for legal separation, most people resort to informal separation or even abandonment (Chant and McIlwaine 1995: 14). Olivia yearns for an official ending to her marriage: "I haven't seen him for years, but he's still my husband legally. It's not fair. We adopt everything of American laws but divorce. My sister says maybe I should go work in Canada and get citizenship there, so I can divorce my husband."

Single motherhood is one of the major forces that push women overseas. Among the fifty-eight Filipina informants in this research, three are widows, and eleven became single mothers after their husbands committed adultery. Like most female heads of Filipino households, Olivia receives no financial support from her husband. That was why she decided to work abroad again: "My husband doesn't pay a cent for my children! So I have to work abroad again to make money! It's not easy for women to find jobs in the Philippines. But it's easy for women to find jobs abroad. You can be a helper, a caretaker, and so on."

As Olivia points out, the labor market in the Philippines is marked by sectoral segregation and wage differentials along the gender line. The ideology of female domesticity in the Philippines constrains women's participation in the productive labor force (Israel-Sobritchea 1990). Women's employment is usually limited in the categories that resemble "wife-and-mother roles" such as household jobs on plantations and professional jobs in nursing and teaching (Chant and McIlwaine 1995; Eviota 1992).

Some other women work overseas to escape domestic violence, negligence, or the infidelity of their husbands.[8] Divorce is not uncommon in Indonesia,[9] where women tend to get married at young ages.[10] Six Indonesians in this study (out of thirty-five) are divorced. One of them is Muslimah, who got married at seventeen. Before giving birth to her daughter, she worked in a factory in Jakarta and then took a domestic helper job in Singapore for two years. She decided to go overseas again when she was in her late twenties because her husband had an affair with a neighbor. After her divorce, heartbroken and ashamed, she ran away from the scandal in the village to the foreign land of Taiwan:

> If I stayed in Indonesia, I would feel sad every day. Seeing my husband with another woman [*sighs*] . . . It was really painful. So I came to Taiwan. I want to make a lot of money. So my husband would feel . . . perhaps he would feel bad knowing that I have money . . . well, his [new] wife is pretty but she has no money. I want to earn money. It's OK that I have no husband, but I want to live a good life.

The income earned in overseas employment is a source of confidence for migrant divorcées, and, more practically, it offers economic security for single mothers and their children. Rokayah is another Indonesian divorcée from an East Java village. She married a soldier when she was sixteen and gave birth to a boy at eighteen. Her parents arranged this marriage. The husband was addicted to gambling and neglected his family. For two years Rokayah worked as a nanny in Jakarta, going home twice a month. In her late twenties she came to work in Taiwan, holding the same nanny job with a wage five times what she earned in Jakarta. When I asked her if she ever considered entering another marriage, she firmly shook her head: "If I get married again and the husband is not good, my son would suffer. I want to make money so he could go to school. I don't want my child to grow up without knowledge."

To support their children's education, especially at expensive private schools and colleges, migrant mothers sacrifice in that their children grow up without the physical company of a mother. Molina from the Philippines said in tears: "At night I cry sometimes. I'm thinking: I am taking care of others' children, who is taking care of my children? All these years, I am not there for them. My children always ask me, mama, why are you always leaving? I said I always leave but it's for your future."

When migrant women are taking care of others' children, who is taking care of their children? Many depend on grandmothers, aunts, sisters, and other female kin to be caretakers, and in some cases the husbands quit their jobs and become full-time homemakers.[11] There are also a significant number of migrant women who seek nonfamily members to care for their children. Some consider hired help a better solution than kin care-takers, as they feel emotionally unable to evaluate or criticize relatives' labor performance. Moreover, kin caregivers are not necessarily cheaper than waged workers, because migrant parents are obligated to provide them with financial paybacks.

Molina and other migrant women I met were enthusiastic to show me their children's pictures (often carried in their wallets) and to offer de-tails of their children's activities. This is a way to display their "maternal visibility" (Garey 1999: 29), even though they were hardly participants in those memorable events displayed in the photos—the festival dance, beauty contest, graduation ceremony, birthday party, and so forth.[12] Mi-grant mothers, socially defined as the primary caregiver, are vulnerable to the social blame that associates their physical absence with abandoning or disowning their children. Such criticism could come from relatives, hus-bands, or even their own children. In Rokayah's case, her ex-husband maneuvered such social blames to sabotage the mother's reputation in order to win the son's favor. I visited Rokayah in Java after she returned home for about a month. I was surprised to learn that she had not yet visited her son, who lived with her mother in Kalimantan. Rokayah sadly told me: "My son does not want to talk to me. My ex-husband told him that I had a boyfriend in Taiwan. I did bad things in Taiwan. My son is angry at me [*sobbing*] . . . How could I do bad things in Taiwan? I was working all the time, to save money for him!"

The pain of family separation and the fear of displacement are even more drastic for undocumented migrant workers, who overstay their visas and have no chance to visit their families during their entire stay in Tai-wan. Evelyn, a single mother from the Philippines in her early forties, has been doing part-time cleaning jobs since she "ran away" from her contract employer five years ago. She is a very active figure in the migrant commu-nity and a popular friend for her generous and warm personality. She had been recently diagnosed with a brain tumor but had no insurance to pay for further treatment. This condition had forced her to reduce her work-load as well as the remittances sent to her two children in the Philippines.

Evelyn had not been able to visit her children since she went undocu-mented. Before I departed for my field trip to the Philippines, she ex-citedly told me, "Maybe you can meet my children there!" During my stay in Manila, I did not get any messages from Evelyn's children. One day around midnight I received a phone call from Evelyn. She was upset and wept on the phone: "My children never called you, right? You know what day is today? It's Mother's Day! They don't remember this day or even my birthday! I am very sad so I called you in the Philippines. I'm not going to send them any more money. I'll see if they will think of me when they have no money." Evelyn talked about her children in an earlier interview:

> I feel very upset about my children. They don't talk to me. This one . . . I left her studying in college but now she got married and has a son already . . .
>
> *How old is she?*
>
> Twenty years old. She never told me she got a boyfriend! She never told me.
>
> *Why don't they talk to you anymore? Are they mad at you or something?*
>
> I don't know . . . I am sacrificing my life for THEM! I never get involved with a man. I need a companion also, but I never think of that. I think only of my family. I don't want them to become like me. I am suffering for my marriage. But my children, they don't understand me. Sometimes I have no job! I have no money to give to my landlord. Sometimes I am hungry. I have no food . . . I never ask them for help.

Deeply hurt by her children's suspicion that she stays overseas to enjoy herself, Evelyn defends herself by underscoring her chastity ("I never get involved with a man") and altruistic motherhood ("I am sacrificing my life for them"). Despite her efforts to portray herself as a "martyr mom"—one who suffers overseas for her children and grieves in the process of mothering from afar (Parreñas 2005)—the physical separation over time has obstructed her children's faith in her motherly virtue, and her illness hampers her ability to mother them with regular flows of remittance.

Scholars have written about how migrant mothers achieve transnational motherhood: they expand the definition of motherhood by developing the belief that they can fulfill their maternal responsibilities through being a breadwinner overseas (Hondagneu-Sotelo and Avila 1997), they send letters, phone calls, and text messages to their children on a frequent basis, and they rely on generous remittances and expensive gifts to establish concrete ties with their children (Parreñas 2001). In addition, migrant mothers try to maintain the day-to-day reproduction of their households in virtual presence, for which I coin the term "transnational homemaking."

Migrant mothers often send packages of goods—called *balikbayan* boxes in the Philippines—to their families back home. The contents usually include souvenirs from host countries, hand-me-down clothes and toys from employers, and such items as soap, lotion, and packaged food. Once I accompanied Tiwi to ship a bulky, heavy package to her family in Indonesia. Her friend said to me, mocking Tiwi as an "irrational" gift-sender: "You know what she put in there? She sent shampoo, toothpaste, and even several packs of juice!" Tiwi responded in defense, "But I'd like my daughter to try this Taiwanese brand of juice." By sending the packaged fruit juice, the favorite of her employers' children, the migrant mother would like to share with her family the exotic components of her overseas life as a way of compensating for her absence from her daughter's childhood.

Actually, many of the grocery items that migrants send are available in their home countries. According to the calculation of Deirdre McKay (2004), it is more expensive to send a box of goods from abroad than it would be to send the money to purchase these items in the local market. These in-kind remittances, selected against the formula of economic calculation, represent a symbolic performance of domestic labor for migrant mothers. McKay notices that it is mostly women migrants who send these *balikbayan* boxes, and she argues: "In choosing items for the box, they are doing a kind of transnational grocery shopping that reproduces their domestic identity in their family at home" (2004: 19).

In addition to transnational grocery shopping, migrant mothers can serve the role of transnational homemaker by planning the family menus for the week (Parreñas 2005) and supervising the daily expenses of their husbands or children. For instance, Trinada, a Filipina working in Taiwan, worries about the financial management at home and hence tries to keep an "eye" on her children, one in high school and two in college, despite her physical absence:

> ocw [overseas contract worker] children are like that. They get pregnant. They go to drugs, because they have a lot of money. Their friends said, "Your mother is an ocw, you must be rich, you pay [for] this, you pay [for] that." So I asked my children to send me all the receipts for their expenses. Then they won't waste their money. [*Receipts for everything?*] Yes, everything, the eggs, the movies, the books, everything.

Although migrant mothers can no longer attend to the details of family life or conduct the domestic chores themselves, they manage to participate in the mundane routines of household reproduction with the assistance of the transnational flows of goods, information, and messages. Transnational homemaking helps them maintain the roles of spiritual housekeeper and long-distance nurturer and, consequently, reconstitutes the boundaries of home and family across borders.

"WE'RE JUST LIKE OUR MADAMS"

Another way for migrant mothers to expand the definition of motherhood and justify their separation from the family is to mark a similarity between themselves and their female employers. During my interview with Juliet, a Filipina who left her children to work in Taiwan, I asked how she felt about working overseas and she simply answered, "It's OK. Many women work outside. We're just like our madams." She identifies with a modern version of employment womanhood, which describes her employer, a bank manager, as well as herself, an overseas domestic worker. By drawing such a comparison, migrant mothers perceive that they are just like other employed women who leave children behind to pursue market wages. The only difference is that they have traveled farther to cross borders.

The previous chapter demonstrated that female employers are structurally positioned in a relationship of competition with their market surrogates for the wifely and motherly status. Migrant domestic workers also compare themselves with female employers. Their intimate observation about the employers' family lives provides them with privileged knowledge by which they evaluate female employers while framing their own ideals of womanhood. By situating themselves on the same platform as their employers, migrant women render the boundary between maid and madam fuzzy and seemingly elastic.

I heard similar rhetoric mostly from Filipina migrant workers, especially those who have advanced degrees and held white-collar jobs in the past. By positing a fuzzy maid/madam boundary, they manage to reconcile the personal anxiety entailed by their path of downward mobility. A Filipina migrant, Trina, marked an occupational proximity between herself and her employer: "My employer used to be a stewardess. Stewardess is like a maid. That's why she can understand my work." Although Trina was unaware of the sociological thesis about the historical continuity of reproductive labor across the public and private sectors (Glenn 1992), she refused to view her work as a downgraded job and argued for her standing as equivalent to that of the stewardess employer.

Some migrant domestic workers also draw a similarity between themselves and their employers based on the fact that they are "remote madams" back home. Several Filipina informants said to me, in a proud or embarrassed tone, "You know, I have a maid in the Philippines!" One of them is Christina, a college graduate and a former teacher. She hired a live-in domestic to take care of her children while she was working in Taiwan. Despite holding a similar occupation now, Christina drew a clear distinction between herself and her maid: "My sister was laughing, you have a maid in the Philippines, but you are a maid in Taiwan! I said it's different. They are undereducated. Not everyone can work abroad. You have to be very serious, very determined."

These migrant women hold an ambivalent status in being an overseas maid yet a remote madam. Rhacel Parreñas (2001: 72) situates their intermediate status in the multi-tiered "international division of reproductive labor": while they gain increased wages by caring for the children of middle- and upper-class women in industrialized countries, they transfer their own household and childcare labor to poorer women in the home country. Local domestic helpers are women on the bottom of the hierarchy who possess the least economic and cultural capital; they are either not sufficiently qualified or cannot afford the costs of seeking employment abroad.[13] For overseas domestic workers, becoming a "madam" at home marks their upgraded social status among village fellows and brings psychological compensation for their sufferings in the host country.

Migrant domestic workers tend to be more critical of those female employers who are not working outside the house. "They have no job but watching me," said one informant. In their eyes, homemaker employers neither achieve the gendered duty of caring for one's own family nor accomplish the ideal of career womanhood. Migrant women consider their homemaker employers idle yet demanding: "She wakes up late. She reads the newspaper, watches TV, goes to the club, and supervises my work!" Some workers pity homemakers for their lack of financial independence: "She has to ask for money from her husband and he checks the use of every amount. She has no control of her money. Sometimes she even borrows money from me!" While making critical comments about homemaker employers, migrant women legitimize their own practice of employment womanhood as a morally adequate and financially secure model.

Migrant women who have not built their own families consider home-maker employers to be a bad model. A single Filipina, Jovita, told me, "I don't want to become my employer. She told me, 'You cook something for my husband and I am going out for mahjong!' That's bad. She doesn't cook for her husband. She doesn't take care of her children. I don't want to become a wife like that. I want to cook a warm and nice dinner when my husband comes home after work." While criticizing her employer for a failure in the domestic role, Jovita romantically imagines her future in the framework of the traditional ideals of housewifery and motherhood. Yet, in reality, it is not easy for her to achieve what she perceives a good wife and a good mother should be.

In addition, migrant caregivers are often critical of what they perceive as their employers' neglectful and substandard parenting (Hondagneu-Sotelo and Avila 1997). They blame their employers for prioritizing career over children: "their parents are too busy. They don't have time to talk to the children." Further, they criticize some parents for laziness and selfishness. Rutchelle, a Filipina mother of two in her thirties, has been working for a Taiwanese household for over two years. In the church, I frequently saw her along with two Taiwanese children, one girl of five and one boy of four. I assumed that their parents were busy at work but Rutchelle corrected me, "No, the parents are at home. But the children want to be with me." I asked the boy, Tommy, what his parents were doing that day. He replied, "They're sleeping. Mommy was drinking last night." Rutchelle shook her head, "I don't understand why they sleep so much."

In contrast to the "irresponsible parents," several migrant women told me, with pride or excitement, about their emotional closeness to the children under their care. A Filipina worker quoted what the children said to her upon the end of her contract: "We don't want to stay here. We want to go to the Philippines with you!" As ties with their children back home are loosening, migrant mothers seek emotional rewards in the job of substitute motherhood. They confirm their motherly capability with the evidence that their employers' children prefer them to the biological mothers, despite the fact that they have also left their own children to work.

In such a situation of "diverted mothering" (Wong 1994), migrant caregivers are trapped in an emotional predicament. They have to assure female employers that their temporary presence will not shake the status of biological mothers (shoring up the mother-caregiver boundary), but they also feel traumatized if their emotional ties with the employers' children are only ephemeral. For instance, Rutchelle tried to comfort Tommy's mother, who sometimes feels jealous about the children's attachment to the migrant nanny: "I told her it's OK. I am only a housekeeper. I am here only temporary. The children have two Filipinas before. They forgot them. Helen, the last one, my boss showed him [Tommy] the picture. He doesn't know her." I checked with Tommy, "Who is Helen?" Indeed, he shook his head. I jokingly said to Tommy, "Helen would be upset if she knew you don't remember her." Rutchelle then grabbed the boy in her arms, saying with confidence. "But he will remember me forever!"

FILIAL DAUGHTERS, OLD MAIDS

Many studies have focused on migrant workers who are mothers themselves, ignoring another significant group: single migrant women. Almost 40 percent of Filipinas in this study are single (twenty-two out of fifty-eight). The proportion of single Indonesian migrants, a relatively young population, is even more dominant. In this study, 60 percent of Indonesian informants (twenty-one out of thirty-five) are single, most in their early twenties. Like married women who emigrate to unburden themselves from domestic constraints, single women view going abroad as an opportunity to flee from paternal control over unmarried daughters. Jovita has a college degree and used to work as a secretary in Manila. She left her family to work in Taiwan when she was twenty-four to experience freedom from her parents and adventure in a foreign land:

> When I applied the job abroad, my parents didn't know. I didn't tell them until I was leaving. They couldn't do anything, since the paper was already processed. They were worried, because I didn't have the experience working in the house and they didn't know what kind of employer I would have . . . I never thought of going abroad. I was from the provinces. The highest mission I had was to work in Manila. I just wanted to run away from home. You know, just like other single women looking forward to freedom. But now, I have freedom only on Sundays!

The freedom granted to a live-in domestic worker is limited, as Jovita discovered. Nevertheless, overseas employment still provides single women with an option to establish economic independence from their parents. In Indonesia, arranged marriages are still common and parents tend to arrange early marriages in order to protect family reputation (Jones 2002). Some young Indonesian women launch themselves on the overseas journey to defer their entry into marriage and withstand pressure from their parents. Nani is a twenty-six-year-old Sundanese, who grew up in a farming family in West Java. With no interest in farming, she went to Jakarta, working as a waitress after junior high school. When she was twenty, Nani took a domestic helper job in Saudi Arabia instead of becoming a farmer's wife. She recalled the family dispute back then:

> My dad and my mom said, "You cannot go to Arab." I said, "Don't worry. No matter what happens, Allah will watch over me." Everyday, I argued with my parents, "May I go to Arab? May I go to Arab?" They said, "Don't go to Arab. Get married." I don't want to get married at such a young age. I would suffer! I saw people getting married younger than twenty. They got a divorce. I don't want that.

Nani told her parents that, by working overseas, "I make money for you, not for myself." Because single women are not yet tied to their own nuclear families, remittance usually serves as a means of filial tribute to their parents. In my observation, Indonesian single women usually remit some money back to their parents and save a substantial amount in preparation for setting up a new home after marriage.[14] In comparison, Filipina migrants, as single daughters and elder sisters, are burdened with stronger financial pressure from their extended families.

Scholars have described the Filipino family as "residentially nuclear but functionally extended." Although the nuclear family structure has become dominant as a result of urbanization and economic change, the cultural values of mutual assistance and reciprocal exchange among extended kin, known as *utang na loob* (debt of the soul) in Tagalog, are deep-rooted despite the distances over which family members migrate (Chant and McIlwaine 1995: 15). Single adult daughters are expected to provide financial assistance for extended family members; the most common form is to sponsor education of younger siblings (Medina 1991).

Mercy, a single Filipina in her early twenties, started working abroad after finishing one year of college. There are twelve daughters and two sons in her family. Eight of the daughters have worked overseas for various periods of time and they take turns to support the extended families and younger siblings. Mercy recounted how she first started working overseas: "My sister called me and asked me if I wanted to work in Singapore.

I said OK, because I want to help my family. My sister said: 'Don't worry, we have five sisters working here.'" Mercy remits almost all her monthly wages back home. Without the slightest complaint, she views this as her share of family responsibility: "My sister is getting old, she needs to save money for herself. My sister supported my education before, so I support my younger sister's college now. We have an agreement. It's my turn now."

In Mercy's case, the decision of migration is a family strategy that defines the moral worth of dutiful daughters by way of their contribution to and sacrifices for the collective benefits of the extended family. Yet, for other migrants, remittance to parents and extended kin may not be an honorable duty but a never-fulfilled obligation. One Sunday I met Jovita after she had just received a letter from her family. She showed no excitement but seemed upset. Amy, Jovita's best friend, tapped her shoulder and said, "Well, they must have written to ask you for more money." Jovita said in dismay: "My mother, my sisters, they always ask me to send more money. They ask me why I don't send all the money home. I send NT$10,000 a month! I [have to] leave some for myself." After a deep sigh, she continued: "I told myself—I will just stay to finish this contract, because I am already old, feeling tired."

In addition to financial pressure exerted by her family, another thing that worries Jovita is the uncertain future after her contract in Taiwan ends. She wonders if she will be satisfied with the poor wage level in the Philippines. Another Filipina, Nora, shares a similar concern. Despite graduating from a prestigious college, Nora found it difficult to locate jobs commensurate with her qualification: "I can't find work easily because I am over-aged and my education is over-qualified." When I pressed her to explain what she meant, she pointed to age discrimination experienced by women in the labor market:

> In the Philippines, when you find a job, they don't like women [who are] too old. They want women twenty-one years old, beautiful, smile and how to say that, "ordinary" . . . [When Nora applied for jobs after returning from Singapore at the age of thirty] they said, "Wow, you graduated from this university?" Then they said, "Sorry, we can only give you 2,000 pesos."

Each month Nora remits half of her monthly wage to her sisters and mother (her father died when she was young). From time to time she sends money to other relatives in response to their requests for funds with which to purchase appliances or to renovate their houses. Now she is paying her youngest sister's tuition and other expenses in college. When I asked her if she would encourage her sister to work abroad, Nora said no, explaining that she tries to satisfy the sister's financial requests in order to protect her from the hardship of working overseas:

> The life working abroad is too hard . . . I know my sister, she cannot cook, cannot do any housework. [*Does she want to come?*] Yes, she wants to. I told her, "If you have a job there, a family there, [stay there and] I can buy you what you need." I just bought her a motorcycle. I told her, "Don't work abroad. It's too hard."

These single daughters, bearing the financial burden for their original families, feel that they have no choice but to continue working abroad. In this way, they are also concerned about the delay of or hindrance to their marriage. Rosemary told me about her friend, Manny, who is single, in her late twenties, and employed to take care of a newborn baby. Manny's employers are so occupied by their multinational business that they leave Manny and the baby alone at home most of the time. Rosemary described what happened to Manny:

> They [the employers] trust her very much. She's happy, because she loves the baby very much. It's like her own baby. When the mama comes home, the baby doesn't like her [the mama] and just cries. Manny's contract is going to finish soon and the employer said, "We want you to stay forever." Manny said NO—"If I stay here forever, how can I get married and have my own baby?"

Manny's words indicate the conflict between assisting in the maintenance of the employer's family and the worker's desire to build a family of her own. Women's single status is usually associated with the social stigma of spinsterhood, whose equivalent term in Tagalog, *matandang dalaga*, figuratively means "womanhood partially fulfilled" (Hollnsteiner 1981). Despite the stigma of old maid, some Filipina workers prefer to remain single because of a perceived incompatibility between the life of working overseas and the traditional concept of family life. Fey has been working overseas for eleven years, since the age of thirty. She talked about her perspective on marriage and her future plans:

I saw my friends who leave their family and children to work abroad. That's not good. If you are alone, nothing worries you. So single is better. I want to work as long as I can, until sixty years old maybe. I will save some money and I will go back to the Philippines. I already bought a house there.

Other Filipina workers refuse to enter marriage for more radical reasons. Trina, at the age of thirty-eight, has been working in Singapore and Taiwan for over ten years. There are twelve daughters and two sons in her family and eight of the daughters have worked overseas for various periods of time. When I asked Trina if she was interested in marriage, she shook her head and said in a determined voice:

> No need [to get married]. I am a breadwinner now. I see my sister's life after getting married. I don't need that. She stays home, wasting her education. Her husband works overseas. She has to do cook, do wash, do everything! I don't want to marry, because after that you only stay home and cook food for your husband! Just like a maid! I am a maid. I know that! So why bother to marry?

Trina's remarks pinpoint the continuity between unpaid household labor and domestic work. She considers the social position of a housewife as merely an unpaid version of a maid and thus prefers her current economic independence and individual freedom as a single waged domestic worker. With the money earned overseas, she has purchased a piece of land on the outskirts of Manila and invested in a *sari-sari* (neighborhood grocery store) with sisters and cousins who are also single. Through extended kin networks, these women create a community of mutual support, an alternative to the traditional nuclear family. I turn now to another strategy single migrant women use to deal with the pressure of marriage—they seek international marriages to escape the downgraded status of (old) maid.

FROM FOREIGN MAIDS TO FOREIGN BRIDES

After a Sunday mass, I found some Filipina workers in the backyard of the church secretly passing around a flyer, trying to avoid the attention of priests and nuns. The flyer, boldly titled "Heart of Asia: American and European Men Want to Write to You," started with this paragraph:

Our international pen pal club gives you the chance to correspond with American and European men. These men have good jobs, nice homes and higher education. But they are missing something in their lives . . . They are looking for someone who is loyal, sensitive and caring; someone who shares their traditional values about home, family and relationships. They are seeking someone to respect and appreciate. They are seeking YOU.

This international pen pal club and many other similar agencies are based in Hong Kong, the city with the largest population of Filipina domestic workers in the world. International marriage has long existed in the Philippines given the almost century-long U.S. army presence (Enloe 1989). Colonial history and white supremacy continue to shape the cultural logics of love and desire in the contemporary Philippines (Constable 2003a). Modern technologies, especially mobile phones and the Internet, have facilitated the blossoming of transnational romances. The most popular destinations for Filipina brides are the United States, Australia, Germany, and England (Eviota 1992). Recently, the demand for foreign brides has come from men in wealthier Asian countries including Japan and Taiwan. A growing number of Taiwanese men have turned to China, Vietnam, Indonesia, and the Philippines for potential mates.[15] Here I focus on the link between overseas domestic employment and international marriage to demonstrate how migrant women negotiate available options given the structural constraints in their overseas experiences, which can span the categories of labor migration and marriage migration.

Previous studies have challenged a popular myth that most Filipina brides are poverty-stricken or sexy bar girls from Manila or the American base town of Angeles City. Fadzilah Cooke (1986) interviewed 104 Filipinas who married Australian men and found that more than half of the women were in professional or clerical occupations, the two dominant occupations being teaching and nursing. This profile is similar to that of overseas Filipina workers. The affinity between overseas employment and international marriage is no surprise, given the exposure of migrant workers to foreign culture and transnational connections. Working overseas brings them opportunities to meet foreigners and easy access to international marriage services. In addition, migrant workers, after staying abroad for a long time, often find it difficult to readjust to the lifestyle and material conditions back home. The feelings of displacement drive them farther away from home toward immigration. Many apply for jobs in countries such as Canada that grant permanent residency to migrant workers; another shorter route to naturalization is to marry a foreign pen pal or host national.

International pen pal services are the most common medium through which Filipina migrant workers connect with potential foreign mates.[16] In this way Luisa had received correspondence from eight men in the United States and Europe. Luisa frequently showed me the pictures, letters, and tapes she received from them. One of her pen pals was an African American man from Texas. She told me, "He's ugly, but he is the only one serious about marriage. I don't mind he is black. I care about if he is green [if he has a green card]!" Luisa's best friend, Imelda, also had frequent correspondence with a number of international male pen pals. Although she had processed a job application in Canada, Imelda was worried that her high school education would not qualify her to apply for Canadian citizenship in the future. She told me, "If I want to get residency in Canada, I have to go to school [college]! [It's] too hard! It's easier to marry a pen pal."

Another, less popular, route to international marriage is to meet Taiwanese men through personal networks. Most Filipina migrant workers consider marriages to Western pen pals a more impressive path to social mobility than marriages to men in the South; they associate the latter with less-educated Filipinas who could only find foreign mates through commercial agencies, or with Indonesian and Vietnamese migrant workers, who cannot master the English language or Western lifestyles. Marrying a host national, nevertheless, helps migrant women bypass work restrictions imposed by host states upon noncitizens. Fey's sister worked in Taiwan as a domestic worker on a tourist visa in the 1980s. Through the referral of another Filipina bride, she married a widowed Taiwanese man almost twenty years older than she. Fey commented on her sister's marriage:

> *Fey:* This man told my sister, if you want to marry me, you can stay
>   longer. I objected. I said, "You don't know what kind of person he
>   is!" But my sister wanted to marry him, because she wanted to stay
>   in Taiwan.
> *PCL:* How's their marriage?
> *Fey:* Not good! He keeps all the money. He has a pension from the
>   government, but he only gives her a little allowance, so my sister

has to do part-time [domestic] jobs. Now he's in the hospital. My sister is taking care of him. He has three children with the first wife. They seldom come to see him. But the father lets those children take care of his saving. My sister doesn't know how to read or write Chinese, so the children take all the money! So now, if he dies, my sister will have nothing!

Helen [overhears and comments]: This is a waste of love!

Fey [shakes her head]: No, this is not love, just help.

The widely accepted myth that marriage is grounded solely on romantic love leads to an accusation that foreign brides maneuver marriages to obtain citizenship. Whereas the modern meaning of marriage is centered on love and intimacy, the conjugal institution has long been a relationship of interdependence and exchange on economic and social terms. This is especially true for people with limited social resources, whose marriages are often "not love, just help." Marriage in the Philippines is traditionally considered a means to social mobility for women; the desirability of the husband is partly measured by the status upgrade he can offer (Medina 1991). Seen in this light, international marriage is a recent form of the old-fashioned tradition of "marrying up" (Cooke 1986). What is new is that the assurance of social mobility in an international marriage is grounded on the economic disparities between the countries of the groom and the bride.

In the eyes of Filipina migrants, Western and Taiwanese men become more desirable mates when compared to Filipino men who are trapped in the poor homeland and offer little promise of economic security and social mobility. The latter even present the risk of becoming "demasculinized" and "domesticated" husbands who depend on their wives working abroad. Luisa explained to me why she preferred marrying a foreigner to a Filipino: "I don't want to marry a Filipino. They have no money, low salary. What if he says to me: 'When will you go back to Taiwan? And send me money?' I will kill him!" Besides the worry about the dependent husband, she was also concerned about her disadvantage in the local marriage scene: "It's not easy for me to find a Filipino. Because I have worked in Japan, in Taiwan, people think I am an urban, fashionable city girl. They think I must be materialistic, but I am not." Filipina migrant workers, especially those who work as entertainers in Japan, become less desirable wives for Filipino men as well. After residing in metropolitan cities in foreign countries for years, these women are assumed to be too "liberated" and unlikely to conform to the rural lifestyle and traditional norms of femininity. Filipinas employed in Japan as hostesses, singers, and dancers in bars and hotels—so-called *Japayuki*—are commonly maligned as prostitutes in Japan as well as in the Philippines. The prostitute image of Filipinas is so pervasive that all overseas Filipinas become moral suspects for their potential association with the sex industry (Suzuki 2000).

Filipinas have quite a different image in the eyes of Taiwanese and other foreign grooms. They consider Filipinas—associated with religious devotion and traditional family values—better wife candidates than Taiwanese and Western women who are "liberated" from the traditional gender roles. Rosamaria, a Filipina who is married to a Taiwanese bus driver, remarked matter-of-factly: "You know why Taiwanese men want to marry Filipinas? Because Filipinas clean the house very well, listen to the husband and mother-in-law, and take good care of the children." International marriage indicates a crisis of masculinity not only for Filipinos but also for foreign grooms. These men, who are mostly widowed or divorced, lower-class, and not preferred by women in their countries, try to regain their masculinity by "rescuing" foreign women from poverty. They fulfill their nostalgia for a pre-feminist family romance by constructing an ideal domestic sphere sustained by the household labor of servile foreign wives (Tolentino 1996: 67–71).

The experience of overseas domestic work even becomes a positive qualification for women applicants in the international marriage market. One Sunday at Holy Spirit, a group of Filipina migrants were reading and discussing an application form for an international pen pal club. Helen found a question embarrassing to answer and asked those who had applied before: "How did you answer this? What's your *profession?*" Luisa bluntly answered, "It's OK to say caretaker or domestic helper. They like that because they are all old and they like people who can take care of them." Here the continuity between unpaid household labor and paid domestic work presents another irony for migrant women. The feminization of domestic labor as a cultural logic trivializes women's labor and skills in the professional field of domestic service, but it increases the value of domestic workers as potential wives (and unpaid caregivers) in the market of international marriage.

Indonesian women, compared to Filipina migrants, have less linguistic capability to correspond with English-speaking foreign pen pals, and the Muslim tradition discourages them from marrying a pagan. Yet it is not uncommon that migrant workers, Filipinas and Indonesians alike, receive marriage proposals from their Taiwanese employers, who are usually middle-aged divorced or widowed men. Romantic intimacy is involved in some cases, but in others, marriage proposals serve as an extension of labor contracts when migrant women are hired to take care of the men's frail or ill mothers. Nora, the nursing graduate introduced earlier, received a marriage proposal from her employer right before her contract was about to finish. After Nora rejected this proposal, she and another Filipina, Rosemary, chatted about the proposal:

> *Nora:* He [the boss] said, "You can stay here, because my mother likes you and you like my mother."
> *Rosemary* [speaking to PCL]: They want to marry her [Nora], because his mother likes her working here. So I told her, no, this is a lifetime.
> *Nora:* Right, if you get married, they will say you stay home, don't go out . . .
> *Rosemary:* And you don't get paid! [*all laugh*]

Most migrant domestic workers, like Nora, are keenly aware that if they accept an employer's proposal, they will continue to perform similar domestic labor, only in the name of family obligation rather than employment. The workload placed on a wife may even be intensified since the "labor of love" offered by a family member is supposed to be incommensurable (thus unpaid) and incessant (no days off). A migrant worker who becomes a foreign bride will forfeit the wages, rights, and benefits previously sealed by her contract. Whenever a Filipina worker mentioned that her employer's relative was asking her for a date, I often heard responses from other migrant women such as this one: "You have to be careful! Maybe they just want a free domestic helper and caretaker!" Helen pursued correspondence with an American man and received his proposal after a few months. She took some time to consider and finally turned it down for this reason: "When you have a husband, you have to provide all the service, cooking, cleaning, massage . . . for free! Being a DH (domestic helper), at least you got paid."

Despite its monetary gains, waged domestic work is generally stigmatized as being unskilled, demeaning, and not a real job—to recall Helen's embarrassment regarding how to answer her "profession" when joining an international pen pal club. By contrast, unpaid household labor is granted more moral value and social recognition (a respectable wife and mother). This is why some migrant women find more nonmaterial benefits in an international marriage than in waged domestic work. Luisa's American pen pal planned to visit Luisa and her family upon her return to Manila for vacation, and they would discuss the possibility of marriage at that time. I told Luisa to be careful about marrying someone she barely knew. "I know," Luisa sighed deeply, "but I am tired of cleaning toilets!"

In fact, Luisa will not stop cleaning toilets after she gets married, but she will clean her own toilets instead of other people's toilets. Her housework will be socially slotted in the category of "labor of love" rather than that of waged labor; that is, she will lose monetary gains for her domestic labor but receive emotional value and social recognition instead. Agencies recruiting workers for domestic service in Canada even describe international marriages as a potential gain of labor migration in their marketing plans. One advertisement quoted a marriage proposal from a Canadian employer: "Why be a Nanny; marry me and my children will call you Mommy" (McKay 2003: 46). Migrant women like Luisa enter an international marriage not only to seek a partner who can promise economic security and permanent residency in a wealthy country but also to pursue a romance with the elevated status of "the lady of the house." They can detach themselves from the stigma of "maid" and "nanny" and become "honey" and "mommy" who better approximate the hegemonic norms of domesticity and motherhood.

Along with other researchers, I observed that migrant women "do not only marry to emigrate, but they also emigrate in order to achieve the desired goal of marriage" (Constable 2003b: 175). Some migrant women embark on the journey of labor migration and later chart the route of international marriages. There are also women who emigrate as foreign spouses because legal channels of labor migration are unavailable.[17] Ethnographic findings demonstrate that the boundaries applied to categorical forms of migration such as "marriage," "contract work," and "family reunification" are rather fluid (McKay 2003: 25). In real-life stories, migrant women combine multiple forms of migration to negotiate their life chances and gender identities; they not only transgress geographic borders but also transcend the boundaries between maid and wife, and nanny and mommy.

MAKING BOUNDARIES FUZZY

While female employers tend to demarcate a rigid line between maid and madam, the boundary between private homemaking and waged domestic work is rather fuzzy for migrant women. The feminization of domestic labor provides opportunities for them to move across multiple positions involving different forms of labor that are nevertheless all defined as women's work. Their migratory trajectories indicate a fluid line between "maid" and "madam," more exactly, a structural continuity across paid and unpaid domestic labor in association with ambiguous exchanges between money and love.

Migrant women who are housewives in home countries become major breadwinners as overseas domestic workers. Despite their financial gains, they lose moral credibility in failing the reproductive responsibilities in their own households. To reconcile the predicaments incurred by transcending the gender boundary of breadwinning, migrant women reconstitute the meanings and practices of domesticity and motherhood. They deliver love and care through remittance, groceries, and text messages to achieve transnational homemaking and long-distance motherhood.

Despite the apparent status hierarchy in an employment relationship, migrant domestic workers situate themselves as being equivalent or even superior to their female employers in the moral map of womanhood. By deeming themselves similar to madams who are employed outside the home, migrant mothers legitimize their leaving their own children behind for the future of the family. By criticizing homemaker employers, migrant workers claim their own superior capability in wifely and motherly performances. By entering international marriages, single migrant women wish to escape the downgraded status of (old) maid and elevate themselves to the status of housewife.

The social view that domestic labor is an exercise of women's endowments and moral duties has serious consequences for the conditions of waged domestic workers. The public/private boundary is a fuzzy line in the intimate environment of live-in domestic work. The fusing of labor contracts and marriage proposals may be an extreme case. Yet, in general, migrant caregivers desire some emotional ties to their wards so they can retrieve meaning in this downgraded job and ease the pain of separating from their own families. Accordingly, migrant women are trapped in an unsolvable equation between money and love associated with their paid and unpaid mothering work. They have to pay substantial emotional and monetary costs to be a "good" mother, either a transnational or substitute one.

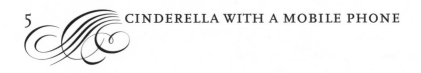

After a Sunday mass, I went out with Luisa and several other Filipinas for lunch. We went to an American chain fast food restaurant, where crowds of migrant workers were chatting over Cokes, fries, and burgers. Noticing that Luisa carried a bag with clothes in it, I made fun of her for being such an early shopper on Sunday. She shook her head and explained to me, with slight embarrassment: "No, those are the clothes I have to change [into] when I go home. When I go out, I want to look smart, fashionable, and intelligent." Tapping on her ivory silk blouse, she said, "In these clothes. I'm like a business manager. Those clothes," she pointed at the bag, "I bought in the market, for NT$100! I look like a 'floor manager' in those!" After a big laugh, she continued with a wry smile: "Before I go home, I change. I take off my make-up. I change my mini skirt. I look like a totally different person at home. You know, just like Cinderella."

This chapter examines how migrant domestic workers during their overseas journey experience spatiality on multiple geographic scales: the employer's household, the city, and the host/home country. The concept of spatiality captures "the ways in which the social and spatial are inextricably realized one in the other"; in other words, space is no passive arena but is realized through the ways people conceptualize and experience time-space relations (Gregson and Lowe 1995: 224). The same space can hold distinct meanings and capacities for its various dwellers. Residing with employers, migrant domestic workers occupy a marginal space at "home" and their privacy is easily invaded given the conflation of workplace and residence. Unlike professional expatriates who enjoy the privileged metropolitan lifestyle, lower-end migrant workers are the underclass in the global city, granted limited access to public space and facilities.

Erving Goffman (1959) uses the metaphors of "front" and "backstage" to theorize the situational and context-bound performance of everyday life. I find them illuminating in describing the double spatiality of the global Cinderellas. I further expand his concepts by attending to the constellation of power in the representation and constitution of social space. In this view, the sculpting of spatial boundaries constitutes a site of everyday struggles for both employers and workers in the geography of control and resistance.

This chapter will present a series of constructions of spatial boundaries on multiple scales. Employers and residents in host countries attach distinct meanings and uneven significance to various spatial realms—within the private houses of employers and across public areas in host cities. Their representations of space, which accord with the divides between front and back stage, mirror the hierarchical social order that excludes and marginalizes foreign workers. The front/backstage schema also describes how migrant workers negotiate self-presentation and identity performance across spatial settings in the presence of various audiences—employers in foreign lands or villagers back home.

Inasmuch as space is implicated in the enforcement of labor control and racial segregation, space is a medium through which migrant women assert agency empowering themselves. The global Cinderella does not merely leave a glass slipper, awaiting the coming of a prince as her savior. I will demonstrate how migrant domestic workers reconstitute the meanings of social spaces in connection with the transnational flows of goods and people. They utilize everyday technology, mobile phones in particular, to loosen geographic constraints at work and operate transnational networks. They "privatize" the public spheres by turning train stations into their picnic sites and home floors. And they "ethnicize" the urban landscape in host countries through asserting linguistic resistance in their collective presence on Sundays and building commercially vibrant and spatially unbounded communities.

HOME AS THE WORK FRONT

A Taiwanese employer commented on her foreign employee: "Our maid is not perfect at all. Her only merit is honesty. Because we are out of the house working the whole day, we leave the entire house to her and we leave the children to her. To be honest and trustworthy is more important than anything else." Like her, many Taiwanese employers are worried about security of family assets and the vulnerability of children in a chaotic world. Their concerns are aggravated by distrust of migrant domestic workers, which parallel the public anxiety over the presence of foreign workers in a society with recent and limited exposure to ethnic diversity. To protect their "safe haven," employers ironically turn their homes into a field of discipline and surveillance. Their conducting of labor control goes beyond the job performance of the worker to extend to her private life and moral character, with the imposition of temporal management and spatial monitoring.[1]

Domesticating the Alien

The deployment of home space confirms status distinction between employers and workers on a daily basis. The old-fashioned "upstairs, downstairs" model in particular symbolizes the master-servant segregation (Ozyegin 2000). In Taipei and other Asian cities, the living space of most households is rather modest. It is uncommon to see spatial arrangements such as separate entrances, separate stairwells, outdoor toilets, or servants' quarters. Compared to a mode of total segregation, employers conduct more subtle, yet often more intrusive, spatial control in a compact residence.

Some employers set explicit rules to delineate the territory that domestic workers may enter. More often, the two parties develop a tacit agreement that the family and the maid have unequal rights to the use of household space. When I asked employers if they felt any inconvenience living with a nonfamily member, many gave an answer similar to this one: "Not at all! Because she knows how to be invisible! Whenever we watch TV in the living room or have guests over, she just hides herself on the balcony. She is well disciplined."

The spatial components of a residence contain different functions and meanings in family lives. The living room and dining room are reserved for the social activities of the family; they also constitute a front region where the family receives and entertains guests. In contrast, the spaces deemed appropriate for a domestic worker include the kitchen and the balcony. In these backstage regions, she cooks and does laundry to maintain the daily cycle of the family. Other than these areas, the bathroom, her bedroom (if she has one), and the children's playroom are the settings to which she has more access.

In many cases, workers stay in the same room as young children or patients in their care so that they can assist on a standby basis. These living arrangements seriously intrude on the privacy of workers and can amount to emotional and labor exploitation, as these two examples show:

> Here I have no privacy at all. In the beginning, they came in the room without knocking on the door and I was only wearing shorts or even panties. [Sometimes] I want to sleep and they get in and talk to her [the paralyzed patient]. I cannot sleep. Even in the middle of the night, whenever she wakes up, I wake up. All she needs, I am the one.

> I sleep with the child. The only place I can take a rest is the bathroom. I always go to the bathroom on the top floor. Nobody uses that one. After I clean it, I sit there, crying! I pray, "Lord, I want to go back to the Philippines!"

For surveillance reasons or because of a shortage of space, some workers are asked to sleep on a sofa bed in the living room or in a Japanese-style room with tatami mats and fusuma doors. To protect their privacy and safety, domestic workers manage to "territorialize" or "backstage-ize" the open space in which they sleep. For example, one worker hung clothes in her Japanese-style room in the evening to make the not entirely opaque fusuma door less translucent. Another worker sleeping in a living room moved the coffee table at night so that she could hear if someone tried to cross the barrier and enter her "domain" for sleeping.

The private home of employers is a workplace for migrant domestics that can be wired with mechanisms of surveillance. The possibility of child abuse and mistreatment haunt many employers, especially when both parents work elsewhere during the day. These employers often rely on devices or agents to monitor migrant caregivers. Some try to supervise the situation at home when they are at work by making frequent phone calls or surprise visits. Some ask their homemaker neighbors to keep an eye on workers or entrust security guards in their building or housing community with the job of preventing workers from going out without permission. More intrusive methods of surveillance, such as installing a secret recorder or video camera in the house, are rare, but not unheard of.

Grandparents are most often included in the surveillance of domestic workers. Several employers reported that they would not have hired a migrant worker without the presence of grandparents at home, typically with comments like this: "How can you feel at ease when you leave the children to a stranger—and a foreign stranger? But in my case, my mother-in-law lives together with us. It's better to have someone at home to watch." Employers within nuclear families may request grandparents who live nearby to pay periodic visits during the day. Others drive their children together with the migrant caregivers to the grandparents' house before work and pick them up after work. Some employers feel awkward about conducting surveillance in the intimate sphere and attempt to obscure their monitoring practices. They disguise their surprise visits as retrieving something left behind at home, or grandparents will drop by to check on the worker for the reason that they "miss the grandchildren."

Keeping the Wild in Custody

Albeit mostly working alone at home, migrant domestic workers have access to certain exterior space. They commute to spots related to their job duties such as supermarkets, hospitals (accompanying their wards), schools and parks (picking up and hanging out with the children). Garbage collection is another occasion for migrant domestic workers to leave the houses and meet other migrants in the neighborhood. These are their backstage areas where they can take a break from the observation of employers and connect with their national fellows. As it is, employers conduct surveillance not only to regulate the home space but also to control worker access to space outside the home.

As discussed in chapter 1, the CLA is greatly concerned with the problem of "runaway" foreign workers, and employers are held liable for it. To prevent workers from disappearing, which would lead to the freezing of quotas, many employers take it upon themselves to oversee a worker's mobility. The worker's passport is usually kept by the employer or agency during her stay in Taiwan, despite the fact that the CLA outlaws this practice. Most agencies suggest that employers not allow their workers to have Sundays off, especially during the first three or six months of a contract. Some employers require that workers take a day other than Sunday off as a measure to distance them from the larger community of migrant workers. In extreme cases, workers are not given house keys or are prevented from leaving their employer's residence on their own.

Other employers adopt more covert measures to monitor a worker's whereabouts. Some check the worker's room or personal belongings during her day off to look for any unusual signs that suggest the worker might run away. Some request information from the telephone company detailing the numbers of the worker's local calls in order to learn more about her social life. These employers looked embarrassed when describing these actions to me, but they rationalized their intrusion into the worker's privacy by viewing themselves as moral guardians. "We are not intruding, we are just concerned," said one employer.

Some employers ask their migrant employees to work on Sundays because of a special need, such as the care of a newborn baby or an invalid patient. However, others make this request for purposes of control. Shu-hwa explained, "We don't mind paying her [the worker] overtime at all. We just don't want her to go out, messing around with too many friends. It's better to stay home. Doing no work is fine." It is common thinking among Taiwanese employers that granting rest days to migrant domestic workers will inevitably have negative consequences: "We're afraid she might *bian-huai* [go astray] once she goes to church and socializes with other Filipinas." "We have specified this in the contract—no day off. We don't want them to be polluted at church."

What do employers mean by the expressions "going astray" and "being polluted"? What are the real concerns behind these perceived threats? The first reason for employers to confine workers is to distance them from the migrant community, which is considered a dangerous source of "pollution." The Catholic Church and church-based NGOs in Taiwan are major providers of legal information and assistance to migrant workers.[2] During Sunday mass and the social gatherings that follow, migrant domestic workers compare notes on employers, offer mutual advice, and swap tactics of resistance. When expressing worries about the "pollution" of the migrant community, employers are actually concerned about workers becoming more aware of their rights and more active in negotiating terms.

Employers are also troubled by a scenario in which migrant domestic workers might "go astray" if they meet boyfriends on their day off. Many workers reported experiences such as "my Ma'am always asks me if I meet other men in the church" or "they don't like me to go out every Sunday, because they are afraid I will do nasty things." These employers consider dating a migrant boyfriend to be a sign of moral degradation in migrant women, which may lead to pregnancy or "running away." Mindful of the criminal acts committed by some migrant domestic workers and their boyfriends, some employers worry about a connection between dating and kidnapping or burglary.[3]

Peggy is one of them. She terminated the contract of her Filipina worker when she discovered that the maid was dating a Filipino man. She believed she faced a dilemma between respecting the worker's rights and easing her own anxiety about her son's safety. She said: "I know she has the right to go out on a date. We probably shouldn't have forbidden it. My husband also told me this." Downcast for a few seconds, she kept her chin up and justified her rule: "But I was so panicked and worried about my son. He slept next door to my maid. You know, every night I would wake up several times and check to see if my son was still in his room."

Besides the "no dating" policy, migrant domestics are usually forbidden to receive visitors in the employer's house or to sleep over at their friends' houses, even on their days off. The discipline of migrant women is similar to the surveillance by a patriarchal family over the virtuous behavior of daughters. In the eyes of employers, female ones in particular, the threat of migrant women serving as potential seductresses or troublemakers rationalizes the imposition of moral control and even intrusion into a worker's privacy. These measures of spatial monitoring reinforce the subordinate status of migrant domestic workers in the family life and fortify moral boundaries in racial as well as gender terms.

BACK STAGE ON SUNDAYS

For migrant domestic workers, the most Cinderella-like role reversal accords with the front/backstage boundary between workdays and days off. In the front region—the employer's residence or under the watch of the employer—they display deference, avoid confrontation, and play the role of "good girl" to reduce employer concern. Sunday outings, which disrupt the normal routines and social relations at work, constitute the most important backstage arena for migrant domestic workers.

Migrant worker "weekend enclaves" have appeared in several Asian cities, such as at the Lucky Plaza in Singapore, the Central District in Hong Kong, and Chungshan District in Taipei. The Singaporean geographers Brenda Yeoh and Shirlena Huang (1998) describe them as "counterspaces" constructed by migrant domestic workers in challenging the dominant conceptions of public space; these weekend enclaves situated in public ironically provide migrant women with more personal freedom and privacy. I further explore the backstage activities of migrant domestic workers in Taiwan: they reclaim autonomy, privacy, and cultural differences at the Sunday carnival, and they reverse the hierarchical order symbolically through gossiping and ridiculing their employers' English.

Cinderella Going Out

Migrant domestic workers usually spend their Sundays performing the following routine: in the morning Filipino migrants gather with their *kababayans* (compatriots) at church and attend mass. Afterward they go shopping, have lunch, and send remittances and packages to friends or family in the immediate area. Indonesian domestic workers usually meet friends at Taipei Railway Station, hang out in the surrounding area, or catch a train to neighboring Taoyuan County. In the afternoon, migrant workers are also found in nearby parks and tourist spots, having picnics and taking photos. Some go to discos, dancing to electronic music and sweating their work stress away; others spend time in karaoke bars, singing favorite tunes from home. After a tiring day of touring the city, they hang out in fast food restaurants or on the floor of the train station before returning home in the evening.

Off-day dressing vividly illustrates the shift in identity from the front to the back stage. Although I have never heard of Taiwanese employers requiring domestic workers to wear uniforms, some rules on appearance do apply.[4] Most employers prohibit workers from wearing make-up, nail polish, or perfume at work. The typical style is a simple T-shirt with slacks or Bermuda shorts. Female employers would raise their eyebrows if workers wore V-collar shirts, skirts, or mini shorts. This dress code marks the difference between workers and employers, and in particular maids and madams. The "simple and covered" rule aims to suppress the femininity of workers and reinforce their class subordination.

When going out on Sundays, migrant women leave their employers' domain of control as well as their homes. They dress up in blouses, tight jeans, or short skirts; they put on glittering necklaces, dangling earrings, and high heels; and they pamper themselves with mascara, lipstick, and nail polish. With these material markers they project an urban, fashion-

FIGURE 5. *Indonesian migrant workers picnicking in a park*

conscious image with a reference to heterosexual femininity in drastic contrast to their appearance at work.[5] In this way, migrant workers not only disassociate themselves from the role of the maid but also attempt to diminish the hierarchical difference between "madam" and "maid" on the front stage. They often compliment each other's appearance on Sundays by saying, "Wow, you look like our madams!"

Their backstage activities on Sundays are a dramatic contrast to their deferential behavior at work. Although domestic workers cannot refuse used items handed down from employers on the front stage (Rollins 1985), shopping on Sundays becomes a way for them to feel empowered backstage. Many migrant workers spend a substantial amount of time and money shopping for a variety of items, including clothing, jewelry, and expensive appliances like DVD players and mobile phones. Sunday is also a feast day in which migrant workers enjoy generous amounts of food of home-country style. In the employers' houses, the maids have to match the tastes of employers and lack the autonomy to cook the kinds of food they like. Some even suffer from hunger or humiliation from the limited portions or variety of food they are given by employers.

Through a collective presence on the urban back stage, migrant workers achieve a sense of social belonging and solidarity. They use the Sunday gatherings to circulate legal information, express grievances, and offer emotional support to each other. They cry on each other's shoulders and color the gray mist of work routines as a maid with humor and laughter. For instance, while having a picnic with a group of Filipinas in a park one Sunday, Nora joked about her job: "I didn't know how to dance before. But after I worked as a domestic, I came back to the Philippines and my sister said, 'Wow, you know how to dance now.'" She then imitated mopping floors with an exaggerated swing of her buttocks, saying, "Because every day I do this, I lost all the fat on my belly!"

Passers-by could easily recognize a carnival atmosphere in the Sunday gathering of migrant workers. With singing, dancing, food sharing, and sometimes drinking and smoking, they turn parks and other public spaces into their picnic sites and festival grounds. These leisure activities not only deviate from their work routines but also depart from their ordinary lives back home. A sense of anonymity in overseas lives frees migrant women from parental control and conservative norms in villages. In addition, the carnivalization of Sunday activities creates utopian moments in which migrant workers can temporarily escape oppressive relations at work (Wu 1997). The physical activity of dancing in particular helps migrant workers release emotional stress. An Indonesian migrant told me that she spent most of her days off at the disco during the first year of her stay in Taiwan because "I was unhappy. I went dancing and I forgot about it."

The festival day nevertheless has to end. Most employers stipulate a curfew for the migrant worker's day off. It varies from six to nine o'clock. One Sunday evening, while Claudia and I sat on a sidewalk bench to kill the last hour before her curfew, I rubbed my legs, sore after a whole day of walking through the city. I said, "You folks are amazing. Every time I go out with you, I am totally exhausted. I cannot believe you leave the house at 6 a.m. but are still energetic until the last minute before your curfew!" Claudia softly answered: "You know what the truth is? We are tired, but when you think that you have to wait for another six or more days to see these people, you don't want to go home! Then you live it up! You don't feel tired anymore. It's like Cinderella. Next day, you go back to another life."

Like Cinderella, who goes back to the kitchen when her carriage turns

FIGURE 6. *Filipino migrant workers dancing in a disco*

into a pumpkin, at the end of the Sunday carnival, migrant women have to take off their make-up, turn off their mobile phones, and change from their fancy clothes into deferential aprons. In chapter 6 I discuss in more detail how migrant workers handle the transition between front and back stage as a practice of boundary work.

Backstage Linguistic Resistance

Gossiping is one of the common backstage activities of migrant domestic workers. On weekdays, they have to compliment their employers and pretend to be stupid. On Sundays, they exchange funny stories about employers and reveal family secrets, such as finding a condom in the pocket of a boss's shirt when doing the laundry. They also criticize the manners and taste of the employers. For example, one Filipina domestic worker once asked me, "Fried rice: you say *chaofan,* right?" After I nodded, she proudly announced to her compatriots: "We Filipinos eat fried rice for breakfast, but my employers want *chaofan* for dinner. And they say we Filipinos are poor? We eat real dinner, not fried rice! And Taiwanese think they are socialites?" Another time when I joined a gathering of Filipina migrants, Judy talked about her boss: "Taiwanese men are no good. Some of them are gross. My boss likes to eat betel nuts. He spits on the floor all the time!" She imitated the way he spat and everybody laughed.

Rina Cohen (1991: 204) points out the significance of collective gossiping and joking in such a group: "The joking and laughing serve not only as tension-release mechanisms for individuals, but also allow the participants to reinterpret experiences, share in mutually reassuring communication, and provide solidarity and support by transforming individual experiences into collective experiences." By gossiping about their employers, domestic workers reposition themselves from being the object of surveillance to its agent. In mocking and critical tones, they temporarily invert the hierarchy: they become the evaluators who claim some kind of superiority over their employers. The most acute example of this among Filipinas is linguistic resistance. As I have noted earlier, college-educated Filipina migrants have better English skills than many Taiwanese employers. This situation creates a contested space in the power dynamics of employment relations.

One Sunday evening, a few Filipina workers and I were having a picnic in a park. Lazily sitting on the grass, Grace and Carlita chatted about speaking in English with their Taiwanese employers in comparison to their previous employers in Singapore:

> *Grace:* I feel more comfortable speaking English here [in Taiwan].
> *Carlita:* In Singapore, they correct our English. Because they learn British English, but we learn American English, more similar to here. In Singapore, they don't say "vase" and "God" [*in an American accent*]. They say "varse" and "Gord" [*in an exaggerated British accent*].
> *PCL:* They think your English is wrong?
> *Carlita:* Yes, they think we are wrong and we should speak in their way.
> *PCL:* So when you said you feel more comfortable speaking English here, this is because English is similar here or because people here speak English worse than you?
> *Grace:* Of course it is the second reason [*laughs*] . . .
> *Carlita:* My employer said, "Oh, you speak very good English." I am thinking, "No, I speak lousy English." They ask me to speak slowly, but I think I already speak very slow!
> *Grace:* My employer's friends also said to her, "Oh, it's very good you have someone teach English free of charge!"

Many Asian host societies, including Hong Kong, Malaysia, and Singapore, were part of the British colonial empire. British English remains powerful in these societies in the postcolonial era. A bilingual education system has been in place in Singapore since the 1950s, and the use of English in both official and family settings has become widespread among younger generations of Singaporeans.[6] In Hong Kong, before the handover of power from Britain to China, English was the official language and was used at all levels of education (Crystal 1997).

As shown in the conversation above, Singaporean employers hold the view that there is a "correct" accent or "standard" English, which comes from Britain. This view reflects an internalization of colonial linguistic habitus, although what they speak is actually a Singaporean emulation of the British accent. In this way, however, Singaporean employers establish their authority by insisting on the superiority and legitimacy of their linguistic performance in contrast to the Filipinas' "mispronunciation" (American English with a Filipino accent).

In Taiwan, English has never been a dominant language, a condition that increases the relative value of this linguistic capital and enlarges the gray area of this symbolic struggle. Some Filipina domestic workers gain a sense of cultural superiority over their Taiwanese employers, given their command of English, a language they consider to carry more economic value and cultural currency. As they embrace the symbolic hegemony of this global language, they devalue other languages in a way similar to the manner in which their employers belittle Filipino dialects. The Chinese lessons I gave at Holy Spirit covered the basic vocabulary of Hoklo (Taiwan's primary mother tongue, especially among older generations and in rural areas). Helen was among the Filipina attendants who complained about how hard it was to learn this Chinese language. She said, bluntly:

> I don't understand—Why don't people here speak English? Those ladies in the department stores, they are pretty and dressed in fashion, but they can't even speak English! I don't know what they learn at school. They are wasting their time, and now we have to waste our time to learn this stupid language!

When chatting with friends on Sundays, Filipina migrant workers often ridicule the poor English or funny accents of their Taiwanese employers. Nicole Constable (1997a: 177) reported a similar observation among Filipina migrant domestic workers in Hong Kong, in which several workers would develop a "quiz" on the special skills a domestic worker needs in interpreting her employer's poor English. The following examples are two of the many jokes I heard circulating among Filipina migrants in Taiwan:

> One day they [the employers] went out and I stayed home by myself. They called from outside: "Jamie, you go sleep first. Don't wait for us. We will come home eleven years [eleven o'clock]." I yelled on the phone: "Eleven years? But I'm here only for three years [the length of a contract]!"

> My employer called from the office and said, "Luisa, twelve hours, don't forget to eat my children!" She actually meant, "twelve o'clock, don't forget to *feed* my children!" [*laughter*]
> *Oh my God. Did you correct her?*
> No. Some employers don't like that. So I just answered: "Don't worry! I already eat your children!"

These jokes are rich with information about the workers' daily labor conditions and social interaction with employers. When sharing these jokes with fellow workers, migrant domestics reinterpret the working experiences from their own perspective and caricature the job scripts imposed by employers as unsuccessful assignments full of grammatical errors. Many ridicule the ways employers give work instructions, for example, "divorce [divide] the chicken and pry [fry] it when oil is dancing [boiling]." Another common topic is the consequences of misunderstanding when employers are incapable of issuing instructions in English. For instance, one employer asked her maid to *throw* some letters (put letters in the mailbox), and the maid dutifully dumped them in the garbage.

To some degree, these backstage jokes may "temporarily reverse the pattern of dominance and subservience between employers and workers" (Constable 1997a: 176). However, the exchange of jokes and laughter is mostly hidden back stage. In front of their employers, migrant workers tend to follow the script of deferential performance, while cautiously exercising linguistic resistance in disguise. They consciously avoid correcting their employers' errors in English to avoid a confrontation that might risk contract termination. Vanessa described her "never argue with the boss" strategy when talking about an outspoken friend, Carina, who was dismissed by her employer:

> You remember Carina? She likes to argue with her employer. She corrects her employer's English. I told her: whatever they say, you accept it! Don't correct them! They said you "drop" the soup. They meant "put it down." Carina said to them, "Ma'am, not right." That's why they don't like her! Never argue with your boss! They don't like you to be the higher place. I know everything, but I don't show it to my boss. I just bow and nod, [saying] yes and no.

IMMOBILE WORKERS, MOBILE PHONES

Having described the double settings of front and back stage in the lives of global Cinderellas, I now examine how migrant domestic workers counteract geographical constraints with the use of mobile phones. The wireless technology facilitates synchronous communication transcending spatial divides and creates a sense of "simultaneity of place and time" as a marked feature of global modernity (Pertierra et al. 2002).

When I started the second phase of my fieldwork in the fall of 2002, I was greatly surprised at the prevalence of mobile phones among migrant workers.[7] Nowadays the total of cell phones in use worldwide has exceeded the number of fixed phone lines (Accountancy 2003). Taiwan is one of the frontiers in this technological revolution. Its proportion of mobile phone ownership is the highest in the world.[8] Nor are migrant workers left out in this rapid expansion of mobile communications. The mobile nature of this technical device parallels the transnational mobility of migrant domestic workers, yet contrasts sharply with their homebound circumstances.

To a certain extent, mobile phones allow people to engage in communication that is "free from the constraint of physical proximity and spatial immobility" (Geser 2004: 3). Yet, rather than celebrate the liberating effect of cell phones, I argue that mobile information technologies have demonstrated what Doreen Massey (1994: 149) calls "the power geometry of time-space compression"—different groups and individuals are placed in very distinct ways in relation to moves and connections facilitated by time-space compression. The "mobility" created by wireless technology is differentiated by social inequalities among phone users—along the divides

FIGURE 7. *Two Indonesian migrants at Taipei Railway Station on Sunday*

of class and citizenship status in this case. The ways migrant domestic workers use mobile phones accord with their particular experiences of time-space relations as live-in workers and transnational subjects.

As such, the use of mobile phones provides a strategic site for exploring the lives of migrant domestics across the front and back stage. The mobile phone is a means for them to negotiate privacy and to display their consuming power. It helps them offset or resist enforcement of labor control, but it can nevertheless become a tool of surveillance for employers. Moreover, wireless technology has created a virtual meeting place, which allows migrants to build networks, maintain family ties, and rejoin the world of romance.

Negotiation of Privacy

Some migrant domestic workers use mobile phones with their employers' permission or even encouragement. These employers accord this in order to prevent the workers from using their landline phones, which avoids the possibility of overcharging for international phone calls. Employers might also prefer workers to use a separate line to keep family privacy more intact. Phone calls from strangers represent a nuisance or a disturbance that trespasses boundaries of intimacy.

Other workers are prohibited from owning or using a mobile phone. Their employers do not allow them to make or answer phone calls at work. One migrant worker quoted her employer as saying: "Why are you talking? You talk; you don't work." Although domestic workers are confined to the house for long working hours, employers have no guarantee that they will not be idle. Some employers expect their workers to make a constant effort in the household during working hours. The act of "playing with the phone" (in the words of one employer) is considered a distraction from work. In some cases, the children of employers were given spying duty: they reported to their parents if caregivers used their phones during the day.

Employers may forbid migrant workers from using mobile phones for more strict purposes of labor control. They try to prevent workers from making connections with other migrants, suspecting that migrant networks could activate information exchanges about their rights and increase the chance of "running away." In other words, these employers view telecommunications as disruptive to maintaining a worker's geographical immobility. Ironically, some other employers permit their workers to use mobile phones for the same reason. They do not want their migrant employees to use public phones for fear that workers would "hook up with boys" or "fool around with neighbors" when staying out on a frequent basis.

Despite objections from employers, many migrant domestics use mobile phones surreptitiously. They turn on their phones late at night or switch the phone to the silent, vibrating mode during the day to answer calls. This is a "cellular back stage" that migrant domestic workers secretly build to protect their private lives from employers' intrusion. For those workers under the tight control of employers (no days off, no outings), mobile phones are the only means by which they can reach the outside world. These conversations help them relieve exhaustion and loneliness after a long working day. Yet several workers told me that they had to whisper under quilts when talking to friends at night. They lowered their voices to avoid disturbing the sleep of their care recipients who stayed in the same room and tried to shield their conversations from employers generally.

In some cases, mobile phones can be used to monitor the movements of workers. Some employers lend phones to the workers so that they can be reached outside the house. Phone calls then become an intrusion into the private sphere of migrant workers, creating a work-related "cellular front" in their backstage settings (such as outings on days off). Sometimes on Sundays workers receive phone calls from their employers, who ask them to come home early for the sake of the children or the elderly. To avoid this extra workload, some workers choose to hide their phone numbers from their employers. When employers asked about their contact information, they simply answered: "Don't bother. I change the numbers all the time."

Prepaid Cards and Text Messages

In several respects, the ways migrant workers use mobile phones are distinct from the patterns of use by Taiwanese in general. First, migrant workers usually use prepaid cards instead of subscription to a regular account. Telephone companies in Taiwan usually require that subscribers who are not citizens need the company of a Taiwanese citizen as a guarantor upon their application.[9] This poses less a problem for foreign professionals and teachers, who can obtain a guarantee from their companies or schools (Hsu 2004). However, few household or factory employers are willing to endorse their migrant employees. Migrant contract workers, given their class and citizenship status, have no other option but to use prepaid cards, the rates for which tend to be more expensive than for a monthly subscription.

The media has coined the term "foreign laborers' cards" (*wailao ka*) to describe the prevalent use of prepaid cards among migrant contract workers. The police are concerned that some Taiwanese use foreign workers' personal information to obtain cell phone numbers for the purposes of criminal activities; it is difficult to trace these phone records during police investigations.[10] The chief of the Criminal Investigation Bureau commented on a recent kidnapping of a female college student: "If the suspects were not using a 'foreign laborers' card,' we could have caught them earlier and the victim might not have died."[11] After this event, the regulation on purchases of prepaid cards, especially by foreigners, tightened.[12] It not only aims to prevent the use of mobile telecommunication as a tool of crime but also indicates an implicit public anxiety about the fleeting presence of migrant workers and their phone numbers.

Second, given the expensive rates for mobile phones, migrant workers often use another cheaper service: the Short Message Service (SMS). Apart from its low cost, SMS provides users with the option of delaying a response until a more appropriate time. This lack of intrusiveness is critical for migrant domestic workers, who are often unable to answer the phone when at work or within the view of employers. SMS, with an asynchronous mode of communication, enables migrant domestics to maintain back-stage communication while operating on the front stage.[13] They can turn off the ring but keep the mobile phone on, so they can receive texts from friends and reply to them later.

Because the length of a text message is strictly curtailed, SMS users tend to use homophones, abbreviations, and other shorthand expressions to save space and money. Scholars have noticed that young users, in particular, create slang and new words that are understood only within small groups (Ling and Yttri 2002). Likewise, migrant workers have developed common linguistic codes to facilitate rapid communication with family and friends. These "group specific linguistic habits and codes" (Geser 2004: 13) mark group boundaries and bolster a sense of in-group identification. For example, "u go out sndy?" stands for "Are you going out this Sunday?" "hapi 2 c u, gudnyt" stands for "Happy to see you. Good night."

Migrant workers in Taiwan often mix English, Tagalog or Bahasa Indonesia, and romanized Chinese in their messages. For example, "i just 1 2 say, cie cie, slmat" stands for "I just want to say, thank you (Chi.), salamat (Ind.)." Such multilingualism indicates their liminal positioning across a

FIGURE 8. *Display of prepaid cards on sale in a migrant shop*

number of cultural territories. In the beginning, I had great difficulty in deciphering these codes, and I continue to be amazed at how clearly migrant workers understand each other despite their very spontaneous methods for romanizing Chinese. The latter demonstrates that migrant workers manage to obtain a command of the Chinese language as a practical kit for daily survival.

SMS not only facilitates communication on a person-to-person basis but also provides a broadcasting tool for rapid, wide, and cheap distribution of public information (Lasen 2002). Text messages offer a vital platform for the exchange of information among migrant domestic workers who are isolated at work or have no days off. Information is posted about news from home and migration policy updates in Taiwan. In addition, migrant domestic workers circulate chain messages that carry jokes, short poems, and pictures consisting of characters included on the keypad of the handset. Through these creative pieces and humorous words, migrant workers cheer each other up against a backdrop of boredom and loneliness at work.

Current events have proved that SMS has great potential for arranging collective action at low cost.[14] This capacity for collective mobilization is especially significant in the Philippines, where around one hundred million text messages are sent on a daily basis.[15] Overseas Filipino workers are even more intensive SMS users. During the outbreak of the Iraq War in 2003, Philippines embassies in the Middle East region resorted to this means of telecommunication to keep in touch with Filipino communities (Asis 2004: 14). In Taiwan, although collective activism is limited among migrant workers, the exchange of text messages creates a public platform in the burgeoning development of migrant organizations.[16] Migrant members use text messages to inform each other about group meetings and announce forthcoming activities to those who are constrained by work and cannot join the meetings.

Finally, mobile phones can be a substitute for other electronic devices that are in short supply among some migrant workers. They use cell phones to listen to radio programs or check emails when a radio or a computer is not available or not allowed by employers. Some mobile phones contain an inserted camera. This function allows migrant workers to take photos useful in particular circumstances. For instance, in January 2005 a group of Filipina migrant workers used their phone-camera to document the difficult working conditions in their factories; these images turned into critical evidence for their petition to the CLA for more appropriate job transfers.[17] The mobile phone, a compact multitasking device, serves as a critical tool of everyday technology for migrant workers to grapple with spatial constraints and deficits in resources in their daily lives.

Consuming Modernity and Nomadic Intimacy

Consumption is an important means of self-expression and identity marking. The purchase of a mobile phone, an item that is easily displayed, becomes critical for migrant workers who wish to show off their spending power. Phone models popular among migrant workers are usually quite recent releases that are compact and expensive. One Indonesian migrant explained that they have no choice but to follow this rule because of peer pressure: "All of us have small mobile phones. If you buy a big one, people will laugh at you: 'Is this a shoe? An alarm clock?' So you have to buy a small one."

Many migrants purchase cell phones not only for their own use but also for their family members back home. Updated models are a must-buy gift when migrant workers return home permanently or on vacation. In addition to the symbolic function of "conspicuous consumption" (Veblen 1912/1994), the purchase is practical because many households in Indonesia and the Philippines are not wired with landlines. The market for mobile phones has grown rapidly in these two countries. In the Philippines, twenty-two million (of a total eighty million) Filipinos have cell phones, but there are only 6.7 million available landline telephones and only half of these phones are subscribed.[18] In Indonesia, the number of mobile phone users increased by 60 percent in 2003 and today totals more than twenty million, or 9 percent of the population. According to market estimates, this number is expected to rise to sixty million by 2008.[19]

With this wireless technology, transnational migrants are able to maintain "nomadic intimacy" (Fortunati 2001) despite their diasporic nature. Transnational family ties are built on the many phone calls and text messages circulated across borders. Some migrant mothers even send daily messages to their children. In a study conducted in the Philippines (Pertierra et al. 2002), a man whose wife works in Hong Kong calls him twice a day, in the morning and at night; he said that he felt as if "she is just around." This study found that mobile phones have a positive impact on cross-border marital relations, because couples can share intimate moments during voice calls; their intimacies sometimes take place in a graphic form, such as that a wife likes to end her phone calls with detailed instruction for her husband to kiss her from head to toes. In addition, mobile phones allow transnational couples to monitor each other for the prevention of extramarital affairs.

However, the convenience of wireless technology comes at a great cost. Most migrant workers spend a significant amount of money on phone calls and text messaging. According to a survey by Hsu Wei-ching (2004), the average amount spent on phone cards per month is NT$1,637, second only to food (NT$2,001). Some migrants I know spend as much as NT$5,000 per month on their phone, which is one third of their monthly income.

The building of "nomadic intimacy" among migrant workers is not limited to connections with family and other relatives back home. Some also use mobile phones to expand their connections and explore the possibility of romance. Several Indonesian women I know found Indonesian boyfriends who were working in other countries such as Malaysia and Saudi Arabia. Some couples were introduced through referrals by migrant friends. Magazines that target overseas migrant workers also publish personal advertisements with contact cell phone numbers. A few migrant friends of mine developed long-distance relationships through transnational telecommunication. Some even discussed the prospect of marriage after meeting one another back in their home countries.

To sum up, mobile phone technology can empower people through facilitating communication, but the benefits of emancipation are mediated by the social positioning of phone users. The increase in freedom and autonomy often comes hand-in-hand with growing personal responsibility and exposure to new forms of social control.[20] The ways in which migrant workers use mobile phones (prepaid cards or text messaging) are indeed a reflection of their marginal status as noncitizens and their employment conditions in the host country. Employers may encourage migrant employees to own a mobile phone or prohibit them from using one, in both cases to increase control over their working conditions. Migrant workers, nevertheless, do assert agency through the purchase and use of mobile phones. By contacting fellow migrants and their transnational family through the air, live-in domestic workers lessen the constraints of spatial segregation and physical distance.

MARGINAL INCORPORATION IN THE CITY

The communities of migrant workers in Taiwan do not appear as a spatially confined and constantly active ethnic enclave. Their activities are intermittent—dormant on weekdays and active only on Sundays—and their members are fluid—most migrant workers do not reside in the community but only visit as consumers on their days off. These features of communities, again, reflect how migrant domestic workers experience particular time-space relations in Taiwan under the regulations imposed by host families and states—more specifically, their live-in condition and transient residence.

Given these constraints, Filipino and Indonesian domestic workers have developed communities of their own. The infrastructure of the communities rests on the support of other transnational migrants, including missionaries, ethnic Chinese, and marriage migrants from Southeast Asia. Based on the transnational flows of goods and people, these business-oriented enclaves accommodate the social activities and consumptive needs of migrant contract workers. These migrant communities tend to be segregated along national lines. Such ecology emerges out of scale economy, but it also mirrors a relationship of market competition between migrant groups. In the following, I introduce the distinct spatial patterns of Filipino and Indonesian migrant communities in Taipei. Both demonstrate complex spatial practices that incorporate and marginalize migrant workers at the same time.

Chungshan: A Holy Site with Business Niches

St. Christopher is a modest Catholic church located on Chungshan North Road in Taipei. This church has offered mass in English ever since American soldiers were stationed in Taiwan in the 1950s. The neighborhood, filled with American-style bars and restaurants, is still frequented by Western expatriates. This landmark symbolizes Taiwan's past dependence on the United States as well as Taiwan's present transnational ties. Since the early 1990s, St. Christopher has become the most popular gathering place for Filipino migrant workers on Sundays. In addition to an English service, the church now offers mass in Tagalog in response to the increasing number of Filipino churchgoers. According to the estimate of a Filipino missionary, at least three thousand people attend mass there every Sunday.

The surrounding area, known as Chungshan by migrant workers, has acquired nicknames like "Little Manila" and "Philippines City" among Taiwanese. Tagalog characters are seen on many signboards of Filipino grocery stores, delicatessens, karaoke clubs, and remittance and cargo services. On Sundays the streets are flooded with Taiwanese and Filipino vendors selling all sorts of commodities, including Filipino newspapers, magazines, CDs, videotapes, Tagalog romance novels, clothes, underwear, jewelry, cosmetics, luggage, sheets, typewriters, and even used computers. Migrants can also purchase homemade Filipino food and take advantage of low-cost services such as hairdressing, manicures, and hair perms in the alley behind the church.

Trading on the street saves rent and avoids tax but the informal economy also has its downside. Street vending is outlawed by the city government, and police patrols rack the nerves of migrant workers, legal and illegal alike. Under these circumstances, most retailers and services in the alley have recently relocated to the second floor of a nearby shopping mall,

FIGURE 9. *Filipina migrants posing for photos in front of St. Christopher church*

FIGURE 10. *Filipino migrants hawking food in the alley behind the church*

Wan-Wan Plaza. This mall had been unsuccessful in attracting Taiwanese customers and used to have many vacancies, but it has now become vibrant after an inflow of migrant businesses.

After being incorporated in the formal economy, migrant businesses become less accessible to foreign contract workers, who have no cultural resources or legal position to work outside their contract jobs. Most establishments in the Chungshan area are owned and managed by ethnic Chinese (*huaqiao*) or Southeast Asian women who are married to Taiwanese men (so-called foreign brides). These "outsiders within" in Taiwanese society import goods through transnational networks to reproduce a home-country lifestyle that accommodates the circular flow of guest workers. Some business owners also utilize migrant contract workers as their distributors of goods. By selling Internet phone cards, mobile phone SIM cards, or Levis jeans to their compatriots, migrant workers can make some extra money as part-time entrepreneurs.

Most stores in this plaza are open on Sundays or weekends only. So how do the owners cover rent and other costs when their stores are open for such a short time? One solution is to raise the price of food and services. Migrant workers are not at all discouraged by the inflated prices. Jessie, a

FIGURE 11. *A Filipino specialty shop*

Filipina-Chinese delicatessen owner, said in an interview: "They [migrant workers] can only eat their home-country food one day a week, so they don't care how much they have to pay." The other solution is to set up a partnership with a local business. A few diners managed by Taiwanese that serve local customers become Filipino delicatessens only on Sundays. One Filipino karaoke club rents space on Sundays from a local community organization.

Jessie came to Taiwan over ten years ago by entering an arranged marriage to a local man. Thanks to the business niche created by the recent inflow of Filipino migrant workers, she successfully runs a delicatessen and wins recognition from her husband and parents-in-law because of her financial gains. As Lisa Law (2001) has argued, the sensory practice of home cooking creates a sense of familiarity in the imagining of place and enables migrant workers as national subjects. Marriage migrants like Jessie play a critical role in the cultural economy of migration, in which food is a significant marker for identity negotiation (Wang 2004). Their culinary skills and knowledge, which may not be appreciated by their husbands' families, contribute greatly to the reclaiming of cultural differences and ethnic identities in migrant communities.[21] The company of migrant customers also heals the homesickness of Jessie, who feels alienated in Taiwan despite her Chinese descent. She said, "They are like my brothers and sisters. I feel like back to my hometown on Sundays."

Taiwanese business owners have also recognized the rich profits to be made from the consumer pool of migrant workers. They have created a stratified market that serves both Taiwanese and migrant customers, albeit with distinct products or in different time brackets. Low-priced clothing chain stores, such as Giordano and Hang Ten, have opened outlets in this area. Special sales are held on Sundays and offer out-of-season or defective stock at discount prices. A few discos target Filipino migrant workers as their major customers on Sunday afternoons, a time not popular among Taiwanese partygoers. These clubs even provide free shuttles to transport migrant workers directly from the church to the clubs. In a similar vein, nearby "love hotels" offer discount prices for rooms on Sunday afternoons, a promotional strategy that targets migrant couples.

For Taiwanese people, the Chungshan area is a business district known for wedding photography. Glamorous wedding gowns are displayed in the shop windows only one or two blocks from the St. Christopher church. It is common practice for Taiwanese couples to take photographs before their wedding, a ritual that allows brides-to-be to experience the vanity and pleasure of being a queen for a day (Lee 1999). The Western fairy tale of an opulent wedding and a beautiful bride is, however, incompatible with the stigmatized images of Southeast Asian migrants—impoverished, backward, and uncultured. Local stores and residents in this neighborhood have aired grievances about the noise and mess caused by migrant workers. They are concerned that the image of "Little Manila" or "Philippines City" will bring about a decline in business and real estate prices, especially because Sundays are the busiest day for wedding photography studios and real estate agents (Wu 2003).

The collective presence of Filipino migrant workers in the Chungshan area has transformed the consumer-cultural landscape of Taipei City. Migrant workers use shopping as a way of celebrating their financial improvement and contesting their feelings of indignity and powerlessness at work. They are sought-after consumers for low-priced commodities and downtime services. Local businesspeople embrace foreign workers to maximize profits, and transnational entrepreneurs reunite with their working-class compatriots to maintain business niches. Nevertheless, migrant workers are welcome only as visiting consumers rather than permanent residents, as the presence of these ethnic others is still considered a taint on the public appearance and cultural presentation of the neighborhood.

Train Stations: Nodes of Flows and Networks

Unlike Catholic churches, which occupy a central position in the spiritual community and political mobilization of Filipino migrants, mosques play no such role among Indonesian migrant workers in Taiwan. The activities of Indonesian domestic workers on their day off are more decentralized and spatially fluid. Taipei Railway Station, the primary site of their gathering, serves as a node of personal flow, social networking, and chains of activities.

Taipei Railway Station is a modern six-floor building that contains public facilities like toilets, phone booths, shops, and food courts. This fully air-conditioned building shelters migrant workers from the discomfort of summer heat and winter rain in Taipei. They usually sit on the floor of the ground-level lobby, chatting, napping, sharing snacks and homemade ethnic food, or reading Indonesian magazines purchased from the grocery store upstairs. When hungry, they feed their homesick stomachs at the Indonesian delicatessens. When bored, they go shopping in the underground Metro Mall or hang out in small dance clubs and karaoke bars run by Indonesian Chinese in the nearby streets.

An invisible yet firm line divides migrant workers and Taiwanese passengers in the first-floor lobby. Most Taiwanese hurry through the hallway to buy tickets or catch trains. When passing by, they avoid eye contact with the migrant crowd. The spacious lobby, well lit and with a high ceiling, has virtually no seating. The waiting areas are located underground. The design of the station, built in 1989, aimed to create a sense of flow as well as to discourage homeless people from congregating there (Wu 2004). This spatial image has, nevertheless, been modified with increasing use of the station by migrant workers. The station has become a picnic site and temporary shelter where migrant workers spend an average of six hours on Sundays, according to one survey.[22] They turn the lobby into their home floors and replicate their former lifestyle to overcome social and cultural alienation in a foreign country. An Indonesian migrant said:

FIGURE 12. *Gathering of migrant workers at Taipei Railway Station*

FIGURE 13. *Indonesian migrants and the author (third from right) picnicking on the station floor. Courtesy of Lo Jung*

Taiwanese think this is no good. Sitting on the floor, it's dirty. But it's OK with us. We sit on the floor at home . . . Here, we eat Indonesian food, we talk in Bahasa Indonesia, we buy Indonesian goods. It seems that we were in Indonesia, not in Taiwan anymore.

For migrant domestics who are isolated at work, the station is a central node that allows them to enter the flow of fellow migrants. Most Indonesian domestic workers take only one or two days off each month. Therefore, they don't necessarily take the same day off as their limited number of friends do. Many try to meet new friends in the train station so that they will have company on their rest days. Often they will run into "classmates" who were recruited by the same agencies in Indonesia and with whom they spent months together at the training center before coming to Taiwan. They also "territorialize" space in the train station by using the numbers on the wall (area markers such as B20) to mark particular corners at which friends can gather on a regular basis.

Taipei Railway Station is a major hub for local transport from which migrant workers can take the Mass Rapid Transit (MRT) rail system or buses to many tourist spots across Taipei. It is also a convenient place for migrant workers from various cities to gather on Sundays. From there, they can also easily visit nearby cities, in particular Taoyuan and Chungli, where large numbers of migrant factory workers reside.[23] Many Indonesian domestic workers in Taipei take a train ride (forty minutes) to Taoyuan on most Sundays. Taoyuan has become a major migrant enclave serving as an extension of Taipei Railway Station. In addition to offering cheaper rent in this region, Taoyuan makes for a popular spot to gather because of its proximity to industrial areas where male migrants work and reside. As the majority of Indonesian migrants in Taiwan are women, it is common to see couples in Taoyuan consisting of a Thai man and an Indonesian woman, who communicate with each other with their limited Chinese vocabulary.

Walking out of Taoyuan Railway Station through an underground tunnel, one enters an exotic wonderland filled with vendors selling phone cards, mobile phone accessories, and cheap toys. Taiwanese developers long disregarded this area behind the station, but it is now filled with three-story complexes of migrant business—the first floor a delicatessen, the second floor a karaoke bar, and the third floor a dance club. There one can taste satay and phat Thai, purchase coconut milk and shrimp crackers, and meet potential mates on the dance floor. Some restaurants also provide satellite television sets that show synchronous news and programs from Thailand or Indonesia (Wang 2004).

These multi-functioned stores provide a secluded backstage setting that shelters migrant workers from the inspective looks of Taiwanese. The gatherings of migrant workers in public space have attracted complaints from urban residents. One criticism particularly targets squatters in Taipei Railway Station, which is designed as a front stage on which the city displays an image of modernity to visitors. When one Taipei City councilor conducted a survey of Taiwanese people in the train station, 76 percent of the 272 respondents said that they were either "disgusted" or felt "bad" about the noise and mess made by migrant workers there on Sundays. Ninety percent of those polled viewed the phenomenon as a "negative subculture" that would ruin the image of this city landmark.[24]

Taoyuan, in contrast to Taipei, is a relatively backstage region in the scheme of national development. While Taipei stands as a metropolis for financial and service industries, the industrial parks of Taoyuan suffer from water shortages and air pollution. This satellite city has accommodated the relocation of industrial plants from the overcrowded and overpriced metropolis. The dispersal of migrant businesses from Taipei to Taoyuan follows a similar spatial pattern. Moreover, the migrant enclave in Taoyuan is located behind the main public thoroughfare. In other words, it is the backstage part of a backstage region; it is the marginal part of a marginal city.

Indonesian workers feel less excluded in Taoyuan in comparison to the metropolis. In Taipei, Indonesian migrant workers usually shop at the underground Metro Mall. Few of them ever visit the major department stores just across the street from the railway station. One Indonesian informant told us that she "feels scared of getting into it. Things there must be very expensive." This far-beyond-my-class image is framed by the architecture of one department store in particular, which is located in the second-tallest building (fifty-two floors) in Taipei. Some workers who were adventurous enough to walk into the department store felt discriminated against by the sales staff: "They look at us in a different way. They smile to Taiwanese, welcome them. But not to us, they think Indonesians are maids, are poor people."

The CLA once proposed relocating migrant workers to places of less public visibility, but no such proposals have turned into practical plans. After more than a decade of recruiting migrant workers, Taiwanese have gradually accepted their presence as long as they remain on the margins spatially as well as socially. The spatial locations of Indonesian workers' Sunday activities clearly symbolize a pattern of "marginal incorporation": they gather at the corners of Taipei Railway Station; they eat and dance behind the prime public area in Taoyuan; and they shop underground rather than in skyscraper department stores.

MOVING ACROSS COUNTRIES

Another spatial formation that accords with the front/backstage distinction and situates the identity formation of migrant workers is the transnational social space composed of both home and host countries. In front of the audience back at home, their family, friends, and villagers, migrant workers are cast in the role of "overseas heroes" who are assumed to have achieved material gains and undertaken a pilgrimage to modernity during their overseas journey. The dark secrets of their working experiences—filled with hardship, suffering, and alienation—are often hidden backstage and shared only with migrants in the host country. Some migrant domestic workers, mostly downwardly mobile Filipinas, even conceal or obscure their job descriptions in Taiwan from their friends and acquaintances in the Philippines. One informant said:

> I met a Filipina on the street in Taipei. She's my neighbor in the Philippines. She was an instructor. She asked me not to tell people I saw her in Taiwan. Many people don't even tell their family and friends what they are really doing here. They don't know we are just washing dishes and dogs!

When I first requested an interview from Marilou, a twenty-nine-year-old college-graduated Filipina, she asked me: "Are you going to publish it in the newspaper? Last time some reporters came and wanted to take a picture of me. I said, no-no, I don't want my friends in the Philippines to see me mopping floors in Taiwan!" Weeks later, Marilou told me she had to do more "aerobics" (the secret code for part-time cleaning jobs among Filipina domestics) recently because she just sent US$100 to sponsor her high school reunion. I asked why she had to send money given that she could not attend the reunion, and she answered: "They asked for a donation for school renovating. OCWS [Overseas Contract Workers] are major donors. Because we work abroad, they think we earn more money, we should donate more."

Displaying material gains is the most effective way for migrant workers to maintain the glamour of working abroad in front of their peers. In addition to the regular demand of remittances from family members, relatives and friends also make monetary requests on an irregular basis for purposes such as renovating houses, sponsoring a nephew's education, supporting an ill relative, or attending a school reunion. Migrant workers find it difficult to refuse these requests because they lose face if they fail to satisfy these demands. A large amount of their savings is spent in purchasing expensive consumer items and gifts for relatives and neighbors upon their return back home. The baggage claims in the international airports in Manila and Jakarta are always stuffed with large cardboard shipping boxes, containing television sets, CD players, DVD players, and other appliances.

However, to maintain a glamorous lifestyle at home is not easy for returned migrants. Judy, a single Filipina in her late twenties, explained why many of her siblings have been working overseas across countries for years: "They bought a lot of appliances, car, house. [And] they stay in the Philippines for a long time without income. Then they have to sell the car. They want to work abroad again, and they have to borrow money again." Judy considered the circular migration trajectory as an unavoidable fate, because: "Stay in the Philippines, you sacrifice. In Taiwan, at least you earn money and you can buy whatever you like. You can bring some money home and start a business." However, when I asked how many people actually start a business, her bright tone turned somber: "That I don't know."

"Starting a business" is a phrase widely used by migrant workers to describe their future plan. The business usually refers to traditional investments in commercial sectors and equipment, such as jeepneys,[25] tricycles, taxis, sari-sari (small grocery stores in the Philippines), delicatessens, and other petite retailing businesses. Very few of the migrants in my study plan to invest in more diversified economic activities or to use their skills or training acquired by working overseas. Raul Pertierra (1992: 17) points out two factors that explain returnees' preference for such investments: first, investments of this type serve as status symbols validating returnees' affluence in an underdeveloped economy; and, second, they satisfy the demands of family members to share or manage the money together. When a returned migrant purchases a profit-making vehicle, it is usually her brother or husband who becomes the driver or runs the business.

Returned migrants tend to stay unemployed, at least for some time, upon their return, as a way to verify their financial gains and advanced status in the local community (Pertierra 1992: 17). The aspiration of starting a business often fades in the end, because their savings are exhausted by the debts incurred in the migration process and the monetary requests of relatives.[26] In February 2002, two and half years after my fieldwork with Filipina migrants, I went to the Philippines to visit some of my informants. Many of these returned migrants were unemployed and in the process of applying to work abroad. Quite a number of them had relocated to Hong Kong, Israel, and Canada as domestic workers. A Filipina friend wrote to me from the Philippines to request possible job opportunities in Taiwan. When I asked her why she aborted her plan of settling down in the Philippines, she replied to me in an e-mail:

You ask me why I need to go back to work abroad. I supposed not to go back but, if it is the only way that we can earn money with a bigger amount then no choice but back to the usual. If you're an ex-abroad, it's really difficult to adjust to the lifestyle here in the Philippines. It seems that you're not content with what you earn here. You will say too little I'm not used to it. Then the temptation enters your mind—why not go back abroad if there is an opportunity?

The satisfaction with "livable" wages is always relative to life expenses mediated by social and individual expectations. After these homecoming migrants become accustomed to the wages and leisure styles in host countries, they often find it difficult to live on a meager income in the home country. Not to mention that they have to start at the entry level, because their knowledge and skills are considered dated after working overseas in unskilled jobs for a significant period. Marilou is an "ex-Taiwan" or "ex-abroad"—migrants who used forged documentation to circumvent the admission regulation enforced by Taiwan's government.[27] At the end of her second contract, she was worried about her next step:

What are you going to do? Will you come back to Taiwan?
No. I have enough experience with Taiwan already—five years! My employer asked me to change name [and come back]. I said I am tired of changing names. I am afraid when I go home, I don't know what my name is anymore!
So will you stay in the Philippines?
I don't know. [In the Philippines], I will have to start from the bottom again. And think about the salary. It's very difficult, after we have got used to here.

To avoid starting over in the labor market in the Philippines, Marilou decided to look for job opportunities in the global market, particularly in Canada and Hong Kong.[28] Many also feel alienated from the family or displaced from the environment upon their return. As a result, they tend to engage in movements across host countries. During the trajectory of circular migration, they are usually unable to move out of the "occupational ghetto" of domestic service (Glenn 1986). The story of deskilling through immigration remains prevalent in Canada, although migrants who entered the country through the Live-in Caregiver Program are able to take on any employment after working in a Canadian household for twenty-four months (Pratt 1999).

The most likely path to upward mobility for migrant women is to climb the ladder of host countries when landing the next job of domestic service overseas. The destinations of Asian migrant domestic workers can be divided into four tiers based on the wages offered. On the bottom of the hierarchy are the Gulf countries, where human rights and benefits for migrants are meager but the threshold of entry is low.[29] The second tier includes Malaysia and Singapore, where wages for migrant domestic workers are slightly higher than the ones offered in the Middle East.[30] These two destination tiers usually attract migrants with limited finance and education; the religious affiliation particularly drives Muslim women from Mindanao and Indonesia to work in the Middle East. The third tier includes Taiwan and Hong Kong, where migrant wages are protected by a minimum wage.[31] Migrant workers to these two countries are usually moderately qualified candidates with previous overseas experiences. The top end of this hierarchy is Canada, where migrant domestic workers are offered higher wages[32] and most importantly, opportunities for permanent immigration.[33]

The amount of wages is the primary factor that shapes migrants' preferences for different host countries, but they also consider the affordability of placement charges, which tend to rise with wage increases. The hierarchical order of host countries thus becomes a ladder of mobility in the chronological paths of migration. Many migrant workers in Taiwan formerly worked in the Middle East, Singapore, or Malaysia; they were thus able to pay the high fees to Taiwanese brokers with the capital they had accumulated in the previous overseas working experience. While working in Taiwan, they are saving money and seeking opportunities to move up to a better host country.

Migrant workers often consider overseas jobs only a temporary solution to financial difficulties, and they expect to start a business after accumulating sufficient money. They imagine that they will enjoy a relaxing life after the drudgery of overseas work, even harboring a "fantasy of reversal" to be personally served by their own domestic workers once they return home (Parreñas 2001: 172). However, not many of them are able to move successfully beyond the status of "foreign maid." In order to preserve material comfort that is difficult to sustain on an average income in home countries, many returnees are driven back and forth to the flows of migration. Their overseas journey becomes repeated, circular, and relatively permanent. They move from country to country, from house to house, only farther and farther away from home.

"FRONT" AND "BACK STAGE"

The spatial positions and experiences of migrant domestic workers present multiple ironies. The workplace of migrant domestics is a private home that becomes a terrain of control and surveillance. The living space of migrant workers is in the corner of global cities shadowed by the glamour of cosmopolitanism. They use mobile phones to build transnational links and diasporic communities while they are confined to a rather immobile living condition. They are hired to maintain the social reproduction of the host family and country, but the city as a site of collective consumption provides them with few resources.

My analysis expands Goffman's theatrical concepts of "front" and "back stage" to connect micro interactions with the structural forces of power disparity. The metaphors of front and back stage illustrate the distinct social perceptions regarding various spatial realms; such conceptualization of space mirrors and materializes the social order that excludes or marginalizes migrant workers. In employers' households, the living room is at the front, reserved for the family and guests, while the kitchen and balcony are categorized as "maid space" or backstage areas. The hierarchically organized urban landscape also contains a differentiated capacity for the accommodation of migrant workers. Taiwanese object to the congregation of migrant workers at Taipei Railway Station for fear of tainting the frontal image of the global city. And yet less public complaints are directed at the distribution of migrant businesses behind Taoyuan Railway Station, the backstage part of a backstage region of Taiwan.

The concepts of front and back stage also describe how migrant workers negotiate multiple identity performances across spatial settings. In front of the employers, migrant women "act like a maid." Only on Sundays are they able to take off the deferential apron and put on the self-proclaimed image. In front of their families and relatives, migrant workers perform the role of "national heroes" by showcasing their material gains and overseas adventures. Their suffering and alienation are well kept secrets to be circulated only among migrant friends in the host country. To maintain their advanced status in the village, many returned migrants feel they have no option but to leave home for another assignment of overseas work.

I also stress that the front/backstage boundaries are permeable and the meanings of space are contingent, subject to reassignment and resistance. Employers can turn the private zone of the bedroom into an unbound workplace for caregivers who cohabit with their wards. Migrant workers can "privatize" public space on Sundays and make it a provisional home for the gathering of migrant friends. With the use of mobile phones, domestic workers establish a concealed "cellular back stage" within their working environment, but employers can insert a "cellular front" by calling the workers on their days off to extend surveillance and control. The next chapter will further discuss how spatial boundaries are deployed in the daily interactive scripts with which employers and workers negotiate social distance from one another in different patterns.

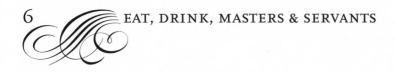

"Like one of the family" is a phrase that is often used by domestic employers and some workers to describe their relationship with the other party. However, this relationship is featured by an ironic combination of personalism and asymmetry (Glenn 1986). A sense of personal intimacy analogizes employment relations as family ties while substantial social distance exists between employers and employees. Nevertheless, interactions across social groups do not always undermine but often enhance distinctions between them. Gul Ozyegin (2000: 11) puts it concisely: "The threat of mixing is countered by established rituals." This chapter takes a deep look at how employers and domestic workers affirm, contest, and reconstitute social differences and the public-private boundary in their daily interaction with the other party.

Previous literature has captured a variety of dynamics in the interactive scripts of employers. Judith Rollins (1985) observed that white employers in Boston play the role of "benevolent mothers" as a way of confirming the inferior status of colored workers. Pierrette Hondagneu-Sotelo's (2001) interviews with employers in Los Angeles resulted in broader findings. Although maternalistic acts are still prevalent among wealthy homemaker employers, middle-class double-earner families have neither time nor energy to cultivate personal ties with domestic workers. They maintain a distant relationship with part-time housecleaners, or they deploy "strategic personalism" with live-in nannies only to ensure the quality of care work.

Workers also negotiate the social distance with their employers in distinct ways and for various reasons. Latina day workers and part-time cleaners in the studies of Mary Romero (1992) and Leslie Salzinger (1991) "upgrade" this occupation by establishing a businesslike contractual relationship. However, Jennifer Mendez (1998) interviewed cleaners employed by a bureaucratic agency and found that many workers actually prefer private employment, in which they have the autonomy of selecting employers and can obtain personal favors. Turkish maids and doorkeepers interviewed by Gul Ozyegin (2000) even strategically elicit the class guilt of their employers to generate favors and raises. In addition, newly arrived migrants in Europe tend to choose live-in work to minimize expenses and alienation in a new country (Anderson 2000: 40). Many live-in workers crave personal contact with their employers, viewing personalism as an avenue for employers to show respect for them as people (Hondagneu-Sotelo 2001).

This wide range of observations demonstrates that neither employers nor domestic workers are monolithic groups. They develop different preferences and strategies given their particular social positions, job descriptions, and employment conditions. To further explain the variations in attitudes and strategies among employers and domestic workers, I develop two typologies to synthesize their different approaches to boundary work. These frameworks are characterized by their concerns over two major types of boundaries. The first type is *socio-categorical* boundaries that consist of class and nationality-based ethnic distinctions between employers and workers. The second type is *socio-spatial* boundaries that circumscribe the province of domesticity and organizes the public-private divides.

The boundary work in domestic employment relationships is situated in the domestic politics of food, space, and privacy. The previous chapter examined the deployment of home space as a field of exclusion and incorporation in everyday domestic lives. Food management is another crucial mechanism by which employers define the marginal status of domestic workers in the family (Colen 1986; Lin 1999).

Eating meals is a daily ritual for maintaining family ties. Mealtimes provide a routinized setting for sharing information, coordinating activities, and transmitting social norms and cultural values among family members (McIntosh 1996). The consumption of food in a household also marks status hierarchies among family members according to age, gender, and economic responsibility (Delphy and Leonard 1992). For example, women and children often eat separately from men, get smaller portions or food of lesser quality, and the food is often chosen to suit the taste of the head of the household. In a similar vein, employers mark family boundaries through the arrangement of eating meals—who is included at the dining table, where to sit at the table, who eats before or after whom—as well as the distribution of food—who gets more food, better quality and a larger variety, and whose tastes or needs are prioritized.

Privacy, defined as a state of "social inaccessibility" (Zerubavel 1981: 138), is established through guarding access not only to physical space but also to personal details. Domestic workers can easily access family secrets of their employers and learn about their quarrels and even their sex lives. Employers might either loathe the presence of an outsider in their home or actively disclose personal information to the worker. Workers might perceive the role of confidante either as evidence of personal ties with their employers or as an extra job requirement and emotional burden. Although the protection of privacy concerns both employers and workers, privacy is nevertheless a right unequally distributed along class lines. As Barry Schwartz (1968) points out, the privacy of upper ranks in an organization is ensured structurally by the mediation of a lieutenant stratum; the privacy of lower ranks is more easily invaded since members of the lower rank enjoy less control over those who may have access to their privacy. In other words, the negotiation of the private zone is intertwined with the struggles over class and ethnic inequalities.

I identify three major structural factors to explain the distinct preferences of employers and workers toward certain types of boundary work: first, *class positioning*—the disparity or similarity between the employer's class position and the worker's previous background; second, *job assignment*—the ratio of care work to housework involved in the job content;[1] third, the *temporal-spatial setting* of the employment—how much extra time and space the employer has and how much time the employer and worker spend together at home. These structural factors construct a complex map that coordinates a variety of subjective dispositions shaping the interactive dynamics among employers and migrant domestics.

EMPLOYERS' BOUNDARY WORK

I begin with employers' boundary work, because they have the upper hand in shaping the interactive scripts of an employment relationship. Basically, employers are negotiating two primary sets of boundaries during their interactions with domestic workers. They weigh to what extent

TABLE 4. *Typology of domestic employers' boundary work*

	Family Boundary		
	Inclusion	Exclusion	
Highlighting	Maternalism	Distant Hierarchy	
	— — — — — — —		*Class/Ethnic Divides*
Downplaying	Personalism	Business Relationship	

they want to include or exclude domestic workers in the family and they also consider whether to highlight or downplay hierarchical difference between themselves and domestic workers. Drawing on these two dimensions, I divide employers' boundary work into four categories: maternalism, personalism, distant hierarchy, and business relationship. It should be borne in mind that the categories in my typologies are Weberian ideal types. In reality, they are more like a continuum along which individual employers lean toward one or more approaches of boundary work in shifting contexts. Also, boundary work does not necessarily describe intentional acts of employers and workers; more often, the parties act on some tacit knowledge that frames their understanding of selves and others.

Distant Hierarchy: "You Are Not My Guest. You Work Here"

I drove over an hour to the house of Mrs. Li, located in the northern hills of the Taipei basin. This area used to accommodate high-ranking officers in the U.S. army during the 1950s and 1960s and later became a suburb of upper-class Taiwanese families. Mr. Li owns an investment firm with local and overseas interests. Mrs. Li, now in her early forties, became a full-time homemaker after getting married. When I reached the front door of their three-floor house, a Filipina came to answer the door. She led me through to the living room, where a generous array of snacks on expensive china plates awaited me. Mrs. Li showed up a little later, greeting me with a warm smile. She never introduced the worker to me, although she called her in a few times, in a raised voice and an affected English accent, to replace the hot water for my tea during the interview.

A relationship of distant hierarchy is grounded in the deferential performance of domestic workers, which may be linguistic, gestural, spatial, or task-embedded (Goffman 1956; Rollins 1985). In Taiwan, domestic employers are addressed with respectful terms like "Ma'am" and "Sir," while migrant workers are called by their first names or even assigned similar-sounding Chinese names if the employers cannot pronounce their original English or Muslim names. Some job requirements are aimed at making a ceremonial display of the worker's subservience. For example, some Taiwanese employers request the Filipina worker to answer the telephone, although they themselves are at home and the worker speaks little Chinese.

The consumption of food is another matter that symbolizes class hierarchy in an employment relationship. Both domestic workers and employers complained to me about this issue, the workers calling the employers "stingy" and the employers calling the maids "greedy." To some employers, especially women, the power to distribute food among household members signifies their control over the domestic sphere. Mrs. Li, for instance, confidently explained to me her rules of "food management":

> My principle is that you are not our guest; you work here. I don't want you to take any food without my permission. This is my house. You have to follow my rule, so I can have everything here under my control. Although I'm very strict in this aspect, once in a while, I will buy some sweets for them and put them on their desks. But without my permission, even a piece of candy is not allowed.

What concerned Mrs. Li was not food per se but the control of its distribution. Food management in domestic employment involves, first of all, what to eat and whom it is for. Status distinctions between employers and maids are displayed by a hierarchical distribution of various kinds of food—expensive versus cheap, meat versus vegetable, subsistence meals versus snacks, and fresh food versus leftovers. Some employers even use separate refrigerators in the house to store the family's food and the maid's food. Second, there is also a division in terms of how to eat and where to eat. Employment agencies often suggest that their employer clients have migrant workers eat separately—at different tables or in different rooms, with different plates or after the employers finish. This advice not only reflects a racist prejudice that views migrant workers as uncivilized and unhygienic; eating separately is also a daily ritual that symbolizes, in the words of my interviewees, the "master-servant distinction."

After the interview, Mrs. Li proudly gave me a tour of their newly renovated house. She reluctantly showed me the maid's room after my persistent requests. It was a small room with plain furniture and a tiny window. A work schedule and guidelines were posted on the wall. The room dramatically contrasted with the main part of the house, where antique furniture and elaborate paintings were nicely displayed in spacious rooms. The floor plans of upper-class residences embody a map of spatial deference. A servant's quarters or the maid's room, usually of a limited size and with bad ventilation, can be found in less visible areas such as the attic or basement.

The employment of housemaids and the purchase of their deferential performance constitute a status marker and a means of "conspicuous consumption" (Veblen 1912/1994). But this status attribution by domestic employers is not necessarily an intentional process. As Pierre Bourdieu (1977) argues, the cultivation of "habitus"—the systems of durable disposition internalized and shaped by members of the same class—requires a slow, lengthy process of embodiment. Like Veblen, Bourdieu pinpoints the significance of consumption in the reproduction of class distinctions, but he emphasizes processes beyond the reach of individual intentions or consciousness: "status signals are mostly sent unconsciously, via the habitus, or unintentionally, because of the classificatory effects of cultural codes" (Lamont and Lareaur 1988: 164).

The old rich, who have lived in the luxury of domestic service all their lives, tend to embody more class habitus indicated by their condescending verbal expressions and distant body language toward domestic workers. Emily, a twenty-nine-year-old mother of a newborn baby, lived with her parents-in-law. Her father-in-law was a retired banker and two migrant domestic workers were employed in this wealthy household. Emily invited me to join them for lunch after our interview. While we were eating, the domestic workers were left in the living room to take care of the crying baby. Emily looked uncomfortable with this arrangement while her mother-in-law seemed quite accustomed to the marginal, invisible status of the domestic worker. After the meal Emily apologetically explained their distinct employer styles to me by drawing on their differences in upbringing and class disposition:

> Probably because my mother-in-law has a longer history of hiring someone in the house, she hardly talks to them [domestic workers]. It seems kind of natural for her to ignore them. I guess if you have had a maid since you were a child, you've gotten used to a position like that. But I am not. Because I am not from a rich family, I am more polite to her.

Most upper-class employers had experience with hiring *obasans*, middle-aged local domestic workers. Many shifted to migrant workers not to reduce employment costs but because they were dissatisfied with the job performance and attitude of local workers. Mrs. Chu, the wife of a chief executive officer in her mid-forties, has been a domestic employer for over two decades. She described how she finally came to the decision of hiring a migrant worker three years earlier:

> I heard many bad things about Filipina maids. I dared not try. At that time it was already very difficult to find live-in Taiwanese. The last *obasan* I hired charged me a lot and that one was quite arrogant. She didn't take your orders at all . . . One day a friend came to my house. She didn't even bother to answer the door. She just sat there and murmured, "Who's that?" So I had to open the door myself. My friend came in and saw an old woman sitting there—the *obasan* didn't bring the guest a cup of tea or anything—and my friend asked me, "Is that your mother-in-law?" I said to myself, "OK, this is enough. I can't bear this anymore."

The confusion of maid and mother-in-law in the eyes of family guests was the last straw that pushed Mrs. Chu to give up local workers. Hiring a foreigner, whose physical appearance displays more visible difference, lowers the risk of misrecognition and keeps the status distinction intact. Most employers found it much easier to request deferential performance from foreign domestics than from local *obasans*. Employers who hire migrant workers across national groups also reported a higher satisfaction with Indonesian workers in this aspect, as they tend to display more deference than Filipina workers in their verbal and body languages.

Not only do workers from various ethnic groups interact with employers in different ways but the employers find themselves acting differently toward local and migrant domestic workers. Mr. Tang, a sixty-year-old retired small business owner, explained the difference: "Because we have different nationalities—she's a foreigner. A Taiwanese maid, although she's a maid, she is Taiwanese. I am Taiwanese. We grew up in the same place, so the distinction is not that clear. We somehow treat her with more courtesy. But the Filipina maid is different. She's Filipino, not Chinese."

When hiring a compatriot domestic worker who is "one of us," employers feel somehow obliged to view them as equal and treat them with respect despite the class divide. Yet the "foreignness" of migrant domestic workers seems to justify a pattern of distant hierarchy. There are actually institutional factors that buttress the alleged "naturally" different attitudes of employers. Local workers can maneuver social networks to negotiate positive terms for their work: they can gossip about "bad" employers in the street market to damage the latter's reputation, and they can discourage friends from working for these employers. By contrast, migrant domestics have no local connections as safety nets, and state policy endorses their transient and marginal status.

After replacing local *obasans* with foreign workers, Mrs. Chu noticed a better protection of her family's privacy and social reputation:

> It's easier to protect family privacy when you hire a foreign maid. If you hire a Taiwanese, she knows the language and your neighborhood. She can gossip about your family! If you are a celebrity, she could ruin your name. Some even sell the news to tabloids! You don't have this kind of problem with foreign maids. Whatever you talk about, she can't understand anyway.

In comparison with local workers, migrant domestic workers are less an intrusion into the employers' family life because of their unfamiliarity with the local language or networks. The employers could easily sustain a distant hierarchy given migrant workers' isolation from the host society and culture. The longer the employers have been hiring live-in maids, the more accustomed they become to the latter's "invisible" existence. Their spacious residence accommodates sufficient physical space, as well as considerable social distance, between masters and servants.

Maternalism: "I am Her Custodian in Taiwan"

I met Mrs. Ho and Atik in the airport before I flew to Indonesia for fieldwork. Mrs. Ho approached me with the story of her poor maid, who wanted to carry an electric rice cooker back home to Indonesia but could not afford the overweight fee charged by the airline company. I agreed to help out by checking the rice cooker under my name. Mrs. Ho was grateful and told Atik, "This lady is very nice and she will take care of you on the plane." The family accompanied Atik until she walked into the customs gate. I was touched when seeing them hug each other and say goodbye in tears. A few weeks later, I arranged to interview Mrs. Ho and found out that what underlies their intimate ties and family analogy is still an evident status hierarchy, only in a softened tone and obscured format.

Mrs. Ho, now in her late forties, got married in her sophomore year and quit college soon afterward. Despite lacking a degree, she owns a restaurant in Taoyuan and runs some retail business on the side. She hires Atik to take care of her frail mother-in-law and to clean the restaurant on the side. At the beginning of chapter 2 I quoted Mrs. Ho's description of her feeling upon meeting Atik on the first day. She used racialized terms such as skin color and smell to portray what she perceived as the physical distinctiveness of foreign workers. Her mind was occupied by doubt and panic about hiring such an ethnic other at home: "I was thinking, Oh my God, an outsider, a black person, is going to live in my house for two or three years. What should I do?"

Mrs. Ho managed to overcome her fear for the "disdained alien," as she described: "I am easygoing enough to dissolve my doubts. Soon, we treat her like part of the family." This dark-skinned family member has no full entitlement, after all. During the three years of her stay in Taiwan, Atik had no days off and was discouraged from contacting people outside the family. Wherever Atik went, Mrs. Ho sent a member of her restaurant staff to accompany her. These rules of spatial control aimed to isolate Atik from other migrant workers. Mrs. Ho considered the building of migrant networks very "dangerous": "When they go out, they crowd together and teach each other bad things—how to steal, how to loaf on the job, etc. You cannot do bad things on your own, but if you have each other, like family, to support you, you have confidence and guts to do anything."

To "protect" Atik from the "bad" influence of the migrant family, Mrs. Ho "adopted" her into the Taiwanese family and introduced "safe" migrants for her to make friends with. While depriving Atik of her rest days, the patronizing employer took her along on family outings and dinners. Mrs. Ho has some friends and relatives who also hire Indonesian domestics, and the employers would bring the workers to meet each other and hang out together. (In another example, Peggy and her friend, both hiring a Filipina domestic worker, take their migrant employees to movies every other month. The employers drive the workers to the theater, pay for their tickets, and pick them up right after the movie finishes.)

Maternalistic practices, as Mary Romero (1992: 110) phrased it, define workers as needy, immature, and inadequate to master their own lives, while affirming the employers' perception of themselves as generous, thoughtful, and superior guardians. Maternalism not only validates the employer's class status but also strengthens her sense of racial superiority and accords with "women's supportive intrafamiliar roles of nurturing, loving and attending to affective needs" (Rollins 1985: 179). In particular, migrant domestic workers, who are alone in the host country and trapped in the live-in condition, serve as inferior protégés and surrogate daughters for their employers.

Mrs. Lai is a forty-one-year-old single mother who hires a Filipina worker, Julie, to help with housework and care for her aging mother-in-law. Julie had once run away to MECO (the Manila Economic and Cultural Office) in Taipei,[2] complaining that Mrs. Lai had restricted her activities and taken away her right of taking days off. Mrs. Lai was furious and defended herself by saying that she was actually a "good" employer. She explained to me why she had to watch out for Julie, who was actually only four years younger than she:

> Last time she said she wanted to go to visit friend in Yilan. I said no. I couldn't let her go out by herself. I am her custodian in Taiwan. If something happens, how can I face her parents? The agency told us we shouldn't lend her money, but I still did. When she went home for vacation, we bought her a lot of clothes and gifts . . . Yes, I don't let her off on Sundays. That's because I'm afraid she might make some bad friends in the church. We're also worried that she would be bored, so we bring her along whenever we go to dinner or shopping.

Employers like Mrs. Lai and Mrs. Ho appoint themselves as substitute mothers or custodians of their foreign employees, thus claiming a necessity to intervene in the workers' private lives. These employers arrange travel plans for a worker's vacation, request details of the worker's social activities, and withhold a portion of wages as "forced saving" or "compulsory deposit."[3] The last measure, although euphemized as a well-intentioned one, implies a racist stereotype about Southeast Asians—"They don't know how to save money," said one employer. In the eyes of maternalistic employers, the lack of capitalist work ethic and financial management explain why Southeast Asians have not achieved economic success as Taiwanese have, or, at least, these hapless qualities are characteristic of these nationals given the underdevelopment of their countries.

In parallel with the employer's intrusion on a worker's privacy, employers sometimes intentionally disclose their personal lives to domestic workers. For example, Jovita, an outgoing Filipina worker in her late twenties, described her homemaker employer:

> She talks to me a lot, maybe because she doesn't trust her friends. At least I won't talk to any of her friends. She often complains to me about her husband. She told me they never make love anymore! Yeah, we Filipinas know all the secrets in the family.
> *So you two have a close relationship?*
> Yes and no. She's a good actress and I am, too! Maybe when she talks to her friend who also has a Filipina, they are chochochocho [talking] about me. But it's OK. I talk to my Filipina friends, too. I'm very talkative. That's why she likes me. She can only talk to her Filipina in the house. She is lonely.

This kind of volunteer confession is most common among female homemakers, who request the attentive ears of their "home sisters" to ease their own isolation and loneliness. Their secrets are especially safe with migrant domestic workers. Compared to local workers who may gossip around, migrant workers are "trustworthy" confidantes because they are temporary in Taiwanese society and totally excluded from the employer's social circles.

As Judith Rollins (1985) and many others have reported, benevolent maternalism is most clearly illustrated by "gift-giving"—employers give away second-hand or discarded items, especially old clothes, as "gifts" to domestic workers. Leftovers are another kind of "gift" often passed to migrant domestics. Some Taiwanese employers bring home the leftovers for the domestic workers after a meal at a restaurant. Although the employers perceive this as a well-intended gesture ("We think she would like to taste this"), many workers do not appreciate it. For instance, Trinada, previously a real estate agent in the Philippines, explained, "Some employers go out for dinner and bring leftovers. You ask them why and they said 'I have a Filipina.' That's not good. I don't eat leftovers. I feel disgraced. We are not rich, but we don't eat leftovers."

Workers respond to the gift giving of employers in different ways. Some workers detest this act as a means of humiliation, but other workers view personal favors as a payment in kind, something they deserve under the patronage of employers. How the workers feel—appreciation or aversion—also depends on the value of the discarded articles. Despite the distinct feelings workers harbor in their hearts, in front of employers they have to accept the "gifts" with gratitude. And this gift exchange is one way only: the recipient is not expected to reciprocate the favor (Rollins 1985: 192–93). Nevertheless, employers, on the higher end of power hierarchy, may request to have these "gifts" returned. Jovita described her experience:

> All my clothes are from her. She bought so many things, all expensive. Then she threw them away in a bag. She said I could try [them on]. If I like it I can keep it or give it to other people. Sometimes when she sees me wearing her clothes, she said, "I don't know why I threw that out, it still looks nice." Then I said, "Well, you can have it back." [*Did she ever take it back?*] Sometimes. Once she said, "Do you still have the bag I threw away last time? Can I borrow it just once? Because it fits my clothes tonight." I laughed in my heart and said, "Sure, they were yours anyway."

This example further reveals the power asymmetry in the practice of gift giving in domestic service. The recipient (worker) is not allowed to return the gift, but the giftgiver (employer) may request a return from the recipient and reclaim her ownership of the article. The employer can selectively confide her secrets to the worker and even request the details of the worker's social life, but the worker cannot freely refuse the confession or questions.

In contrast to the mode of distant hierarchy, these employers develop an intimate relationship with domestic workers but adopt an attitude of maternal benevolence to affirm their class and ethnic superiority. Barrie Thorne studied how boys and girls play at school and found that gender "boundaries may be created through *contact* as well as *avoidance*" (1993: 64, emphasis added). By the same token, domestic employers can mark status distinctions through either avoiding or enhancing personal contacts with domestic workers. The abridging of physical distance between employers and workers does not diminish social inequality between them. The increasing contacts framed by the employer's script of maternal benevolence only underscore the superior status of employers and intensify the intrusion into workers' privacy.

"We are Just a Middle-Class Family. . .
We Don't Treat Her Like a Servant"

The prototype of distant hierarchy is domestic employment in wealthy families with a spacious residence and a long-term history of employment. Maternalistic practices are most common among small-business owners and homemaker employers. The following two patterns of boundary work, personalism and business relationship, tend to be exercised by middle-class employers in dual-earner households. Middle-class employers invest less interest in marking the hierarchical difference between themselves and migrant domestics, but they attempt to confirm their middle-class identity by distinguishing themselves from other employers, including both "people above" and "people below" (Lamont 2000a).

Man-jun is a college-educated travel agent in her early forties. She hires a migrant worker to cover housework and take care of her two children, who are nine and three years old. During our interview, she repetitively emphasized her middle-class status and her respectful attitude toward migrant domestic workers:

> Today is no longer the age of authoritarianism. We are just a middle-class family. We can afford a foreign maid and we have the *need*. We don't treat her like a servant. We told the children that you have to say "thank you" whenever you ask her to do something. We know it's an issue of human rights. We have to respect that. Not like the older generations, they think that you have a foreign maid, you have a servant, kind of like an authority, a master.

No matter how they actually interact with their domestic workers, employers like Man-jun project their self-image by underscoring their beliefs in democracy and meritocracy in opposition to authoritarianism and aristocracy. The expanding middle class in Taiwan has been said to be one of the driving forces in the process of political democratization in the 1980s (Hsiao 1989). The cohort of Taiwanese between the ages of thirty and forty-five, the primary population who hire migrant domestic workers (CLA 1999), went through their youth during Taiwan's dramatic political transition marked by the termination of martial law in 1987. Moral values such as democracy, liberalism, and self-reliance constitute the core of middle-class identity in Taiwan.

In their early forties, Jack and his wife are both managers in international corporations. They hire two foreign workers to take care of his ill father and their young children. During our interview, Jack was not shy in bragging about his achievement in contrast to his modest upbringing (his father retired from the army). As a first-generation domestic employer, Jack expressed concern that his family might be destroying the moral principle of self-dependency:

> When people hear we have two foreign maids at home, they all envy us a lot. There is nothing to envy. I don't encourage people to hire a foreign maid. You only do so when there is a need in your family. Employers become lazy, like getting addicted to drugs. It's better to do it yourself. Be self-reliant.

These employers use a need-based narrative to characterize their employment, and they try to downplay status hierarchies between themselves and their workers. In this way, they are, intentionally or not, validating their middle-class identity in contrast to other class groups. Middle-class employers underscore their *achieved* status as over against the heritage-based privilege of upper-class families. They frame their employment relationship as an equal-footing business arrangement in contrast to the feudal tradition of domestic servitude.

In addition, managerial and professional employers tend to distinguish themselves from employers with lower education. They point at advanced education and English skills as the primary markers that impact on their distinct management methods or interactive styles. Some employers consider fluency in English to be a necessary ground for establishing valid authority and efficient management. For instance, Mr. Yang, a business manager in his late thirties, contrasted himself with his uncle in the provinces:

> My uncle's family also hires a Filipina. Nobody in the family speaks English, so they can barely ask her to do anything. She only plays with the kid every day. My aunt even has to cook for her! She offers little help and they have to serve her. My uncle said she's a guest, so they feel embarrassed to ask her to do this and that. That's why I said the rural people do not fit that well with Filipina maids, because they cannot communicate and cannot place demands on the maid.

Another way for professional employers to distance themselves from less-educated employers is to draw on the universalistic discourse of human rights as a legacy of their advanced education. Yi-ling, a thirty-two-year-old journalist, remarked: "We are educated intellectuals. Of course, we don't treat them like master and servant. We always eat together, interacting on the same level . . . Those abuse cases in the newspaper, I think their employers are poorly educated."

When middle-class employers characterize their employment relationships with the moral discourses of need, self-reliance, and liberal values, they cultivate class boundaries not to highlight their difference from migrant domestics—a distinction perhaps transparent enough for them—but to dissociate themselves from "people above" (the old rich) and "people below" (less-educated employers). In addition to the local references of class ranking, they draw on global connection to establish their middle-classhood—to identify with the imagined community of cosmopolitans who share similar linguistic habitus and cultural tastes in a global village.

I do not imply that highly educated employers would necessarily treat their migrant employees with more kindness or fairness than other employers. Instead, they believe or argue that they do—this is how they frame the relationship with migrant domestics by way of the cultural repertoires of middle-classness. To downplay class and ethnic divides inherent in the structure of domestic employment, these employers utilize two distinct approaches: they cultivate a personal relationship to include domestic workers as part of the family, or they maintain a businesslike relationship by viewing their home as a workplace.

Personalism: "I Don't Want to Live in a Status Hierarchy"

Guo-ming is a thirty-five-year-old graphic designer who runs a studio together with his wife, also a graphic designer. They are so occupied by work that they sometimes sleep in the office, leaving their two daughters to the care of the Filipina caregiver. Guo-ming identifies his family as an "average middle-class family" that just make ends meet after paying off housing loans and saving educational expenses for their children. Although their Filipina worker has been a great help in the family, Guo-ming feels quite uncomfortable with a relationship of distant hierarchy:

She has been with us for a couple of years, but she's still very reserved, overcautious.

Could you be more specific? Like what kinds of situations?

Um, for example, she never initiates a conversation with us unless we ask her something, and she always answers very briefly. We want her to sit at table to have dinner with us, but she'd rather eat after we are done. I am really not used to that, but if we ask her to eat with us, she actually feels very uneasy. Then we look at her, we feel uneasy ourselves, too. I keep wondering why she wants to keep some distance from us . . . I don't like the feeling of living in a class hierarchy. This is very different from eating in a restaurant. I don't know why, but being served by a waiter or waitress is much more OK.

Why different? Because this is at home?

Yeah, home is a very private setting, not a public space. So when your home becomes something like a restaurant, doesn't this make you nervous?

Guo-ming does not feel flattered but instead bothered by the reverent attitudes of the migrant worker, such as her way of communicating (never initiating conversations) and her eating preferences (eating after the family is finished). The liberal guilt of middle-class employers is magnified when a status hierarchy is located at home. In the eyes of Guo-ming, home—"the haven in a heartless world" (Lasch 1977)—should be distinct from a public restaurant, which has a more "natural" association with depersonalized hierarchy.

Another employer who shares similar feelings is Wen-jen, a college professor and mother of two in her late thirties. She considers the deferential performance of her Filipina employee, especially her verbal and body languages, not as a status marker but as a source of psychological burden during their daily interaction:

I think it is Filipina maids themselves who act like that. I never request that. Actually it's more difficult for me to get along with them when they are acting like that, like they want to *serve* you. Many things, I just want to do them myself.

Like what?

For example, when I am cooking, to move the food in the pan to a plate, that's no big deal. But she thinks that's something she should do, if you don't let her do it, she becomes really nervous. Or when we are talking, she would say, "Your family is rich, mine is poor. I envy you."

Employers like Wen-jen do not want a drama of social inequality onstage in their everyday family scenes, and they feel uncomfortable when their sweet home turns into a cold workplace. Therefore, they try to establish personal ties with their domestic workers to ease their own discomfort and embarrassment. Many replace the derogatory title of "maid" with terms they perceive as status-neutral such as "babysitter," "caregiver," and "helper." Some even analogize domestic workers as family members such as "sister" or "auntie." They ask the domestic workers to sit at the table with the family while having meals or invite them to join family outings. They welcome the workers into the living room to watch television together with the family, and they seek conversations about the worker's personal background and family life.

Despite the family analogy and kinship metaphor, unmistakable inequalities underlie the relationship between employers and workers. Hon-yin, a forty-year-old nurse and mother of two, told me of an interesting episode, in which the status disparity was too substantial to obscure, even in the eyes of children:

> I told my son, "Lucy [the Filipina worker] works in our house to help mommy take care of your baby brother. You cannot call her a maid" . . . One day my son wanted to buy a toy, I told him, "You already have something similar. This one costs NT$500. Do you know that mommy pays Lucy only $500 a day?" You know what my son said to me? He said, "Then why don't you give her more money?"

Another reason for employers to foster personal relationships with migrant domestic workers is the involvement of care work. Melissa is a thirty-six-year-old business manager and mother of two. She hires a Filipina caretaker, Neda, who has three children around the same ages as Melissa's children. Melissa detected some feelings of envy or deprivation on Neda's part, considering the uneven levels of material comfort enjoyed by Neda's children in the Philippines and Melissa's family in Taiwan. Melissa explained: "Sometimes I feel kind of sorry for her. Because here we enjoy better economic conditions, whatever the children want, we can easily satisfy them. But it's not the same for her children . . . Sometimes when I buy stuff for my children, she has an envious look on her face."

Chao-ju, a lawyer and mother of two, used the narrative of "mutual help" to describe her relationship with her Filipina caregiver. However, the apparent economic disparity between the two parties troubles her sometimes. Chao-ju's family once went abroad for a vacation. Before their departure, she gave the worker an allowance for food and groceries. But the Filipina returned from the market with only a small amount of food and a few pairs of children's shoes. Chao-ju recalled:

> I told her the food was not enough and I asked her why she bought those shoes. She said those shoes were cheap and she wanted to send them back home for her children. I was very sad upon hearing this. So later on when she asked me for a loan to pay off her children's tuition, I gave it to her. Some people say it's dangerous to lend money to maids; they would run away. But I told her: "You come here to take care of my children, so I will take care of your children, too. We take care of each other's children." I think we are two women who need help from each other. I would offer what she needs and she would give me what I need.

In rhetoric and in some practice, Chao-ju turns a relationship of employment hierarchy into a sisterhood of mutual help. Feeling partly responsible for the family separation of the migrant worker, she urges herself to act in sympathy with the mother away from her children. In a similar vein, Melissa finds time to chat with Neda about her feelings of working here and her family left at home. Melissa attempts to comfort Neda's homesickness and check on her emotional stability in a condition of family separation. Nevertheless, Melissa bluntly admits that such emotional engagement is a strategic act mainly for the benefit of her children: "Everything I do for her [Neda] is for my children." Parents like Melissa engage in emotional work to ensure that no unusual problems arise in the lives of caretakers they hire. By incorporating migrant caregivers as part of the family, employers gain confidence in the quality of care service. Fictive family membership can enhance a worker's commitment to the welfare of her employers, as well as the authenticity and sincerity of their emotional labor, their "labor of love."

Employers like Melissa are engaged in a practice of what Pierrette Hondagneu-Sotelo (2001) calls "instrumental personalism" or "strategic intimacy." She elaborates how personalism is similar to yet distinct from maternalism: the latter is a one-way relationship defined by the employer's gestures of charity, but the former is a two-way relationship, albeit still asymmetrical, that recognizes the worker's human dignity (207–8). She also argues that employers personalize employment relationships not to enhance a status hierarchy but to secure good care for their children. I further establish that middle-class employers adopt the attitude of personalism to deal with the apparent class inequality at home—they want to minimize their class guilt, to confirm their middle-class identity, and to ease their discomfort resulting form a conflation of private and public spheres.

The distinction between personalism and maternalism is yet a fine line, given the inherent structural inequalities in an employment relationship. Personalism may be a cure for the loneliness of a migrant worker, but many workers would rather maintain some distance from their employers, who may be caring friends at this moment but turn into condescending madams in the next. Migrant domestic workers do not always favor personalism and neither do Taiwanese employers. Melissa said, "My husband often complains, 'We don't even have time to take care of our children. Now we have to take care of her?'" She then sighed deeply and remarked, "We hire her to help, but actually, she brings us more trouble than help!"

For dual-earner households who suffer from a time crunch, the personalistic aspect of employment is a time-consuming job. Moreover, personal ties with migrant workers could incur unsolicited emotional burdens for employers. May-lien, a mother who hires a Filipina to take care of her three-year-old daughter, described her feelings:

> Sometimes I wish that I didn't understand English. So I wouldn't have to listen to her. It's a pain that I could understand what she says. [*What did she say?*] For example, she misses her daughter, their house is crappy, how much money they need to build a new wall and fix the roof, she just goes on and on . . . I know she feels bad, but there is nothing I can do.

To cultivate a personal relationship with domestic workers could be costly for employers in terms of time and emotional investment. Some employers thus confine the employment relationship within business terms, especially among those who hire migrant workers for the purpose of housework instead of care work.

Business Only: "I Need a Helper, Not a Friend"

I met Jessica for lunch at the café in the high-rise building where she worked. At the age of thirty-two, Jessica has worked in several international banks and has been promoted to the position of manager in her current job. Showing up in a no-nonsense black pantsuit, she told me that she had precisely one hour for the interview. Then she quickly ordered a sandwich and organic fruit juice and started talking about her principle of interacting with her Filipina employee. She mentioned of a friend of hers who was a full-time homemaker married to a business manager. This friend also employed a domestic worker and dispatched many boring afternoons by having tea with the Filipina worker. Later they had a big fight over the issue of lending money and in the end the worker was sent back home. Jessica commented on this story in Chinese spiced with English keywords (indicated in italics):

> I think you have to define her *position* clearly. You need a *helper*, not a *friend*. So you better not have tea or intimate conversation with her. Because once you two talk about things and she has different opinions from yours, then what? You try to dominate the conversation with your identity as a master! It's not *fair*. So I don't treat them like friends. Otherwise, either you will be *over the line* or she will be *over the line*. Maybe one day she will talk to you in a way like, "Hey Jessica, I am too tired today. I don't want to cook!" . . . The rule is clear in our house. After a certain time, it's her time off. I told my son not to bother her during her rest time.

Jessica prefers a businesslike relationship for two reasons. First, recognizing status disparity between employers and employees, she defines the relationship as business-bound with a respect for the worker's private space and rest time. Second, minimizing personal interactions helps her clarify the worker's position (as "helper" rather than "friend") in order to avoid the interference of personal ties in job performance. Employers like Jessica are confident in their English communication with Filipina workers, and they tend to apply their working experiences as managers to the supervision of domestic workers. Another employer sharing a similar line of thinking is Pei-chi, the owner of a family-run computer business in her mid-forties. Sitting in her spacious office, she explained to me the difference between her kind of employer and others:

> Most of my friends have positive employment experiences, probably because most of us work in the computer industry and we all know how to speak English. Those who have negative experiences are less educated people.

Why is such a difference?

Because they don't know how to speak English and they don't know how to establish rules! Not like us. We set up clear rules and nothing would go wrong. So I say, it's the fault of the employers.

Pei-chi went on to illustrate how she set up rational rules to manage the performance of her Filipina employee:

The moment she arrived, I typed up a chart that listed all the chores, what to do from this time to that time. Clean this on Monday, clean that on Tuesday. Daily schedule, weekly schedule, monthly schedule, very clear. In this way, the Filipina maid has a clear idea about her job content. When she is done with it, she can rest. And I could have information about what she has done at home. One Filipina asked me if she could decide what to do each day. She said she must have more to do than the chart. I said, "No need. You just treat this like going to work. Once you are done, you are off."

Both Pei-chi and Jessica explicitly used the metaphors "going to work" and "time off" to describe their households as a workplace. As long as their bureaucratic rules are followed, they make no further requests on the workers and avoid interference in the workers' private lives. Although there is a spatial overlap between workplace and home, these employers manage to draw a symbolic line between the public and private zones. This pattern not only protects the privacy of workers but also safeguards the family lives of employers. I noted earlier that upper-class employers prefer migrant domestics because ethnic stratification helps sustain class domination. In a similar yet distinct way, middle-class employers report that it is easier to maintain a businesslike relationship with foreign domestics than with Taiwanese *obasans*. Employers can easily shut off their family lives from migrant workers via linguistic and cultural barriers, but it is difficult to prevent local workers from intruding the employers' private zones. An-ru, a thirty-two-year-old stockbroker, described the difference:

Our neighbors hire an *obasan*. She minds their family business as she were their mother! A Filipina maid is different. She won't mind any of your business. I think this is much better.

Why is there a difference like this?

The first reason is communication. Second, Chinese think if I am hired by your family, I help with everything in the family. But a Filipina maid just comes here for work. If you don't talk to her, she won't come to you. I prefer this way. When we come home after work, we are exhausted enough. Nobody wants to hear another person blah blah blah.

Younger employers like An-ru sometimes feel pressure from middle-aged *obasans*, who may exercise authority on the basis of seniority to dictate how housework or childcare should be done. An-ru even analogizes the role of *obasans* to that of her mother or mother-in-law. She therefore prefers to hire migrant domestic workers who respect or desire a business-only relationship as much as she does.

The employers who prefer a business-oriented relationship are mostly from double-income households. Time deficit is serious enough for them —they seek helping hands exactly to loosen the time bind between work and family (Hochschild 1997). Hence they wish to maximize their free time after work by minimizing personal interactions with their domestic workers. Besides, a distant yet neutral relationship is more feasible in these households where the employers spend only limited time at home, compared to households where full-time homemaker employers spend the whole day around the workers.

In addition to the time constraint, the spatial setting also has a substantial impact on the ways employers chart their private zones. Unlike upper-class households who own a spacious house, most middle-class Taiwanese households in urban areas can afford only a modest apartment. In the restricted domain of apartment living, there are no quarters for servants to hide in and no physical space to create symbolic distance.[4] Facing the problem of spatial deficit, some employers exclude domestic workers from home space not (just) to demonstrate spatial deference but to protect their family privacy. In other cases, employers have no option but to maintain an inclusive relationship with the workers because of the limited space at home. A-Sue and her husband have recently purchased their first apartment in Taipei. When I asked her about the eating arrangements with her domestic worker, she laughed, saying, "Look at my apartment! It's so tiny. If she doesn't eat with us, where is she going to eat?"

Despite sharing an intimate space with domestic workers, these employers manage to sculpt a line between home as a private domain of family life and home as a public setting of domestic employment. This business-only approach is more feasible when more housework and less care work is involved in the job. It is relatively easy to set bureaucratic rules about cooking, shopping, and house cleaning, but employers feel less comfortable rationalizing an employment relationship that involves care for children or the elderly. It is difficult to account for the "labor of love" as only a "business," after all.

WORKERS' BOUNDARY WORK

Like their Taiwanese employers, migrant domestic workers construct and maintain social boundaries in multiple ways. They may perceive and respond to the social distance between themselves and their employers differently: some recognize and accept the apparent class and ethnic divides, but others object to the divides and identify themselves as equal human beings and class peers of their employers. They also adopt distinct strategies to organize the boundary between the front and backstage areas, a critical spatial deployment in the lives of migrant domestic workers as discussed in the last chapter. Some workers prefer to segment these two areas, but others prefer to integrate them.[5] Along the two dimensions— class/ethnic boundaries and socio-spatial boundaries—I divide boundary work enacted by domestic workers into four categories: seeking patronage, keeping safe distance, obscuring previous positions, and highlighting status similarity.

Seeking Patronage: "Poor Girls Always Get Lucky"

Trina and Maya sat with me on a bench in the churchyard, chatting about their employers. Both of them were rural migrants from Negros and had worked in Singapore and Taiwan as domestic workers for several years. "Poor girls always get lucky," said Trina, in reference to Maya's tactics toward her employer. Maya first came to Taiwan five year ago. After her contract expired, she changed her name and returned to a new employer (the maximum of a legal stay was three years at the time). She gladly told me that she was able to avoid the "forced savings" (wage deduction) after crying and pleading with her employer, saying, "Please help me. I have no money. I owe a lot of money in the Philippines."

Domestic workers like Maya are engaged in what Jennifer Mendez (1998: 129) calls "strategic personalism," through which they obtain alternative "fringe benefits" from their employers in the form of material goods, cash bonuses, and loans. A quasi-feudal pattern of patron-client

TABLE 5. *Typology of domestic workers' boundary work*

	Front/Backstage Boundary	
	Integrating	Segmenting
Accepting	Seeking patronage	Keeping safe distance
Objecting	Highlighting status similarity	Obscuring previous positions

Class/Ethnic Divides

relationship is not very common among the Taiwanese households who hire migrant workers, because of the short tenure of employment under state regulations. Still, some migrant workers, usually among those with less education or from the rural areas, play up their own material poverty to win their employers' sympathy. In particular, those who have previous experience of working overseas can artfully utilize emotional displays to elicit the class guilt of employers. Some talk to the employers about their meager living conditions back home, so they will have a better chance of success when they request loans or advances on their wages. Some display envy when accompanying the employer to shop for toys for the employer's children. Out of feelings of guilt or pity, the employer buys another toy (often a cheaper one) for the worker's children as well.

Newly arrived migrant workers are another group who tend to seek patronage from their employers. During their first year, most migrant workers are burdened by debts and they receive only a small amount of wages after the deduction of placement fees. In these circumstances, they welcome second-hand items from the employers as some sort of payment in kind. During the first few months, migrant workers usually give up their days off because they have little money at their disposal and they want to earn extra wages. Joining their employers' family outings becomes a cost-free opportunity for them to explore Taiwan. They also have to rely on employers for a variety of information and resources, since they have yet to build local connections in the host country.

At the time of their leaving is another moment when migrant domestics feel that they deserve gifts and other favors from their employers. Similar to the situation in which local domestic servants in Java await the coming of gifts and bonuses throughout the whole year until Lebaran or the New Year (Weix 2000), migrant workers view their departure as the time for the deferred payment and gratitude from employers. An explicit example is Atik, the Indonesian worker hired by the maternalistic employer Mrs. Ho, whom I discussed earlier. During my interview with Mrs. Ho, I asked who purchased the electric rice cooker that Atik took back to Indonesia. Mrs. Ho bought it, and, surprisingly, she did so at the request of Atik:

> She asked for it. I also gave her a gold necklace and bracelet. She made requests on my friends and the restaurant staff as well. She said, "I'm going home. I want a watch. I need a rice cooker, a microwave. Could you buy them for me?" She became very gutsy upon the time she was leaving. She dared ask me for money. I owed her 160 K [the amount of forced saving] but she asked for 200 K. In my view, she has been with our family for three years—she sold her youth to us for three years. What a pity! So it's OK to give her more, either as charity or for the sake of our relationship.

As described by Mrs. Ho, Atik was quiet and respectful, never complaining about having no days off and always sitting on the floor while the family watched TV in the living room. Nevertheless, the "docile" Indonesian maid became "gutsy" before her departure. She boldly requested that her employers and even their friends, whoever stood higher on the status ladder, "take care" of her. After contributing her labor to the daily maintenance of the family for three years, she felt that some nice jewelry, modern appliances, and extra payment were her rightful returns and entitlements.

Indonesian migrant workers in general have a higher tendency to accept the status hierarchy between Taiwanese employers and themselves as structurally given, in comparison with better-educated Filipinas, who tend to view the hierarchy more as a contingent situation. Utami is a twenty-five-year-old married woman who grew up in a poor family in Middle Java. Without even finishing primary school, she took her first job, as a housemaid in Jakarta, when she was only ten years old. Utami later sought better wages overseas by working in Singapore for four years and in Taiwan for another three years. Migrant friends in Taiwan consider Utami very "unlucky" in being matched with employers. She is assigned heavy manual labor, including cleaning a five-floor house and washing all clothes by hand. The employers, whose behavior seems to fall into the category of distant hierarchy, treat Utami as an inferior servant. When a whole chicken is served for the family dinner, Utami gets to eat only the chicken head and legs, alone in the kitchen. She is always given cheaper kinds of fruit such as bananas while expensive fruits like apples are reserved for the family. Worst of all, the female employer scolds her when giving orders and always complains about her slowness.

Utami is actually quite an outspoken leader among her Indonesian friends, but she holds her tongue around her employers, despite their rude manners and harsh requests: "I don't say anything. I dare not." Sometimes she jokes about her situation: "I told people my boss is singing every day. She yells at me every day. I take it as if she was singing so I would not feel too bad." To avert confrontation and conflict, she prays to Allah for an end to her sufferings and some changes in the employers' attitude. At first I thought that Utami avoided confronting her employers for fear they might terminate the contract and send her home. She corrected me:

> No, I'm not afraid of going home. I would be happy if I could go home! I told my boss that I don't like it here and I want to go home. I could pay for the ticket myself, but they don't like. So this is not the problem. The problem is that I know who I am and I know who they are. The maid is like the floor and the employers are like the ceiling. They are high; we are low. They are white; we are dark. Different, we are different. So it's useless that you talk to them; they won't listen.

Utami recognizes a grave status difference between her employers and herself. In addition to class hierarchy, she even uses racial terms to mark the distinction. It has been said that Javanese children are socialized to show respect and fear toward those of higher ranks (Geertz 1961). Utami told me that her parents had taught her to be respectful to others, especially those above her. A few times when I saw her on Sundays, she shopped for some ingredients with which to make an Indonesian snack for her employers. I was surprised to hear that Utami did this without the employers' request and that she paid for these ingredients herself. This "niceness" puzzled me. After some time of persistent requesting, I finally learned the hidden message behind this action. When I asked Utami yet again why she did this, she answered:

> I don't know . . . They never bought me anything. Not even slippers. I have been with them for three years and they never bought me any clothes.

So why are you still so nice, making this for them?

I don't know. They like to eat this. So I want to make them Indonesian food. We Indonesians are poor, but rich people have no heart . . . I want to tell them: Do you ever think that we are poor but we treat you with our hearts? You make a lot of money—why are you so stingy to us?

Utami is sending her employer a "gift" with the homemade snack of ethnic flavor. She is inviting her employers into a moral economy, in which the receiving of the gift should make the employers thankful and obliged to return the favor. What kind of favor? Utami is not much concerned about her rest days or other entitlements she is deprived of by her employers. She does not even keep track of the amount of her wage deductions even though most deductions are outlawed practices. What she expects from her employers is some gratitude and recognition for her service and hard work. Unfortunately, the employers completely ignore the unsaid message in Utami's kindness. For the powerful, the giving of gifts is a display of their generosity, and receiving nothing in return from the recipient even marks the superiority of the giver. However, the subordinate send gifts along with her humble wish to the superior—wishing for the return of some warmth, thankfulness, and respect—since they have few resources to demand equal exchanges or challenge the asymmetry of power.

Keeping Distance: "No Extracurricular Work"

During lunch, one Filipina was talking about her previous experience working in Saudi Arabia, where she had meals with several other domestic workers in the servants' quarters. "Wow, that's great," said Olivia upon hearing this. I was surprised at her envy of this spatial segregation that displays a transparent class hierarchy. Olivia explained to me, "It's safer to keep some distance." In fact, Olivia is not alone in holding such a preference. Many migrant domestics do not crave personal bonds with their employers but rather keep some distance from them. I heard many conversations among Filipina and Indonesian migrant workers similar to this one:

Johna [sobbing]: My lady employer has a bad attitude toward me.
PCL: Like how?
Johna: You can see it from her face . . .

Madeline: Don't look at their faces! Just listen to your own heart! They and us are different [*uses her two hands to indicate high and low levels*]. They just act like that. Don't mind them.

Sylvia: Yes! Because they and us are different status, sometimes they don't know [that] what they did hurt us. As long as you know you do good, and they pay your check on time, no extracurricular work! [*Everybody nods, especially Johna.*]

"No extracurricular work" is a common strategy held by migrant domestic workers to cope with their physical and emotional stress at work. When they establish a boundary between work and private life, this kind of detachment provides them with a buffer against the employer's insensitivity to their personal needs and dignity (Dill 1988: 39). They also prefer to minimize interactions with their employers so they can reduce the burden of extra emotional work. When asked if they enjoyed going out to dinner with their employers, many informants answered, "No, I'd rather stay home. I don't want to be a babysitter at the dining table. I want to be a family." Despite the family analogy used by their employers, most migrant domestic workers are keenly aware of their marginal status. Keeping a distance from the employers' family avoids the risk of transcending the line between family and nonfamily.

Although some migrant domestics like to join the employers' family meals, others consider eating together an extra pressure and obligation. Many workers would rather eat alone in the kitchen—a backstage region where they can have more privacy and freedom. When I asked Helen, a Filipina worker, if she eats together with her employer, she answered, "They told me to. Sometimes their friends coming, they told me to eat together, too. But I don't like it. So I pretend busy, I do this I do that, because I don't want to eat together. Too tiring. What am I going to say to them?"

In addition, many domestic workers dislike the invitation to eat at the dining table because they feel obligated to accept food from their employers. One Filipina worker, Elvie, described this situation saying, "My employers want me to eat this and eat that, so I don't like to eat there [at the table]. They want to *see* you eating the things. They want to *give*. They want to make sure you eat it." It is a common practice among Taiwanese that the host picks up a portion of food from the table and places it in the guest's bowl. This act, intended to be courteous, may turn into a coercive measure as perceived by migrant domestics. Similar to what happens in an asymmetrical act of gift giving, the workers are afraid that their refusal of the food will offend the employers.

Another job requirement that domestic workers are reluctant to follow is to be treated as an employer's confidante, especially when the secrets involve tensions between the employer couple. One Filipina worker, Lolita, feels burdened by being sandwiched between confidences of the wife and the husband:

> My lady employer talks to me a lot, even her personal things, like her work, her family, her marriage, everything! She's not getting along with her mother-in-law and her marriage isn't going well. She told me not to marry a husband like hers. And you know what's funny? The husband likes to talk to me about his wife, too! But they don't know the other person also talks to me. If they knew, they wouldn't be very happy [about this]. But I don't want to hear these things. I came here for work, not for hearing this stuff.

When their male employers view them as confidantes, migrant domestic workers even risk becoming a target of suspicion or jealousy from the female employers. Some workers have found out about the extramarital affairs of one of their employers. Whether or not they report the matter to the other employer, they are unavoidably involved in the family drama. By managing to separate the front and backstage regions, domestic workers reduce the risks and burdens in a personalized relationship, marking the boundary to lessen the employers' intervention into their private life.

Obscuring Previous Positions: "I Don't Want Them to Know My Past"

Domestic workers may segment the front and backstage regions not just for reasons of caution but as an active strategy to safeguard their dignity and self-identity. These migrant workers consider themselves the class peers of their Taiwanese employers but see themselves sliding down the class ladder because of personal misfortune or the stagnant economy of their home country. When I asked Luisa if her employer was rich, she bluntly answered, "I don't think so. They have a simple life. They don't go out. I know that, because I used to be rich." Luisa left Manila to work as an entertainer in Tokyo at the age of twenty-one. Later she married the Japanese owner of the club where she worked. Their marriage lasted ten years. After the divorce she returned to the Philippines with two children and later worked in Taiwan as a domestic worker.

Having difficulty adjusting to her drastic downward mobility, Luisa chose to disguise her current job from her acquaintances in the Philippines and to conceal her past from her employers in Taiwan:

> I didn't tell my friends in the Philippines what I am doing in Taiwan. They only know I work. They don't know I am a domestic helper. I feel ashamed. Because I used to be an employer, I don't want people to think I am going down. But actually I am going down [*smiles bitterly*]. My ex-husband doesn't know [about this], either. He called my children and they told him, mama is visiting relatives in Taiwan.
>
> *Does your employer know about your past?*
>
> No. Once, my ex-husband called me from Japan. I just told them that he was my brother-in-law. I don't want them to know.

Several other Filipina migrants with white-collar backgrounds spoke of the necessity of bracketing previous histories and "acting like a maid": "Since we work as a maid, we must act as a maid. If you think that, 'Oh, I used to work in the bank,' you cannot do a good job. You feel down; then you feel conflict." Another says:

> Since you already come here, you shouldn't talk about if you have a car, you have a maid in the Philippines. If you have everything in the Philippines, why do you come here? Keep quiet. Now you are here, you need to follow the rules here. You are a domestic helper; you have to do everything. You cannot complain you don't know how to do this, how to do that.

Luisa obscures her previous social positions from her employers. And, to perfect the "maid" performance, she has to carefully manage the transition from the front to the back stage. Every Sunday, Luisa brings her jewelry, miniskirt, and make-up kit to the church and changes in the bathroom before attending mass. She also tries to shy away from the identity of "maid" after she goes backstage. One Sunday, when we walked through the backyard of the church, where many Filipinas were chatting as usual, Luisa frowned and said to me, "They are talking about many problems here. My employer this, my employer that. I know it's good for you to listen. But I don't like to spend my holiday like this. Monday to

Saturday is already enough. I don't want to hear more complaints about work. I just want to be happy, happy on Sunday!"

By maintaining an impenetrable boundary between front and back stage, domestic workers avert tension between their self-proclaimed day-off image and the "maid" image prescribed by their employers. One Sunday I saw Jovita wearing flamboyant nail polish on her fingers and toes. I joked with her, "Do you wear this in your employer's house?" She flashed a mischievous grin and said, "No way! My employers, if I dress up a little, they would look at me like this." She imitated someone looking her up and down from head to feet. "So when I go out on Sundays, I wish they don't see me at all. Or they would wonder—is this my helper?"

When moving from the backstage area to the front, migrant women try to present a version of their Sunday activities that is deemed "proper" in the eyes of their employers. Some employers regulate their workers' off-day activities by proscribing "no-go" areas or sanctioning "appropriate" places (Yeoh and Huang 1998: 591). A few times I went to discos with Filipina migrants on Sunday afternoons. When we were about to leave, some changed their shirts that had absorbed too much cigarette smoke on the dance floor. They responded to my confusion: "So our employers will think we go to the church! Not the disco!" Jovita told me that sometimes she spent Sunday afternoons in bars, drinking or smoking to relax. Upon her return to her employers' house, she said, "The first thing I do is to run into the bathroom and take a shower. I don't want them to smell me!"

As Erving Goffman (1959: 113) remarks, "the passage from the front region to the back region will be kept closed to members of the audience or that the entire back region will be kept hidden from them." If the worker fails to maintain segregation between their front and backstage settings, their day-off image might shock their employers. Luisa's employer was out of town one Sunday. Instead of carrying clothes to change into later, Luisa walked out of her employer's apartment wearing a silk blouse and high-heeled shoes, with her makeup artfully done and her hair fashionably colored. She described what happened and how her employer responded to it:

My neighbors in the elevator saw me [and] smelled my perfume. And there were rumors in the whole building! They told my employer: "Luisa goes out, like a movie star!" My boss didn't believe it. So the security guard rewound the videotape—they have a video camera in the elevator—and showed it to my employer.

How did your employer react?

She was very surprised! Because I'm not like that on ordinary days. I think she felt insecure after that. She told me: "I don't have many beautiful dresses, because I don't need them. I am always in the house . . ."

What was she trying to say?

She was saying that *I* don't need these dresses, because I am always in the house. I am just wasting my money!

The exposure of Luisa's backstage image—a stylish, classy, and feminine image—constitutes a symbolic challenge to the class superiority of the employer; moreover, it stirs the madam's anxiety. As one Filipina commented of Luisa's employer, "She's afraid you become an attractive woman. Then she will lose her husband!" Luisa finds it difficult or at least risky to merge the front and backstage areas, so she carefully manages her double lives on weekdays and days off by being cautious about how she looks, smells, and behaves. Yet other migrant workers prefer to weave their identities at work and in private in order to underscore their status similarity to their employers.

Highlighting Status Similarity: "I Don't Let Them Disgrace Me"

Nora, single in her early thirties, received a college degree in nursing in the Philippines. She first went to Singapore to work as a nurse at the age of twenty-four. In Taiwan she was hired to take care of an ill grandmother living with a divorced father and his teenaged son. The father was a technician with a high-school diploma. When I visited Nora in the employers' residence, an old apartment with basic furniture, she showed me a picture of herself at her college graduation, which she took with her wherever she worked. I had a hard time relating the young smile in the picture to Nora's face in front of me, so greatly aged it seemed.

In the beginning, Nora felt quite offended when her employers expressed doubt concerning her knowledge of modern lifestyle. "Taiwanese employers think Filipinos are ignorant," she said. "They asked me, 'Do you know how to turn on the television? How to use a rice cooker?' " Nora responded to such insults to her intelligence and dignity with a firm answer: "I said to them, 'No problem for me.' " Gradually, her employers changed their opinions of her, which had a lot to do with the fact that Nora had a higher degree than anyone in the family. Nora told me: "They are proud. They told people I went to college. My boss doesn't say this is my maid. They say this is the one who takes good care of my mother. If they call me a maid, I will feel a little upset. Because people have ego, you want to go up, not go down." Nora then raised examples of how her education equipped her with the intelligent capability to reason with her employers, unlike other Filipinas who only whine about them:

> Many Filipinas complain about their employers. They should have talked to them. If there is a problem, I don't complain. I *talk* to them. Once there were five Sundays in that month, they gave me only four [for overtime pay]. I told them there were five Sundays. Then they apologized and said, "Oh, you are right."

Migrant domestic workers who held managerial positions in the Philippines may define domestic service as skilled work and underscore its similarity to their previous working experience. Ada Cheng (2001) interviewed a Filipina domestic worker in Taiwan, Baby, who had a master's degree in accounting and business administration. Like Nora, Baby is not shy in telling her employers about her education; she maintains a sense of integrity by highlighting the professional aspect of domestic service: "It is work, and I use a professional attitude for it . . . I used to handle everything for my boss, taking notes and keeping track of everything. I am very alert. I keep track of everything. This is not that much difference. It's the same thing working here . . . I have my own program of work, like when to do what, and which to do first throughout the whole day. I do planning" (Cheng 2001: 202).

These cases demonstrate another way for Filipina domestic workers to merge the front and backstage regions—to establish their status as class peers of their employers. Two structural factors explain why Nora could attain a more equal status in this employment relationship. First, her main duty is taking care of a patient rather than household chores. Employers, as noted earlier, are more willing to cultivate a personal relationship with the workers when more care work is involved in their duty. Second, Nora possesses a higher degree of education and more linguistic capital than her employers—she even sometimes tutors the teenaged son in English. Lower-educated employers perceive hiring a Filipina college graduate as a means to upgrade their own status rank. That explains why they are "proud" to have Nora take care of their mother.

Trinada is another Filipina caretaker who falls into this category. She is a forty-four-year-old widow who had a career as a real estate agent in the Philippines. Motivated by a curiosity about the experience of working overseas, she came to work in Taiwan two years ago. The household of her employers includes a sixty-five-year-old ill mother, her son, daughter-in-law, and two adult grandchildren. When I asked her about her employers, she shrugged and said:

> They're OK. The only problem is they don't trust you. For example, if you go home late, they think you do bad things. They said, "Maybe you have bad friends." I said, "Don't say that! You never met my friends. If you say this to me, I can also say, you come home late sometimes, I can conclude you also do bad things outside!" If you always obey, you never get freedom. You cannot always agree with your employer or they will treat you like this all the time. My employers treat me with respect. They say she is the one looking after our mother, not a domestic helper.

Trinada drew on the narratives of equality and mutuality to confront her employers who made a racist assumption about migrant workers—if you say this to me, I can say the same thing about you, too. Trinada and her employers have developed a relatively equal relationship indicated by the way they refer to each other. "They call me *mei-mei*—that's younger sister, right?" she said, "And I call them their first names. They treat me like their younger sister, not a maid." Trinada also intentionally sends out messages to her employers regarding her middle-class lifestyle in the Philippines. "When we go to expensive restaurants, I told them, when I worked in the Philippines I went to similar restaurants, too. So they don't look down on me. I don't let them." Better-educated migrant domestic workers sometimes deliberately initiate conversations with their employers to showcase their cultural taste and knowledge (Hondagneu-Sotelo 2001: 199). Several Taiwanese employers report feeling shocked, yet impressed, when they arrive home to find the Filipina maids watching CNN on television or listening to classical music on the radio.

English is another means that Trinada uses to level the power dynamics in the relationship with her employers. "If what they said is wrong, I told them this is wrong. They ask me about their English, 'Do I say this correctly?' I don't let them disgrace me. I always check. If they say something bad, I always correct." When I asked her if she was ever afraid that her employers might get offended and terminate her contract, she said with total confidence, "No! I am not afraid to lose the job. My salary in the Philippines is even higher! I told them this!"

Unlike Luisa, who conceals her background from her employers, Trinada showcases her middle-class position and lifestyle in the Philippines to her employers. She confronts her employers' authority by challenging their English skills and rejecting their negative comments about migrant workers. She resists the deferential job script and speaks out to enhance her status in the family. As she said, "I don't let them disgrace me." Similar to Nora, Trinada has certain capacity of negotiation because she is employed by a household of average wealth and her job is taking care of their mother.

How do we explain the distinct approaches to boundary work adopted by Luisa and Trinada, despite both perceiving themselves as class peers of their employers? A major difference is related to the stakes involved in challenging employers and losing jobs. Trinada can afford the consequence of open confrontation, because she is "not afraid to lose the job." Being a mother of three grown-up children, she faces lower financial pressure and she still keeps a career alternative in the Philippines. In contrast, Luisa, a single mother with three young children, cannot bear the consequence of losing the only financial source for her family. Therefore, she would rather not risk her job by integrating the front and back-stage areas.

The comparison also reveals another factor that limits domestic workers' options for their approach to boundary work. The way a worker negotiates the social distance from her employers must depend on the way her employers enact their own boundary work. Luisa might have preferred a more permeable boundary between her work and private life, if her employer had adopted a more inclusive, equal attitude toward her, as Nora's or Trinada's employers do. Employers are usually the power holders who take initiatives to frame the dynamics of employment relationships, charting the bounded terrains for the workers to negotiate social boundaries and private zones.

BOUNDARY WORK AT HOME

This chapter has mapped out how employers and workers negotiate class identities vis-à-vis the other party and has compared migrant and local domestic workers to highlight the significance of national-ethnic distinctions in the employment dynamics. These personal encounters across social boundaries are nevertheless confined in a household that conflates the workplace and private zone. The boundary work at home involves a constant negotiation of the definition of family, the distinction between home and workplace, and the deployment of the front and back stage.

With an emphasis on agency and diversity, my analysis of boundary work draws a linkage between actors' structural positions and subjective dispositions. I have established two typologies to describe variations in boundary work and identified three major factors to account for why particular employers and workers lean toward a subtype of boundary work: the class positioning of employers and workers; the ratio of care work to housework in the job assignment; and the temporal-spatial composition of the employment setting.

The employers who would like to showcase their advanced positions on the status ladder tend to underscore their difference from migrant domestic workers. Yet younger generations of employers try to downplay class hierarchy in order to confirm their middle-class identity. Among upper-class employers, those who spend less time at home or have more space in the house are more likely to maintain a distant hierarchy, whereas homemakers who spend a lot of time around the workers often develop a maternalistic relationship. Among middle-class employers, those who hire workers for childcare tend to adopt an attitude of instrumental personalism, while others who seek help with housework favor a business-like relationship to minimize the time-consuming burden of personal interactions.

The above factors also shape variations in the boundary work of migrant domestic workers. Those who view themselves as class peers of their employers usually prefer a permeable boundary between the front and backstage areas. Their attempt to seek equal status with their employers is more likely to be achieved when their primary job is related to care work. Other workers, albeit contesting their employers' superiority, tend to obscure their backgrounds because a segmented approach can better protect their privacy and diminish the risk of confronting the employers' authority. Some workers, usually with less education or a rural background, acknowledge the status difference between themselves and their employers. In particular, veteran migrants know how to manipulate personal ties for their own benefit and new migrants seek patronage from their employers to enrich their resources. Other workers choose to minimize their interactions with employers, so they can limit exposure to extra emotional burdens and the risks of transcending social boundaries. This approach is plausible especially when the workers are employed in a spacious house and when their employers work outside during the day.

These typologies are not mutually exclusive categories but ideal-typical polarities of continuums in reality. Employers may situationally move between the approaches of distant hierarchy and maternalism, or they may fluctuate between a trustworthy personal relationship and a hassle-free business relationship. For instance, sitting arrangements at meals, a critical practice of boundary work, often change in context.[6] In many Taiwan households, eating arrangements vary in terms of the presence of family members. When there are only women and children at home, the domestic worker is allowed to eat at the same table or watch television together with the family. The worker is excluded when male employers or senior family members are present. Various members in the same family can hold distinct attitudes toward domestic workers. It is common that the wife cultivates a personal relationship with the caregiver while the husband acts like a distant master. In other words, the inclusion or exclusion of domestic workers becomes a marker for the multiple layers of family boundaries, which are like concentric circles mirroring status rankings among family members.

A friend who hires a migrant domestic asked me a question after reading this chapter: "So, which type of boundary work is the best after all?" I cannot provide a definite answer to solve his anxiety about how to be a "good" employer because boundary work conducted by employers and workers is interactive by nature. There is greater affinity in pairs of some categories and stronger opposition in other pairs. Patronage-seeking workers would appreciate gifts and favors given by maternalistic employers, while other workers find them humiliating or unwelcome. Personalism-oriented employers feel frustrated when their employees prefer to keep some distance, whereas these workers match better with business-oriented employers or even distant-hierarchical employers. The employers who like to purchase deference would feel offended by a worker who showcases her college degree or English skills; it is more plausible for such a worker to claim her status similarity to personalistic employers, who would like to share a dining table together.

After all, employers have more power to prescribe the interactive scripts than workers, and the former as citizens hold institutional privileges over migrants who are transient and marginalized in the host country. This explains why keeping a safe distance and obscuring previous positions are less risky strategies for migrant domestic workers burdened with the danger of being repatriated by their foreign employers. Boundary work at home is not just a tug of war between the two parties in a local setting; it is a microcosm of identity politics and class struggles embedded in the global context. That is how the personal becomes political, and the domestic becomes global.

 CONCLUSION

During my last six months in graduate school, I sublet a con-
dominium from a couple of professors who were on sabbatical.
Their gorgeous apartment in a quiet suburb offered me luxurious shelter compared with my previous tiny urban nest. Their
mailbox frequently received flyers announcing "Responsible
Cleaners. Flexible Schedule. Reasonable Rate. We are white." A
few times when I looked out through the windows in the study, a
van painted "Dial-a-Maid" was parked across the street waiting
to pick up some cleaning ladies who had just finished their
shifts. From time to time I ran into a couple of women from East-
ern Europe who cleaned for my neighbors downstairs. When I
was distracted from my writing and listened carefully, I could
hear them giggling along with the noise of the vacuum cleaners.

Toward the end of my stay, the owners arranged for someone
to clean their home prior to their return. Since they were paying,
I was in no position to object. In all honesty, I felt relieved to be
free of the hassle of cleaning the spacious apartment. Although
I had met many domestic workers by then, I personally had
never been in a position anywhere close to that of an employer.
This time, I was almost there.

The day came. I made sure that there was iced water and fresh
juice in the refrigerator and I put out some fruit and other
snacks on the kitchen table in case the worker wanted to take a
break. Although the agency told me that the cleaning lady had
keys to get in, I wanted to say "Hi" and have a chat so that the
service would not be another depersonalized relationship. The
bell rang and at the door was a woman in her early forties who
was possibly Polish. I nervously introduced myself and asked
her name. She looked confused and shook her head, saying

only, "No speak English." Throwing me a brief smile, she quickly went into the kitchen and started her work. Obviously she had cleaned this apartment many times before—she knew where everything was much better than I did. I felt like a defeated soldier in a battle for class equality, albeit without the presence of an enemy. I retreated to my room, closed the door, and tried to do some writing. But my stage-managed air of calm could not endure after I heard her cleaning the toilet that I had sat on only ten minutes before. I immediately folded up my laptop and ran to a coffee shop nearby. I dared not return until hours later, when I was sure that she had left my "home."

Migrant women are the primary suppliers of domestic services in cities worldwide. They may be Polish in Chicago, Mexican in Los Angeles, West Indian in New York, Moroccan in Barcelona, Sri Lankan in Kuwait, Filipina in Toronto, and Indonesian in Taipei. After crossing geographic borders, these global Cinderellas find themselves in a live-in condition that ironically combines physical intimacy and social distance, and their care work requires a complex interchange between love and money. Meanwhile, the placement of migrant workers at home strikes double anxieties among employers: home, socially perceived as a private haven sheltered from public chaos, now becomes a field of discipline and surveillance; cultural barriers and social inequalities are so intimately present that they are impossible to ignore. This book reveals how migrant women and their employers in Taiwan—as well as the Polish cleaner and I in Chicago, and many others around the globe—negotiate the invisible yet tangible boundaries at home and in the world.

MORE GLOBALIZED, MORE DIVIDED

The long visits of guest workers have transformed the landscapes in host countries and created a range of transnational social spaces based on the flows of capital, media, and technology. Migrant enclaves have emerged in major cities around Taiwan, and a flow of capital is invested to facilitate the maintenance of transnational ties. Migrant workers use formal circuits and door-to-door services to deliver money and packages; many of the expensive consumer goods they purchased in Taiwan are now under warranty back home. Echoing what Arjun Appadurai (1996: 33) has said, the combination of the electronic media and mass migration has created deterritorialized "imagined worlds." Migrants have access to up-dated political news and celebrity tabloids in their home countries by pur-chasing magazines or logging on to the Internet. They send pirated DVDs of Hollywood movies and Taiwanese TV dramas as gifts to their families. And they live a transnational life by maintaining familial, economic, so-cial, religious, and political ties in both home and host countries (Basch et al. 1994). Everyday technologies such as the Internet and mobile phones enable them to sustain affective links and pursue romances against geo-graphic constraints.

It is true that increasing numbers of transmigrants are living a life be-yond the scope of a single country, but their life chances remain bounded. Scholars warn against a premature celebration of the breaking down of national territories. According to Aristide Zolberg (1991), although many people nowadays cross borders on a daily basis, they only transfer be-tween different territorial memberships enforced by the "bounded states in a global market." Meanwhile, the tendencies of re-territorialization and re-identification have emerged locally (Hall 1997), which results in po-litical and social exclusion based on the cultural imagination of ethnic differences.

This book has demonstrated that the proliferation of international mi-gration has not weakened the sovereignty of nation-states or the gov-ernance of national territories. In Asia, both sending and receiving states regulate the outflow or inflow of international migration. Migrant work-ers, circulating in a bounded global market, are marginalized by a series of legal and political regulations based on the principle of citizenship. In different ways, transmigrants maneuver institutional channels of nation-hood to maximize their chances in the global economy. Upper- or middle-class migrants employ the strategy of "flexible citizenship" (Ong 1999) by holding passports from multiple countries to facilitate their transnational business ties and social lives. By contrast, lower-end migrant workers seek multiple passports from their home nation to help them bypass govern-ment restrictions and increase their number of entries into the global labor market.

Despite crossing geographic borders, migrant workers straddle the fences of racialization and other social boundaries. Transnational mi-grants not only occupy multiple subject positions across different locales but they often experience contested identification. Such conflicts can arise because the workers accept socially demeaning jobs or because they encounter racial discrimination in the new country. Opportunities for people to move across borders have not ameliorated disparities between countries but often consolidate social inequalities along the class, ethnic, and gender divides.

We live in an increasingly globalized, yet more divided, world. My argument contests the common belief that prejudices emerge out of strangeness and lack of contacts across social groups. Contemporary societies may have more exposure to migrants and foreign cultures, but this does not lead to a happy ending of multiculturalism or the disappearance of social bias and discrimination. On the contrary, contact across social divides often stirs up anxieties and uncertainties, prompting a desire to reclaim distinction and exclusion. The encounter between migrant domestics and Taiwanese employers is a microcosm of power struggles and identity politics in the global village. The private household becomes a contested terrain for the reproduction of global inequalities and social boundaries.

AMBIVALENCE AND DISCONTINUITY

"To define something is to mark its boundary" (Zerubavel 1991: 2). Through drawing boundaries we make sense of our surroundings and situate who we are. Social boundaries matter to us not because these mental frames have concrete existence. Rather, differentiation is crucial because social meanings are fluid and multifaceted and the experiential world is full of structural ambivalence. Eviatar Zerubavel (1991) illustrates how social realities consist of the "continuous gradation of differences rather than sharp-cut divisions" (73). And, he argues, the cognitive anxiety over ambiguity among people has widely generated pollution-related taboos and exclusion-based categories that preserve the mental "purity" of a classified order and "the social construction of discontinuity" (74).

Stuart Hall (1997: 47–48) also writes, "[Identification] is always structured through ambivalence. Always constructed through splitting. Splitting between that which one is, and which is the other." The employment of migrant domestic workers by the Taiwanese new rich reveals ambivalent conditions in the feminization of domestic labor, the racialization of foreign workers, the territorial frames of class identification, and the disjuncture between home and family. To counteract such ambivalence, at least four types of boundary-making practices have emerged in this transnational encounter, which involves complex articulations of gender, class, ethnic, and national divides in the making of home and family.

These social boundaries are not only cognitive categories that we use to identify the self in opposition to others; they are also institutional classifications along which social resources are unevenly distributed. To extend Zerubavel's analysis, I emphasize that the social act of boundary making is fundamental to reproducing and contesting social inequalities. Movement across national borders and ethnic boundaries muddles the frames of political membership and social classification, disrupting the maintenance of status quos. Through the interactive practice of boundary making, people cultivate, reinforce, and counteract social distinctions in the politics of everyday lives.

Maid or Madam? The Continuity of Domestic Labor

The opposition between maid and madam wrecks the feminist romance of a global sisterhood. We need a new conceptual lens to identify the commonalities and differences across women. I use the concept "the continuity of domestic labor" to describe how women face similar oppression under the patriarchal division of domestic labor, subject to various constraints given their class, ethnic, and national positioning.

Taiwanese employers and migrant domestic workers bargain with patriarchies in distinct ways. They formulate different strategies to divide reproductive labor between gender, kin, and markets. Taiwanese women outsource part of their wifely and motherly duties to the market so that they can avoid the tensions frequently generated when pushing their husbands to share housework. Migrant women make use of this gendered job niche to secure a higher wage in the global market and become the major breadwinner in their transnational families. Taiwanese daughters-in-law maneuver domestic employment to resist the tradition of three-generation cohabitation and avoid the obligation of serving their parents-in-law. In contrast, migrant women rely on extended kin to maintain their families back home while serving as fictive kin overseas.

I have demonstrated that domestic work is a critical domain in the construction of gender boundaries—womanhood is socially defined by the elements of domesticity and motherhood in contrast to the ideal of breadwinning manhood. In reality, most women transcend this gender divide, voluntarily or by default. Yet the gender ideologies associated with domestic labor remain powerful, whether women do it or supervise other women who do it.

Thanks to hired domestic help, middle-class Taiwanese women are able to take the male path to career achievement. Despite the market transfer of labor activities, the domestic terrain remains inscribed by gender norms. Female employers rely on the "shadow work" of migrant domestics to fulfill their feminized duties of domesticity, motherhood, and filial piety; meanwhile, they are haunted by the anxiety of being replaced by another woman. Female employers establish a rigid boundary between maid and madam to affirm their class-specific and ethnocentric version of womanhood. Their daily practices of boundary work—such as the roping off of cooking and the stratified division of mothering labor—mark the distinctions between wife and maid, mother and caregiver. The lady of the house wants housework to be done, not her position to be taken, by the maid. She invites a migrant nanny to be her partner in mothering, yet only part of it.

Nevertheless, women positioned along the lower end of the class and national spectra tend to make the maid/madam boundary fluid and permeable. Migrant women transcend the gender boundary by becoming household breadwinners. Some argue that they are just like other employed women who leave children behind to improve the welfare of the family. The difference is merely that they have traveled farther. While expanding the definition of motherhood to incorporate breadwinning, migrant women still struggle to achieve "good" mothering in their transnational as well as substitute motherhoods. Not only do they establish a similarity to their female employers; they can also claim to be better mothers than their employers. Some single migrants cross the maid/madam boundary by marrying their foreign employers to pursue the Cinderella dream of "marrying up," shifting from waged work to unpaid service as a wife.

Women in Taiwan, Indonesia, the Philippines and many other parts of the world are trapped in a similar predicament—the privatization of reproductive labor. The maintenance of family welfare is reduced to unpaid kin labor, plus some hired help for those socially privileged. Such privatized institutional arrangements exacerbate the feminization and moralization of domestic labor. The social myths of "women's calling" and "labor of love" manifest anxiety among women as wives and mothers and underestimate women's skills and contributions as laborers. To search for possibilities in building coalition and alliance between maid and madam, we need to treat reproductive labor as a public responsibility and a professional job.

Stratified Otherization—The Racialization of Foreign Workers

I approach racialization as a multi-layered process of stratified otherization. The racialized subject position of migrant domestic workers is situated in opposition to Taiwanese citizens and also in relation to other ethnic others. Foreigners, divided by their class and national locations, are associated with stratified cultural images. The racialization of foreign workers is intertwined with other social processes of boundary making, including the charting of national boundaries, the guarding of private domesticity, and the segmentation of the labor market.

Immigration policy and the regulation of citizenship characterize a nation's distinct understanding of membership coupled with class and ethnic classifications. The state is engaged in nation building while regulating flows of people who penetrate its porous borders. Taiwan's government maintains a closed-door policy toward workers from China and yet recruits Southeast Asians to ensure the visibility of ethnic boundaries and enhance its diplomatic leverage with the Southeast Asian states. Like other Asian host countries, Taiwan's government grants uneven rights to white-collar foreigners and manual-labor migrants. The former are entitled to settlement and naturalization but the latter are prohibited from permanent residence and subject to stringent surveillance. Migrant contract workers are recruited as desired labor within the geographic territory but are rejected as citizens and excluded from the symbolic boundary of the nation.

Employers enforce racialized boundaries in the domestic realm to maintain order and safeguard territory according to the social conception of private domesticity. They regulate the workers' access to home space to fortify a boundary between "disdained" aliens and "purified" households. They control migrant women's whereabouts and personal networks to prevent "pollution" outside the home—the lure of male migrants and the politicization of migrant communities. The racialization of foreign maids is also related to the crisis of female domesticity. To guard their status as wife and mother in the presence of migrant domestics, female employers often draw on stereotypes to amplify ethnic differences, thereby reproducing racism and class prejudice in family life, especially in the upbringing of children.

Recruitment agencies attach nationality-based stereotypes to migrant workers in order to establish segmentation in the migrant labor market. They promote Indonesian women, "the traditional other," as a better model of ideal servants in opposition to Filipina workers, "the Westernized other." They also materialize these discourses by locating workers of "desired" features and transforming their bodies and minds. Through a careful selection of recruitment venues, labor brokers seek "docile" village women subject to surveillance of local networks. By imposing a months-long training project, they claim to have "moralized" and "civilized" the savage to fit the "modern" lifestyle of Taiwanese households. And through "proper" management of dress code, hairstyle, and manner, they present migrant women as defeminized and disciplined servants to the gaze of prospective employers.

The marketing strategies of labor brokers shape the competitive dynamics between migrant workers and obstruct labor coalition across national divides. Filipina and Indonesian workers reproduce racial narratives to mark their superior differences from the other migrant group; consequently, they impose stereotypes and discipline upon themselves, watching their own bodies as an extension of national territories guarded by moral borders. These discourses subjugate migrant domestic workers but they also function as resources that enable the assertion of agency (Pratt 1999). For instance, migrant women may maneuver their images as poverty-stricken subordinates to justify their entitlement to gifts and favors from their employers. They may also develop counterdiscourses to disrupt the coherence of dominant discourses and the functioning of power relations. In sum, migrant women negotiate their subject positions in the discursive terrain of stratified otherization by simultaneously resisting and enforcing the controlling images imposed on them.

Transnational Class Mapping—(De)territorialized Class Identification

When talking about class, we tend to assume an implicit framework of a single nation or society. For transnational migrants, however, the cartography of class is located beyond a single country and across multiple social settings. I use the term "transnational class mapping" to describe the complex class formation in global contexts, in which class process takes place beyond one national territory and yet class boundaries are negotiated in terms of territory-based resources and narratives.

The Taiwanese new rich and middle-class Filipina migrants have taken distinct paths of class mobility as a result of the economic disparity between their countries of origin. With the consumption of imported goods, foreign travel, and migrant labor, Taiwanese employers establish a metropolitan lifestyle on the ground of national wealth. By contrast, Filipina college graduates face deflated wages and underemployment in a stagnant home economy. They seek higher wages overseas but experience downward mobility while working as foreign maids.

This global conjuncture constitutes an anomaly in class theory: class domination based on the ownership of economic capital does not always correspond to the endowment of cultural capital, which refers to educational credentials and the linguistic capital of English in this case. The Taiwanese new rich are eager to convert their money into tools of education and competence in English for their children. Filipina migrants, with their postcolonial linguistic capital, gain relative advantages in the global labor market and hold some bargaining power over less-educated Taiwanese employers. Yet their human capital is still discredited in host countries because of their national origin.

Inasmuch as class positioning operates on a global scale, class boundaries are subject to local negotiation at transnational encounters of people. Taiwanese employers may establish a sense of class superiority over their migrant employees by turning national disparity into racialized differences. Middle-class employers attempt to downplay social disparity in domestic employment as a way of affirming their ideal of behaving like liberal-minded, global citizens. Some Filipina migrant workers highlight their middle-class background to establish their status as class peers of their employers, but others obscure their past to avoid contesting employer authority. Some maneuver their English skills as a symbolic means of resistance, but others ignore the employers' grammatical errors as a way of performing deference.

International migration has created a range of subject positions that allow individuals to negotiate the durability and mutability of class boundaries across borders and locales. Migrant domestic workers, the global Cinderellas, live a dual life in host countries: they are rules-bound servants in employers' residences, yet they are fashion-hungry consumers on their days off; they perform deference on the front stage but mock their employers' English backstage. There is another front/backstage distinction to be made in their cross-border lives: despite facing downward mobility in host countries, migrant workers upgrade their social status back home with the display of material gain. Some overseas maids are "remote madams" who hire local domestic workers back home. Returned migrants often hide the dark side of their overseas experience from their families and neighbors, presenting only the photos of happy tourists and the success stories of homecoming heroes.

Globalization at Home—the Politics of Spatial Boundaries

Globalization does not simply operate on Export Processing Zones or the market floor of international trade. Globalization takes places in our kitchens and living rooms. The household order in developed economies is built on visible or latent labor outsourcing on a global scale. The cheap labor force in the periphery produces affordable appliances that greatly reduce the intensity of housework, or is relocated to take over labor duties as live-in maids and caregivers. The boundaries of home and family are open borders reconstituted by global forces in everyday lives.

Employers and migrant domestic workers face different quandaries and develop distinct patterns in their spatial practices of constructing home and family. When home becomes a site for cross-border contacts, Taiwanese employers safeguard the domestic territory and construct multilayered family boundaries to accommodate the intimate presence of migrant workers. They want to include the workers as part of the family but also attempt to regulate the labor performance in line with the market principle. They want to adopt migrant caregivers as their fictive kin to ensure good care for their children, but they remain concerned about their quality of care and moral reliability. They try to cultivate a personal relationship with the workers to ease their class guilt, but they feel burdened by the extra emotional work and they dislike the encroachment on their privacy at home.

Globalization creates a different disjuncture between family as a circle of intimacy and home as a physical residence for migrant domestic workers. Serving as surrogate family members for their employers, workers must reside separately from their own families. They nevertheless maintain transnational family ties despite their physical absence from the daily household reproduction. Through the frequent flows of goods, information, and messages across borders, migrant mothers are engaged in the practice of "transnational homemaking" to sustain their roles as spiritual housekeepers and long-distance nurturers. Meanwhile, single migrant women attempt to build their own families against spatial constraints by seeking mates through pen pal services or virtual migrant networks. Their journey overseas often turns into a circular trajectory of migration that involves various host countries, different paths of emigration (work and marriage), and multiple forms of transnational households.

Migrant workers also strive to empower themselves in the landscape of exclusion and create a sense of "home" during their stay in host countries. Given the limited privacy available in their employers' residences, they go "public" to expand their private zones and backstage areas. On their Sunday outings, they reproduce a home-country lifestyle with food and other goods available through transnational networks and circuits. Despite their homebound status, migrant domestics go "mobile" to establish wireless networks. Slowly, they develop migrant communities and public spheres, transforming the foreign land into a provisional home.

PUBLIC CARE, PROFESSIONAL WORK, AND CITIZENSHIP

The introduction of migrant domestic workers is a policy that exacerbates the privatization of care. This policy, in excusing the absence of the state and the husband, continues to define housework and care work as a woman's calling and a family duty. The only differences are that it is another woman who is doing the work and the family's duty is to ensure the purchase of quality service. In East Asia in particular, the family is assumed to be the primary institution that guards the economic and social well-being of family members. Most states have not established comprehensive welfare programs. Policymakers praise and encourage three-generation cohabitation as a time-honored solution to childcare and eldercare. This romanticized image of family unity obscures power inequalities along the gender and generational divides. The privatization of care in connection with the principle of familism exacerbates women's subordination to the patriarchal family.

Live-in migrant domestic workers enable many ethnic Chinese households in Taiwan, Hong Kong, and Singapore to maintain the socially perceived ideals of in-home care for children and the elderly. By recruiting migrant women as substitute mothers for their children and fictive relatives for their aging parents, employed women are able to mitigate their motherly guilt and avoid the stigma of consigning elders to nursing homes. This is a global solution to the local norms of familism and filial piety. Ironically, the family idyll of employers is staged against the sober backdrop that migrant domestic workers are separated from their own children and families for extensive periods of time.

Bridget Anderson (2000) has argued that migrant domestic workers enable some middle-class European women to gain access to the public sphere as equals of men. "In order to participate [in the labor market] *like men* women must have workers who will provide the same flexibility as *wives*" (190, emphasis in original). In other words, these women cannot fully exercise their citizenship rights without the flexible labor of migrant workers. Here is another irony: the workers themselves are denied these rights, although "they are helping to give meaning to the notion of citizenship status" (191).

Following a similar logic, Asian governments have introduced migrant domestic workers to solve the care deficit as a privatized welfare program and to push their female citizens into the labor market as part of national development. In the meantime, state regulations, in particular the "guest worker" program, have maintained the status of migrant workers as disposable labor and transient residents. States must ensure the dependency and subordination of migrant workers to facilitate extraction of flexible labor and to sustain their marginal presence in host societies.

To change this situation, we should first challenge the public/private dichotomy and advocate the publicizing of care. Scholars such as Joan Tronto (1993) have proposed that care should be viewed as a political ideal—the practice of care describes the qualities necessary for the achievement of democratic citizenship. To counteract the privatized, familistic model of care, the public should support tax reforms that aim for social justice, while the government should provide affordable institutional care and establish universal welfare programs such as pensions and child allowances. We should recognize care as an essential social right and public responsibility, rather than reducing it to a "parochial concern of women" (Tronto 1993: 180) or the devalued work of powerless minorities.

The second agenda of action is to formalize and professionalize domestic and care work. Because employers do not recognize domestic work as real work, they tend to impose unreasonable demands upon their surrogates (rather than treating them like "employees") and ignore the contract-bound nature of employment. Without adequate social recognition and institutional protection for paid domestic service, a personalized employment relationship can only reproduce an oppressive, family-like hierarchy for these fictive-kin employees. Instead of executing a utopian feminist agenda such as abolishing domestic service, it is more feasible to upgrade the conditions of this work environment and reclaim the dignity and humanity of workers in this field (Hondagneu-Sotelo 2001).

The project of professionalizing domestic work needs to be grounded in changes of institutional regulations that rationalize this occupation. Otherwise, the rhetoric of professionalism could turn into a form of self-discipline in accordance with the discourses of labor brokers. In Taiwan and other Asian host countries, domestic workers are not covered by the Labor Standards Law. Such legal exclusion has intensified the vulnerability of foreign domestic workers in comparison with migrant workers (mostly men) employed in formal sectors. This, again, reflects the state ideology about the feminized and privatized nature of domestic work. In the eyes of the state, the foreign domestic worker is not a worker in the national economy but "an appendage of the household" (Huang and Yeoh 2003: 93).

In addition to legal reform, it is also vital to seek effective strategies to mobilize and unionize domestic workers, whose workplaces are scattered across individual households. Another barrier to the organizing of migrant domestic workers is their transient status and limited duration of stay in host countries. This point leads to the third political agenda for the labor rights of migrant workers. Some inappropriate interventions by the state, such as the regulation of job transfers in the local labor market, should be abolished. As labor equals, migrant workers should be allowed to change employers and extend their residency, conditional upon job availability. In the meantime, the state should strengthen its protection of migrant rights and better enforce its own regulations.

Finally, we need a new framework for the regulation of citizenship and membership. The reality is that the physical presence of "guest" workers in Taiwan and other Asian countries has become relatively permanent, and their active participation in the economic, social, and cultural life of the host country has contested the foundational logic of citizenship.[1] The receiving states should consider opening the possibility of naturalization to migrant manual laborers, or else relax the dichotomous model of citizenship to grant economic, social, and local political rights to noncitizens

(Brubaker 1989). The model of "postnational membership" is another creative political agenda that can be exercised on a supranational level.[2] It will, however, take a long time to achieve this model in Asia, a continent known for its lack of regional cooperation and political unity (Oishi 2005).[3]

We are facing a changing ethnoscape comprising a growing number of business, labor, and marriage migrants who pass through borders on a frequent basis. Personal contacts across social boundaries do not automatically lead to the eradication of distance and prejudice, unless we confront the power relations that permeate everyday lives and engage in institutional reforms to enhance social equality as a political goal. In this increasingly integrated yet fragmented world, we need inclusive immigration policies and reflective cultural attitudes to break down the invisible borders of national parochialism and social discrimination.

APPENDIX A: RESEARCH METHODS

From August 1998 to July 1999 I conducted participant observation in a field site I call Holy Spirit. It is a church-based non-governmental organization that has provided services for migrant workers in Taipei since the early 1990s. Every Sunday, about sixty to a hundred Filipino/as attend the English mass in the morning. Because the church is located in a middle-class residential neighborhood, the majority of migrant churchgoers are female domestic workers. After the mass, about half of them stay at the offices of Holy Spirit, a two-floor building right behind the church. They chat, practice for choir, cook Filipino food, and share lunch together. In the afternoon some stay for bible study, Chinese classes, computer classes, and other activities held by the center. The others go out to remit money, mail packages, shop, and attend other social gatherings.

I joined this community through the referral of the nuns working at Holy Spirit. Later I offered to teach a Chinese class on Sundays and assisted with case counseling on labor disputes and other issues. Volunteer work unburdened me of much of my worries about my fieldwork as only an "exploitation" of information from migrants; it also greatly helped me establish personal relations in the field. All the members of this community were aware of my research, and I frequently attended a variety of their Sunday outings. During the research period, I befriended and maintained frequent contacts with most of the Filipina informants. After I finished the fieldwork, several continued correspondences with me via letters, phone calls, and e-mails.

I conducted interviews with fifty-eight Filipina migrant domestic workers. I reached them through multiple venues to maximize sample variation. The majority (thirty-four) were located at Holy Spirit and four were referred to me by their employers. These women then introduced me to their neighbors, relatives, and friends in other social circles. This allowed me to access workers who have no regular days off or attend other churches. These informants covered various work arrangements and geographic settings. Forty-nine of them were documented live-in workers, three were documented but lived out and worked part-time, and six were undocumented (three live-ins and three part-timers). The majority of them worked in Taipei and other parts of Northern Taiwan, except for five Filipina caretakers who took care of elders in a small town in mid-Taiwan.

I was not always comfortable about requesting individual interviews from migrant workers outside the terrains of their regular activities—which seemed to deprive them of their precious social time on Sundays. I preferred to collect "naturally occurring descriptions" in the course of their ordinary activities (Emerson et al. 1995: 114). I listened to their conversations (or asked them to translate for me if they were conversing in Tagalog) and raised questions to join in the dialogues. Many conversations occurred when we were walking in the street, chatting on the bus, cleaning the church, or having lunch. I jotted notes and wrote them up in detail after I went home. I also conducted tape-recorded interviews with half the Filipina informants, mostly in the office or lounge of Holy Spirit. The interviews ranged from thirty minutes to two hours. Near the end of my research, I held two focus-group meetings at Holy Spirit to discuss the incentives of migration and the impact upon these migrants' families.

I approached the Taiwanese employers on an individual basis and conducted open-ended, in-depth interviews with forty-seven women and four men, including three married couples. All employers were ethnic Chinese. The interviews, lasting from one to three hours, were all tape-recorded and fully transcribed. I found interviewees by using chain and snowball referrals but limited each referral to one person to reach more heterogeneous groups of women. The interviewees were at different life stages and had diverse experiences of employment. At the time of interview, twenty-five employers had been hiring a migrant domestic worker for less than three years, fourteen had been hiring for some time between four to six years, and six had hiring experiences for more than seven years. The average length of employment was four years.

Most of my interviewees resided in metropolitan Taipei but lived in diverse residential locations and were from varied class backgrounds. I drove miles to some luxurious houses on the hills but also walked to old, tiny apartments on the outskirts. I also spent several days in a mid-Taiwan province, interviewing and observing four elders and their migrant caregivers. I interviewed most employers in their residences, where I could observe their interactions with domestic workers on site, but some employers chose to meet in their offices or in restaurants during lunch break or after work to suit their busy schedules and avoid interruptions at home.

I tried to interview male employers, whose voices have been absent in the literature of paid domestic work. I interviewed a few and encountered great difficulty in the process. Some bluntly refused to be interviewed, saying: "I know nothing about these kinds of things. You should just ask my wife." Among those who agreed to an interview, most reported limited knowledge about the workers' personal or job details. As I explain in chapter 3, men's indifference reflects their perception of domestic labor as trivial and feminized. In addition, many consciously maintain some distance from migrant women to preclude their wives' misunderstanding.

It is likely that cases of excessive control were not accessible to me through the method of snowball sampling. When some interviewees referred other employers to me, they often excluded severe cases because, they said, "I don't think she would like to talk to you about this." Some employers rejected my request for interviews; they replied with reasons (or excuses?) like "Sorry. I am too busy" or "I have nothing interesting to tell you." Meanwhile, it was difficult to meet workers who were forbidden by their employers from taking days off. To overcome these potential biases, I reached workers experiencing harsh working conditions when I counseled labor disputes and visited undocumented workers in a detention center. I also collected information about rigid labor control from the interviewed employers and workers who described their neighbors or friends. Because I do not focus on abuses and crimes in domestic employment, such sample bias was not really a primary concern for me. My method located employers and workers in the middle range; these cases suit my focus on the everyday politics of family routines.

All interviews and communications with Filipina workers were conducted in English, since I did not speak any of their native dialects. Luckily, the office director at Holy Spirit is a nun of Chinese descent who grew up in Mindanao and speaks limited Tagalog. Therefore her communications with migrant workers and most activities in the center were conducted in English. This situation allowed me to observe without the help of translators. Most participants spoke English moderately well, but grammatical mistakes like misused tenses and gender pronouns were prevalent. For the sake of clarity, some quotes from workers have been slightly modified without changing their substance.

All interviews with employers were recorded in Chinese and later translated into English by me as they are quoted in this book. Readers should keep in mind that most employers actually speak little or moderate English. All names in the book are pseudonyms. I call older employers by their last names (for men) or their husbands' last names (for women), a common practice in Taiwan out of respect for seniority. I use Chinese first names for younger employers and apply English pseudonyms to those employed by international companies who use English first names at work.

In April 1999 I spent two weeks in the Philippines, staying with several returned migrants and their families in Manila and in Tarlac, a province in the Central Luzon region. I interviewed staff at three manpower agencies and observed recruitment interviews. I also visited OWWA (the Overseas Workers Welfare Administration), POEA (the Philippine Overseas Employment Administration), and five migrant-oriented NGOs in Manila. In the spring of 2002 I took another two-week trip in Manila and Ilo-Ilo, visiting some old friends and getting updates on their current situations and future plans.

The second phase of fieldwork was conducted from September 2002 to October 2003. It is more difficult to reach Indonesian migrant workers than their Filipina counterparts because mosques are not major nodes of gathering for Indonesian migrants (especially for female ones) in the way Catholic churches are in the Filipino community. Hence I located informants in Taipei Railway Station, a popular gathering place for Indonesian migrants on Sundays. With the help of two research assistants, one Taiwanese and the other Malaysian, I approached people who were sitting on the lobby floor and hanging out with their friends. We usually joined in the chatting on the first day we met and set another time for a more formal interview.

We conducted in-depth interviews with thirty-five Indonesian domestic workers. When the interviewee was fluent in Chinese (Mandarin or Hoklo), I conducted the interview myself. With one third of the informants who preferred to speak Bahasa Indonesian, the Malay-speaking assistant conducted the interview and later translated the transcript into Chinese. We tape-recorded most interviews. A small number of informants felt uncomfortable with the recorder, and we took notes for those interviews. About half the interviews involved only one session; with the rest, we built up a longer term of relationship. On Sundays we joined informants for shopping tours in Taoyuan, birthday parties in parks, and picnics on the floor of the railway station. On working days, we kept in touch by speaking or sending messages via mobile phones.

For two weeks in August 2003 I took a field trip in East Java, where the majority of Indonesian migrants in Taiwan came from. I accompanied a migrant friend who was returning home upon the end of her contract. I stayed with her family for a few days and then visited four other returned migrants in different villages. I also interviewed staff at two recruitment agencies in Surabaya and Jakarta, observed a training center for prospective migrants, and visited three migrant NGOs in Jakarta.

During these two research periods, I interviewed seven recruitment agencies in Taiwan and two government officials. I attended a number of meetings held by the CLA to discuss migrant issues with activists and recruitment agencies. I also joined some political campaigns and educational activities held by migrant NGOs. With the help of my assistants, I widely collected statistics, surveys, newsletters, newspaper editorials, and magazine articles. For the history of domestic service in Taiwan, in 1999 I interviewed seven Taiwanese domestic workers and one placement agent who had run the business for decades.

APPENDIX B: PROFILES OF INFORMANTS

TABLE 6. *Ages of Taiwanese employers and migrant domestic workers*

Age	Taiwanese Employers		Filipina Workers		Indonesian Workers	
	Number	Percentage	Number	Percentage	Number	Percentage
21–30	3	6%	15	26%	22	65%
31–40	23	45%	33	57%	12	32%
41–50	13	25%	11	17%	1	3%
Above 51	12	24%	0	0%	0	0%
Total	51	100%	58	100%	35	100%

TABLE 7. *Levels of education for Taiwanese employers and migrant domestic workers*

Education	Taiwanese Employers		Filipina Workers		Indonesian Workers	
	Number	Percentage	Number	Percentage	Number	Percentage
Elementary or below	3	6%	0	0%	5	14%
High school	10	20%	22	38%	30	86%
Junior college	6	12%	17	29%	0	0%
College	20	39%	19	33%	0	0%
Graduate education	12	24%	0	0%	0	0%
Total	51	100%	58	100%	35	100%

TABLE 8. *Occupations of Taiwanese female employers*

Occupation	Number	Percentage
Housewife	7	16%
Small-business owner	11	30%
Full-time worker	19	47%
Business manager, supervisor	9	
Professor, judge, journalist	6	
Public servant	4	
Part-time worker or freelancer	3	7%
Total	40*	100%

*This excludes seven female employers who are senior citizens or patients under the care of migrant workers.

TABLE 9. *Previous occupations of migrant domestic workers*

Occupation*	Filipina Workers		Indonesian Workers	
	Number	Percentage	Number	Percentage
Housewife	14	24%	2	6%
Farming, fishing	0	0%	3	9%
Student	4	7%	7	20%
Small-business owner	6	10%	1	3%
Nurse, midwife	3	5%	0	0%
Teacher	1	2%	0	0%
Other Professional				
Bank staff, real estate agent, supervisor	4	7%	0	0%
Administrative assistant	15	26%	1	3%
Sales clerk, waitress	8	14%	6	17%
Factory worker	3	5%	8	23%
Tailor	0	0%	1	3%
Domestic worker	0	0%	6	17%
Total	58	100%	35	100%

* Last job held in Indonesia or the Philippines before going abroad.

NOTES

INTRODUCTION

1 The UN statistics include international migrants who fall into four categories: permanent migration, temporary migration, irregular migration, and forced migration. Temporary migration is further divided into contract migration and professional migration.

2 There are many articles, theses, and dissertations on migrant domestic workers in Asia, which cannot be listed comprehensively here. See Cheng (2001), Lin, C-J (1999) and Lin H-L. (2000) for the case of Taiwan.

3 *Chaboukan* refers to a girl who was bought and sold at the age of eight or younger. A *chaboukan* was not considered a human being but the property of her master. She had no family name and received no wage, but the master was obligated to arrange her marriage when she reached a certain age (Chuo 1993; Okamatsu 1902).

4 From 1920 to 1930, a period when Taiwan was incorporated into the industrialization plan of the Japanese empire, the number of *shijonins* tripled (from 3,578 to 9,877), according to the surveys conducted by the Japanese colonial government (Bureau of Official Statistics 1924, 1935).

5 Some women's associations, whose members were mostly upper-class Mainlander wives, played the role of matchmaker for the recruitment of domestic workers in the 1950s and 1960s (Chang 1998).

6 Ownership of modern household facilities, such as refrigerators and washing machines, was still limited during the 1960s, but the pace of acquisition increased rapidly in the 1970s (Thornton and Lin 1994: 84).

7 This Japanese term, which refers to "aunt" literally or elder women in general, became a common expression for middle-aged domestic workers in Taiwan.

8 Full-time day workers (9 a.m. to 9 p.m.) are paid NT$25,000 to NT$30,000 per month. (The conversion rate at the time of publication is US$1 to NT$33.5.) Those who work half a day (4 or 5 p.m. to 9 p.m.) earn a monthly wage between NT$15,000 to NT$20,000. If the job covers cooking and cleaning, then laundry and childcare are often excluded. If the worker is hired for the purpose of childcare, she usually provides minimal or no cleaning.

9 The average hourly wage is between NT$300–350 and each cleaning service usually takes three hours.

10 One employer I interviewed had paid as much as NT$45,000 per month for a local live-in worker, which was about three times a migrant worker's wage.

11 This assistance from the United States started in 1951 and ended in 1965.

12 There are a few exceptions who can seek state approval on a case basis: Taiwanese households with triplets under the age of three and foreign executives and managers in multinational companies.

13 See chapter 2 for a detailed discussion of the ethnic composition in Taiwan.

14 See Douglas (1966), Durkheim and Mauss (1963), and Zerubavel (1991).

15 Brubaker and Cooper (2000) suggest that we use the term "identification" to avoid the reifying connotation of "identity." A feasible empirical inquiry turns to "the durability or mutability of identifications across time and across social situations" (Glaeser 2000: 11).

16 Gerson and Peiss (1985: 317) define "gender boundaries" as "the complex structures—physical, social, ideological, and psychological—which establish differences and commonalities between women and men, among women, and among men." Gender boundaries as such are multiple boundaries rather than bifurcated categories.

17 Engels (1942/1972) used the term "reproductive labor" in a broader sense to describe both the production of subsistence and the production of human beings intergenerationally (including biological reproduction). Domestic labor can be divided into two major categories: *subsistence reproduction*, such as purchasing household goods, preparing and serving food, laundering and repairing clothing for family members; and *social reproduction*, including socializing children, providing care and emotional support for adults, and maintaining kin and community ties (Colen 1995; Lorber 1994).

18 I am inspired by Evelyn Nakano Glenn (1992), who views servitude and service work as historical continuities that characterize the racial division of paid reproductive labor.

19 European scholars such as Michel Weiviorka (1994) make a distinction between "old racism" and "new racism." The former refers to classical, inegalitarian racism, which views the Other as an inferior being to be included yet marginalized in the society. The new racism that has emerged in Europe since the 1970s is a model of cultural racism or differential racism; the Other is viewed as fundamentally different, constituting a danger or invader that should be expelled from the society.

20 Robert Miles (1989) cautions about the reification of racial groups in the academic discourses of racial relations. He views racialization as an ideological process that facilitates and obscures class differentiation and exploitation. Immanuel Wallerstein (1991) also argues that the production of ethnic differentiation is an ideological effect of colonialism and the international division of labor. Nevertheless, these Marxist perspectives contain a risk of reducing racism to class domination.

21 Here I follow the ethnomethodological-constructionist approach, which views family as "a socially constructed, situationally contingent cluster of meanings" (Holstein and Gubrium 1995: 896).

22 All names in this book are pseudonyms.

23 Paul Rabinow (1977: 79) says about participant observation: "No matter how far 'participation' may push the anthropologist in the direction of Not-Otherness, the context is still ultimately dictated by observation and externality."

I. A BOUNDED GLOBAL MARKET

1 Office of Statistics, Ministry of Economic Affairs, Republic of China, http://2k3dmz2.moea.gov.tw/gnweb/main.aspx, accessed on 31 July 2004.

2 It should be noted that Taiwan also became a major migrant-sending country in Asia in the 1990s. The number of emigrants from 1990 to 1996 increased more than four times, from 25,500 to 119,100 (Wang 1999: 214). These recent emigrants are mainly middle-class businesspeople, investors, and professionals, whose destinations are usually more developed countries like the United States, Canada, and Australia.

3 According to Tsay (1999), migrant workers made up 7 percent of the total labor force in the manufacturing industry, 11 percent of the construction industry, and 14 percent of domestic workers. Among all manufacturing industries, the textile industry ranked first (21 percent), followed by the basic metal industry (14 percent).

4 The number of domestic helpers has been decreasing since 1996 because some employers forfeited quotas after their children grew older. In contrast, the employment of caretakers has continued to grow; its number by the end of 2006 (151,391) is almost nine times more than the number in 1996 (16,308). Council of Labor Affairs, Executive Yuan, Republic of China, http://statdb.cla.gov.tw/statis, accessed on 1 March 2007.

5 In 1970, 19 percent of female workers were employed in the manufacturing sector, and by 1987 the number had jumped to 42 percent. For male workers, manufacturing employed only 14 percent in 1970 and 32 percent in 1987 (Hsiung 1996: 34).

6 In 2004, among Taiwanese women with a college or university degree, 62 percent were gainfully employed; women between the ages of twenty-five and twenty-nine have the highest rate of labor participation among all age groups (76 percent), followed by women between thirty and thirty-four (70 percent), http://eng.stat.gov.tw/public/Attachment/562210271471.xls, accessed on 1 July 2005.

7 Chronological demographic data show that the increases in nuclear units are associated primarily with the decline of joint households, but the percentage

of stem households containing one or two grandparents has decreased only slightly. The decline in both mortality and fertility rates has also increased the propensity for stem co-residence across generations because older generations have a higher survival rate and the supply of married sons has shrunk (Thornton and Lin 1994: 332).

8 Hong Kong opened a legal immigration channel for migrant domestic workers in 1974, and Singapore introduced the Foreign Maids Scheme in 1978 (Oishi 2005).

9 In Hong Kong in 2004, for every domestic helper to be employed, the employer had to have a household income of no less than HK$15,000 (US$1,900) per month or comparable assets. In Singapore, all applicants seeking to hire a foreign maid have to provide the government with their tax forms; only those with a minimum income of S$30,000 (US$21,429 in 1996) per year will be considered (Huang and Yeoh 1996).

10 According to Nana Oishi (2005), this is strongly related to the gender ideology of the Japanese government, which believes the woman's place is at home and discourages women from working elsewhere. Some policy change has taken place recently in order to supply labor for the long-term care insurance implemented to serve the aging Japanese population. In November 2004, Japan signed an agreement with the Philippines about a plan of recruiting Filipino nurses and caregivers starting from the year of 2006. However, these Filipino caregivers are to be employed by care institutions (rather than by private households) for the provision of home-visit care service.

11 Following a very similar logic, Taiwan's government applies different regulations to Chinese and foreign spouses when applying for citizenship.

12 Similarly, in Hong Kong, mainland Chinese cannot be hired as domestic workers because of fears of administrative difficulty in monitoring their activities since they are indistinguishable from the locals in appearance (Chiu 2004).

13 The Philippines had accused Taiwan of poaching passengers and demanded that Taiwanese carriers reduce their weekly quota of seats. When Taiwan refused, Manila unilaterally scrapped a 1996 air agreement with Taipei and both sides severed air links. The year-long aviation row ended after both countries signed a new aviation agreement on 26 September 2000 (*Taipei Times*, 27 December 2000).

14 *United Daily News*, 10 July 1999.

15 *China Times*, 17, 18 December 2002.

16 *China Times Evening Edition*, 18 December 2002.

17 It was reported in the media that the Thai government had requested all Taiwanese tourists wear surgical masks during their stay in Thailand. The Thai government later denied this.

18 Several of my informants, single and married, were encouraged by recruiters to participate in sham marriages. Indonesian officials also complained to the Taiwanese government about the increasing number of sham marriages that resulted from the ban on labor migration. *China Times*, 19 February 2004.

19 Section 5 in Article III. The Law of Nationality was first issued on 5 February 1929; it was not modified until 9 February 2000.

20 The checkup used to be held every six months. But according to a new regulation in January 2004, the number of medical checkups a migrant worker has to have during a contract is limited to three (after staying in Taiwan for six, eighteen, and thirty months). The government also lifted the requirement of a urine test for marijuana, morphine, or amphetamines.

21 The Department of Health implemented a new rule (the Measures of Inspection and Supervision of Health Examinations for Foreign Persons) on 13 January 2004 that requires all foreign teachers (not including managers, technicians, and other professionals) to get yearly medical checkups (mainly for tuberculosis, syphilis, and HIV) in order to qualify to have work permits renewed. This policy stirred protests from foreign teachers in colleges and universities. The administrators later decided to require medical checkups only from foreign teachers in high schools and cram schools.

22 However, the actual impact of this policy change is still unclear. Legally speaking, an employer cannot fire a migrant worker on the basis that she is pregnant, and migrant workers covered by the Labor Standards Law (such as factory workers, not domestic workers) are entitled to an eight-week maternity leave (but the child would not be a Taiwanese citizen). Yet, in practice, pregnant migrant workers tend to go home voluntarily or after coercion by their employers.

23 Article 59, Employment Service Act.

24 For the rest, 37 percent were permanent workers and 20 percent were classified as "irregular." Statistics released by Philippine Overseas Employment Administration (POEA), http://www.poea.gov.ph.docs, accessed on 17 February 2005.

25 Ibid.

26 In 1982 the Marcos government introduced a strict policy of forced remittance (Executive Order 857), which required migrant workers to remit 50 to 70 percent (for land-based migrants) or 100 percent (for sea-based migrants) of their earnings through Philippine banks. Workers who did not comply with the order would not have their passports renewed and would not be eligible to work overseas. This policy inspired protests among migrant workers all over the world. Under pressure, the penalties were lifted in 1985 (Constable 1997a: 164–65).

27 The Aquino administration introduced a new customs tax law in 1987 (Execu-

tive Order 206), which imposed a 100 percent duty on all appliances brought into the country. Prior to this, migrant workers could bring in appliances tax free (Asis 1992).

28 Statistics released by POEA; see note 24 for the source. The proportions of labor deployment by country were calculated by me.

29 The data for 1980 and 1987 was quoted from Oishi (2005: 64). The 2002 data is based on the Surveys on Overseas Filipinos, National Statistics Office, the Philippines, http://www.census.gov.ph/data/sectordata/2002/of0202.htm, accessed on 28 July 2004.

30 http://www.ncrfw.gov.ph/insidepages/inforesource/inforesource.htm, accessed on 27 July 2004.

31 The 2002 Survey on Overseas Filipinos, National Statistics Office, the Philippines, http://www.census.gov.ph/data/sectordata/2002/of0202.htm, accessed on 28 July 2004.

32 The proportion of single women is often overrated because many workers describe themselves as unmarried in their applications to avoid the paperwork required for married applicants. Besides, some migrants deliberately retain their maiden name in documents to bypass regulations in Taiwan. In doing so, they can revert to their husband's surname later and apply for work in Taiwan again with a new passport.

33 RA8042 attempts to balance the interests of migrant workers and private agencies and ends up limiting the effectiveness of the law (Battistella 1999).

34 The official recruitment system in Indonesia is made up of documented labor recruiting companies, known as PJTKI (*perusahaan jasa tenega kerja Indonesia*). Most migrant workers, however, go to Malaysia using undocumented brokers or middlemen, called *calo* and *taikongs* (Jones 2000; Spaan 1994).

35 The New Order is the term chosen by President Suharto for his regime, which ruled Indonesia from 1966 to 1998.

36 The total number of labor migrants from Indonesia increased from 120,896 in 1995–96 to 235,275 in 1997–98 and 411,609 in 1998–99 (Hugo 2000: 8).

37 Oishi (2005: table 3.2) also found that restrictions for female migrants differ across the region. In India, Bangladesh, and Pakistan, migration for domestic work was once banned; now the ban has been replaced by a steep minimum-age restriction for women (thirty or thirty-five). By contrast, regulations in Indonesia, Nepal, Sri Lanka, and the Philippines are rather relaxed and characterized by a low minimum age.

38 Some pay NT$10,000 during each of the first six months, and others pay monthly service fees in amounts stipulated by the CLA. The money paid to Philippine brokers covers the airfare to Taiwan, but workers have to pay for their medical checkups in both the Philippines and Taiwan.

39 To compete for job offers labor brokers have to pay factory employers a kick-back for every migrant worker brought into Taiwan (Lan, forthcoming). The increased cost is then added to the fees paid by migrant workers. A migrant factory worker can pay as much as NT$220,000 to come to Taiwan.

40 See chapter 5 for comparison of wage levels in different host countries.

41 Victor Fernandez, the head of the Philippine Association of Service Exporters, estimated that 10 percent of Philippine agencies were owned by Taiwanese in 1999 (interview by the author, Manila, 7 May 1999).

42 The CLA used to stipulate that the maximum amount of a placement fee should not exceed NT$7,000. As this official amount was far below the amount actually collected, the CLA approved a new regulation in October 2001, in which an agency can collect a placement fee up to the amount of a worker's monthly wage, plus a monthly service fee (NT$1,800 for the first year, NT$1,700 for the second, and NT$1,500 for the third). Accordingly, the maximum legal placement and service fees collected from a worker during the three years must not exceed NT$75,840.

43 *Industrial and Commercial Times*, 9 November 1995.

44 Newspapers reported that some business associations, which enjoy the privilege of distributing a limited number of quotas among their members, profited from selling quotas (Wu 1997: 29). A construction company was prosecuted for subcontracting a large number of migrant workers to other companies that had no quotas. *United Daily News*, 10 May 1994.

45 In 2005 the minimum wage was NT$15,840 per month; the maximum working hours were eight hours a day and forty-eight hours a week; workers were entitled to one day off a week plus seven days of annual leave. For health insurance, the employer was responsible for 60 percent, the government 10 percent, and the worker 30 percent.

46 The incident occurred when several Thai workers returned to their dormitory on a Sunday night and were barred from entry with liquor and cigarettes. The workers vented their anger by setting fire to a management shack, burning cars and throwing rocks at police. What shocked the Taiwanese public was not only the riot scene but also the media exposure of the inhuman working and living conditions of migrant workers. This high-profile event provoked a public outcry, leading to the resignation of the CLA chairperson, Chen Chu.

47 This is a short expression referring to money borrowed from loan sharks in the Philippines: When one borrows 5,000 pesos, she or he has to pay back 6,000 pesos in a month (a monthly interest rate of 20 percent).

48 The size of the levy, officially called an "employment stabilization fee," is NT$1,500 for the employment of caretakers and NT$5,000 for the employment of domestic helpers.

49 This regulation has been slightly changed since April 2003. An employer will forfeit the quota to replace workers if two or more migrant employees have disappeared from her or his custody.

2. DISAINED ALIENS, STRATIFIED OTHERS

1 Mainlanders (*waishengren*), from various provinces in China, emigrated with the Kuomintang regime largely between 1949 and 1950.

2 Despite emigrating from various provinces in China, Mainlanders are usually categorized as a group distinct from "Taiwanese" (*benshengren*), which consists of the Hoklo and the Hakka. This Mainlander-Taiwanese distinction is nevertheless held together more by sociopolitical experience rather than the ancestral heritage or culture (Brown 2004: 10). For example, "Taiwanese" were largely excluded from political power and national corporations during the martial law period.

3 According to Melissa Brown (2004), foot binding was the only cultural practice that was not adopted by the assimilated plains Aborigines ("We savages don't bind feet"). This marker for the Han-savage boundary, however, faded away after the Japanese government banned foot binding in 1915. Intermarriage, especially virilocal marriage to Hoklo spouses, became more prevalent after the ban.

4 See Chang (2000) for a more comprehensive documentation of the origins and transformation of Taiwanese national identity.

5 *The Pioneer Combat Cops* (*zhan-jing-ji-xian-feng*), 1 May 2003.

6 Misperception of the old and new ethnic others still happens in everyday circumstances. Some Aboriginal friends complained to me that they were stopped by the (Han Taiwanese) police, who assumed them to be foreign workers and wanted to check their identification.

7 *Economic News*, 9 July 1993.

8 *United Daily News*, 7 September 1999.

9 *Economic News*, 10 July 1993.

10 *Free Times*, 9 September 1999.

11 *United Evening News*, 21 July 1999.

12 *United Daily News*, 15 January 1994.

13 *China Times*, 13 May 1998.

14 *United Daily News*, 30 May 2001. The police in Taichung City also released a similar press statement speculating on a connection between the spread of AIDS and migrant workers, *United Daily News*, 5 December 2001.

15 *United Daily News*, 13 July 1999.

16 *China Times*, 14 May 1998.

17 *United Daily News*, 7 December 1999, 29 December 1999, 27 June 2000, 20 August 2001.

18 On 9 November 1995 a Filipina domestic worker, Angelina Canlas, killed her patient and then attempted suicide. She was diagnosed as clinically depressed and sentenced to twelve years for murder. On 8 February 2003 a well-known Taiwanese writer, Liu Shia, died after being attacked by her Indonesian caretaker, who was later diagnosed with a psychological disorder and sent back home.

19 In 2003 the average crime rate among documented migrant workers was 0.08 percent. The crime rate among undocumented migrants is higher (0.40 percent), but it is significantly lower than the crime rate among Taiwanese citizens (0.70 percent). Data provided by National Police Administration of the Interior Department, R.O.C.

20 *The Pioneer Combat Cops (zhan-jing-ji-xian-feng)*, 1 May 2003.

21 *United Evening News*, 12 April 2003.

22 *United Daily News*, 23 October 2001.

23 *United Daily News*, 6 December 2001.

24 These two ways of controlling foreigners—segregation and registration—are similar to the distinct managements applied to lepers or plague victims in nineteenth-century Europe. As Michel Foucault (1977: 198) points out, lepers were locked up as a ritual of rejection and exclusion, while the plague was controlled through the disciplinary projects of spatial allocation and organized surveillance.

25 In 2000 the GER (gross enrollment rate) in secondary education in the Philippines was over 77 percent, in contrast to 57 percent in Indonesia. Statistics releases by United Nations Educational, Social and Cultural Office, http://www.unesco.org/education/efa_report/zoom_regions_pdf/easiapac.pdf, accessed on 3 December 2004.

26 As there has not been any comprehensive survey on this matter, this statement is based on my interviews with labor brokers. In general, Indonesian migrants deployed to work in Taiwan and Hong Kong need to finish at least junior high school unless they have previous overseas experience; workers with lower education are usually sent to Malaysia.

27 The concept of "the linguistic field" refers to a system of specific sanctions and censorship that produces and reproduces linguistic legitimacy (Bourdieu 1991). See Crystal (1997) for more discussion of English as the most powerful global language in the postcolonial twentieth century. Elsewhere (Lan 2003), I have offered an analysis of the symbolic struggles surrounding the English language in the Taiwanese-Philippine migration linkage.

28 Since the establishment of the Philippine constitution in 1935, the postcolonial

government has pursued the formation of a national language based on Tagalog, the main indigenous language spoken in Manila, now referred to as
Pilipino. Yet it was not until the 1970s that the bilingual education policy
shifted in emphasis from English to Pilipino.

29 *China Times*, 31 March 2002.

30 These employers input Chinese words into this palm-sized machine, so workers can read the English translation that shows up on the screen of the
machine.

31 One of the English newspapers, *China News*, offers a Sunday column, *Kaba-
yan*, which publishes letters from Filipino migrant workers and reports news
related to migrant issues. It constitutes a critical public sphere for the Filipino
community in Taiwan.

32 The empowerment of Filipina migrants based on their linguistic capital is
nevertheless limited. The request for English tutoring usually comes from
less-educated employers. In contrast, well-educated employers are concerned
that their children may pick up a "bad," "substandard," or "unrefined" English
accent from Filipina domestic workers. And the assignment of English tutoring could even bring about extra work and unpaid exploitation (Lan 2003).

33 See Lin (1999), Cheng (2001), and Loveband (2004a).

34 I thank Lo Jung for assistance in the web search and chart making.

35 We also browsed forty-eight recruitment agencies' websites in Hong Kong
(searched through http://uk.yahoo.com) and found very similar characterizations of Filipina and Indonesian migrant domestics.

36 http://www.beelief.idv.tw, accessed on 15 July 2002.

37 http://www.885manpower.com.tw, accessed on 15 July 2002.

38 http://www.phr.com.tw, accessed on 13 October 2003.

39 http://www.kc104.com.tw/main-3c.htm, accessed on 13 October 2003.

40 As chapter 1 stipulated, the placement fee charged to an Indonesian migrant
is about NT$30,000–40,000 higher than the amount charged to a Filipina
worker.

41 According to a report of the Manpower and Education Bureau in the Hong
Kong government, the average monthly wage of Filipina domestic workers in
2001 was HK$3,847, while the average wage of Indonesian domestic workers
was $3,073, much lower than the amount of state regulation (HK$3,670) (Wee
and Sim 2005).

42 Filipino migrants had the highest absconding ratio in 1996 (3.6 percent) in
contrast to the rate of 2.6 percent among Indonesians. Yet the rate among
Indonesians rose to 2.9 percent in 2000 and 2.3 percent in 2001. Over the
same period, the rate fell among Filipinos to 1.2 percent in 2000 and 0.9
percent in 2001. Council of Labor Affairs, Executive Yuan, Republic of China,
http://www.evta.gov.tw/stat/9011, accessed on 20 November 2001.

43 The runaway rate of Vietnamese migrant workers was 7.8 percent in 2003 and 10.16 percent in 2004. Council of Labor Affairs, Executive Yuan, Republic of China, http://statdb.cla.gov.tw/html/htm/211050.htm, accessed on 1 March 2005.

44 Recently, some Taiwanese agencies have established similar training programs in the Philippines, but the duration of training (two to three weeks) is shorter than that in Indonesia.

45 All the interviews in this section were conducted in Mandarin Chinese and translated as quoted into English by the author.

46 My interview with staff at the migrant organization KOPBUMI (Defender Consortium of Indonesian Migrant Workers) in Jakarta, 21 August 2003.

47 In such cases the agency often assigns the trainees to local households or the agency owner's family (paid with meager wages) as some sort of internship.

48 Rhacel Parreñas (2001: 174–79) made a similar observation: Filipina domestic workers in Rome and Los Angeles claimed that they provided services of better quality than their African and Latina counterparts.

3. JEALOUS MADAMS & ANXIOUS MOTHERS

1 The daycare of one child by Taiwanese caregivers costs about NT$15,000 to NT$20,000 per month. A live-in Taiwanese caregiver is about twice as expensive and still hard to find.

2 Anthropologists have pointed out the structural constraints women face in a patrilineal extended household as an explanation for the tension between mothers-in-law and daughters-in-law. Because sons are the most critical resource for a woman to validate her family status and ensure her future welfare, a mother has a vested interest in suppressing romantic love between her son and her daughter-in-law as a means to ensure the son's loyalty (Kandiyoti 1991; Wolf 1972).

3 Cameron Macdonald (1998: 31) borrows the term "shadow work" from Ivan Illich (1981), who refers to the invisible reproductive labor that is unpaid, devalued, and feminized but essential in the maintenance of family life and capitalist production.

4 *China Times*, 10 October 1998.

5 Ada Cheng (2003: 178) addresses this point, but it should be added that sexualized images in media representation are also applied to Indonesian women, as I have demonstrated in chapter 2.

6 *China Times*, 2 June 1999.

7 This Chinese term, in opposition to *xiau-nu-ren* (little women), refers to masculine domination in the patriarchal gender order.

8 Breastfeeding, for example, was a job for a house servant who wet nursed her master's children in the past. The physical labor of a black mammy was dis-

engaged from motherhood's spiritual attributes that created a sacred bond between a white mother and her children (Roberts 1997: 56). Yet breastfeeding is now considered emotionally significant in the building of the mother-child bond; mothers who hire caregivers view this practice as a marker designating their motherly status (Macdonald 1998: 47).

9 The total fertility rate in Taiwan has greatly declined from 5.5 in 1962 to 1.2 in 2004. Department of Population, Ministry of the Interior, Executive Yuan, Republic of China, http://www.ris.gov.tw/ch4/statistics/st20-8.xls, accessed on 19 July 2005.

10 Gallin found class variations among Taiwanese mothers-in-law. The mother-in-law in a wealthy family can still enjoy the power to distribute wealth and hence maintain the traditional family authority. In contrast, poorer mothers-in-law depend on their sons to provide economic and social support for them when they become frail. In another study (Lan 2002a), I look at the eldercare practice among Taiwanese immigrant families in California. The social punishment of violating the filial norm in the context of immigration has further decreased, partly because most household income is provided by adult children who settled first in the new country.

11 However, under some circumstances, migrant workers may develop a relationship of alliance instead of one of antagonism with their care recipients. Elsewhere, I have discussed the employment of migrant caregivers among rural elder women in Taiwan. Migrant workers become fictive kin of Taiwanese elder clients who are left behind by their children (Lan 2002b).

4. CROSSING BORDERS & GENDER DIVIDES

1 National Statistics Office, the Philippines, http://www.census.gov.ph/index.html, accessed on 23 July 2004.

2 National Labour Force Survey, Badan Pusat Statistik (BPS-Statistics Indonesia), http://www.bps.go.id//sector/employ/table1.shtml, accessed on 27 July 2004.

3 Over 60 percent of overseas Filipino workers in 2001 were from four relatively developed regions (out of sixteen regions in the whole country). They are National Capital Region (Metropolitan Manila) (19 percent), Southern Tagalog (18 percent), Central Luzon (13 percent), and Ilocos (10 percent). Survey of Overseas Filipino Workers, National Statistics Office, the Philippines, http://www.census.gov.ph/data/sectordata/2002/of0101.htm, accessed on 23 July 2004.

4 The Philippines housed some of the United States' largest overseas military bases from the Spanish-American War until the late 1990s. These bases served as recruiting stations for the U.S. army forces during and after coloni-

zation. After the Philippines gained independence in 1946, U.S. officials inserted a provision in the 1947 Military Bases Agreement granting its navy the right to continue to recruit Filipino citizens (Espiritu 1995: 14–15).

5 In my own experience of traveling in Indonesia, strangers yelled at me with the name of the female actress who costarred with F4; they touched my skin without invitation, commenting, "How fair your skin is!"

6 For discussions of how migrant husbands negotiate their masculine identities, see Gamburd (2000) and Pingol (2001).

7 The Philippine family law before 1988 had a double sexual standard in defining criminal adultery differently for men and women. According to the old law, a married woman can be convicted of adultery for a single act of intercourse. But a married man can have sexual intercourse with a single woman without being guilty of a crime, as long as the single women participated in the sexual act voluntarily and privately. The man is only guilty of the crime of concubinage when he openly cohabits with his mistress (Go 1993: 57–58).

8 This is also found among Filipina migrants in Hong Kong (Chang and Groves 2000: 83) and in Rome (Parreñas 2001: 66).

9 According to Gavin W. Jones (2002), before the 1970s, divorce rates in Indonesia were very high, but they have fallen sharply over the past three decades (2.8 percent in 1995). This decline began with the 1974 Marriage Law, which tightened the procedures required to obtain a divorce.

10 The median age of the first marriage among Indonesian women was 18.6 in 1997, in comparison to 23.3 in the Philippines in 1998. Demographic and Health Survey, http://www.measuredhs.com, accessed on 1 September 2004.

11 According to a survey conducted in the Philippines, 60 percent of married migrant women entrusted their parents with the care of children, 28 percent reported leaving the children with their husbands, 5 percent asked their husbands' parents or family members, and 7 percent hired caretakers outside the family (Paz Cruz and Paganoni 1989).

12 In contrast, quite a number of migrant fathers I met in Taiwan could not recall the exact ages of their children when I asked. They tend to rationalize their losing track of children without much embarrassment; for example, one said: "I haven't been there for years . . . I don't want to go back, [there is] more money and freedom abroad."

13 Domestic service is one of the largest categories of waged work for women in the Philippines (Eviota 1992). Better-off households often hire several domestic workers assigned specialized jobs, including "yayas" (nannies), "helpers" (household workers), and live-out cooks and laundrywomen. The average wage of a live-in helper or nanny in major cities is about Php 1,500 to Php 2,000 per month. The wage rate is even lower in the provinces.

14 This echoes Diana Wolf's study (1992) of female factory workers in Jakarta in the 1980s. Most single daughters sent home only a small remittance and the pressure from parents was not as strong as that experienced by factory daughters in Taiwan or Hong Kong. Rebecca Elmhurst (2002) studied Indonesian factory women in 1994 and 1998 and found a gradual change in their remittance behavior. In 1994 it was rare for parents to make demands on money earned by their daughters from factory work. In 1998, the financial contribution of daughters became increasingly recognized by parents; remittance was mostly used to purchase goods for the daughter's future household and such investment has the effect of raising her value in the marriage market.

15 Twenty-one percent of the women who married Taiwanese men in 2004 were not citizens of Taiwan (ROC). Among them, 38 percent were from China and 61 percent from Southeast Asia. By the end of 2004, there were 94,744 foreign spouses residing in Taiwan, 89 percent of whom were women, mostly from Vietnam (70 percent), Indonesia (12 percent), and Thailand (6 percent). Department of Household Registration Affairs and National Police Agency, Ministry of the Interior, Executive Yuan, Republic of China, http://www.moi.gov.tw/W3/stat/index.asp, accessed on 19 July 2005.

16 When a woman responds to an agency's advertisement published in an English newspaper, her photographs and personal data are later posted on the agency's website free of charge (or for a minimal membership fee). When a male client browses this information on the Internet, he may pay a charge to the agency and request addresses and phone numbers for the women in whom he is interested.

17 During the period when the CLA suspended Indonesian migrant workers, some used forged marriages as a means to enter Taiwan for domestic service. A larger number of Chinese women come to Taiwan to work through the channel of marriage migration. Similar cases are also prevalent in the United States. For example, Eldon Doty, a retired white police officer, and his Filipina wife, Sally, processed a fraudulent divorce and brought Helen Bolusan from the Philippines on a fiancée visa in August 1990. Helen worked as an indentured servant for only US$160 a month until she ran away in February 1993. *Seattle Times*, 1 and 17 August 1999.

5. CINDERELLA WITH A MOBILE PHONE

1 This echoes what David Katzman (1978: 149) says about domestic employment: it is "[the] worker, and not the work itself, [that is] under constant scrutiny." See Hondagneu-Sotelo (2001: chap. 6) for a thorough discussion of how employers deploy multiple strategies to obtain desired work behaviors from domestic workers.

2 See Lan (2005) for a brief introduction to migrant-oriented NGOs in Taiwan.

3 One such incident happened in a city in southern Taiwan on 13 October 1997. A Filipina domestic worker, along with her boyfriend, also a migrant worker, broke into the residence of her former employer, stole some cash, and killed three family members.

4 Wearing uniforms was common for maidservants in the contexts of colonialism and slavery. Some employers in Hong Kong also require their maids to wear uniforms (Constable 1997a: 95).

5 Nicole Constable (1997b) has provided an insightful discussion on the dress of Filipina maids on days off, including a T-bird (tomboyish) style associated with homosexuality.

6 In a 1975 survey, only 27 percent of Singaporeans over the age of forty claimed to understand English, whereas the proportion rose to more than 87 percent among people between fifteen and twenty years old (Crystal 1997: 51).

7 During my fieldwork in 1998–99, very few migrant workers owned a mobile phone. They used Internet phone cards on pay phones or employers' landlines. But during my fieldwork in 2002–2003, the majority of migrant workers had obtained cell phones.

8 *United Daily News*, 20 June 2002. Yet the proportion may be skewed, given the fact that many Taiwanese own more than one cell phone.

9 Some companies allow foreigners to subscribe after paying a deposit (NT$2400–2900) if no Taiwanese guarantor is provided.

10 The police arrested two Taiwanese men who seized more than 2,000 "foreign laborers' cards" and over 200 international phone cards. The men belonged to a crime ring that often approaches migrant workers in their eateries or shops, claiming that they would help the workers remit money home or apply for cell phones. *Taipei Times*, 2 December 2005.

11 *United Daily News*, 17 February 2005.

12 Now all applications for cell phone numbers, including prepaid card numbers, must be submitted in person at the branches of mobile phone companies. The maximum number of prepaid card applications submitted by foreigners is two, and ten for Taiwanese citizens. *United Daily News*, 19 February 2005.

13 Here I borrow insights from Richard Ling and Brigitte Yttri (2002: 165), who studied the use of mobile phones among teenagers in Norway. The mobile phone produces communication networks among teenagers without monitoring by parents and other authority figures. SMS, in particular, enables them to operate on the front stage (e.g., listening to the teacher in class) while conducting backstage communication (sending text under the desk or in one's pocket).

14 For example, in January 2001, Philippines TV reported that then-president Joseph Estrada was found not guilty of bribery and corruption. Because of

information circulated through text messages, within two hours, 200,000 people converged on the streets of Manila, demanding that the president resign. http://www.seeingisbelieving.ca/cell/manila, accessed on 23 July 2004.

15 These numbers were estimated by Nokia in 2002 (Pertierra et al. 2002).

16 There are two burgeoning migrant organizations with the goals of protecting migrant rights and raising consciousness: KaSaPi (Kapulungan ng Samahang Pilipino; Organization of Filipinos) and TIMWA (Taiwan Indonesian Migrant Workers' Association). There are other informal associations based on provisional networks and religious communities.

17 On 20 January 2005, 112 Filipina migrant workers were put up for rehire after the IC company they previously worked for went bankrupt. At the employment center run by the CLA, the workers were chosen by their new employers through a lottery and many were assigned to factories involving heavy machinery and intensive manual labor (*Taipei Times*, 27 January, 2005). The information related to mobile phones was provided by the press release of the Taiwan International Workers' Association.

18 Excerpts from a study by Emmanuel Lallana, "SMS, Business, and Government in the Philippines," http://www.ecademy.com/node.php?id=26936, accessed on 23 July 2004.

19 Siemens Wireless Phone Offensive, http://www.3g.co.uk/PR/May2004/7096.htm, accessed on 23 July 2004.

20 Hans Geser (2004: 16) has argued that the freedom gained from being able to connect to anybody from anywhere comes with the increasing pressure that one has to answer all incoming calls. And the convenience of communication can accentuate the asymmetries of social power: a boss can call employees for work reasons during rest time and parents can exercise more control over the whereabouts of teenage children.

21 Wang Chih-hung (2004: 27) further argues that marriage migrants could cultivate and reinforce the boundaries of ethnic identity by claiming the authenticity of their cooking in contrast to the culinary styles, which have been modified to suit local tastes, in Vietnamese, Indonesian, and Thai restaurants that target Taiwanese customers.

22 Wu Mei-yao (2004) conducted a survey with 209 respondents randomly selected from migrant workers at the train station. The average time they spent in the building every Sunday was 5.8 hours.

23 Chungli attracts more Filipino factory workers to gather on Sundays because of its proximity to a Catholic church and the associated NGO, Hope Workers' Center, while Taoyuan becomes a gathering place for Thai and Indonesian migrants.

24 *Taiwan News*, 11 June 2000.

25 Jeepneys are medium-sized trucks (with seats and cloth covers) owned by private individuals that pick up passengers on regular routes.

26 See Barber (2000) and Paz Cruz and Paganoni (1989) for similar observations.

27 In 2002 this regulation was eased to allow migrants with good records to return to Taiwan for another three-year contract.

28 Hong Kong is a popular sojourn for migration to Canada (Barber 2000: 404).

29 According to the report of Human Rights Watch (2004), the monthly wage of a migrant domestic worker in Saudi Arabia is 600–750 riyals (us$160–200), but unpaid salary is common. Many employers fail to provide their domestic workers with official residency permits, putting them in forced confinement and extreme isolation.

30 Based on my interviews with recruitment agencies in 2003, the wage of a migrant domestic worker in Singapore was S$230–300 (us$153–200) at the start of a new contract. The recruitment fee was about S$1,600. In Malaysia, the monthly wage was RM 380 (us$150) for an Indonesian maid and RM 500 (us$196) for a Filipina maid. The recruitment fee was about RM 1,200.

31 The minimum wage for foreign domestic workers in 2005 was HK$3,860 (us$496), close to the minimum wage in Taiwan (NT$15,840; us$495).

32 In Canada, provincial governments regulate employment relations through the Live-in Caregiver Program. In British Columbia, after 1995, foreign caregivers are covered by overtime regulations and should be paid a minimum hourly wage (scaled to family size) and "time-and-a-half" for work beyond 40 hours a week. The average monthly taxable wage for a live-in caregiver was about $900 in 2004, but employers are able to deduct $325 a month in compensation for room and board (McKay 2005).

33 Domestic workers in Canada can apply to be considered for landed immigrant status following a two-year period on a temporary work authorization. During this time the domestic worker is confined to live-in work with the employer named on the authorization. The government also dictates strict requirements for the entry. These regulations have been criticized as discriminating against Third World women immigrants (England and Stiell 1997: 200–202).

6. EAT, DRINK, MASTERS & SERVANTS

1 Hondagneu-Sotelo (2001: 193) also argues that the extent to which care work is involved has a substantial impact on the preference of domestic workers in Los Angeles toward personalistic employment relations.

2 MECO is the de facto Philippine embassy in Taiwan, because there is no formal diplomatic tie between the two countries.

3 The deduction ranges between NT$3,000 and 5,000, equivalent to one-fifth

to one-third of a worker's monthly wage, NT$15,840. The money will not be returned to the worker until she completes the contract and leaves Taiwan.

4 Seemin Qayum and Raka Ray (2003) also discuss the significance of residential space in their study of the reconfiguration of domestic servitude in contemporary Calcutta. An Indian employer commented on the problem of having a live-in servant in a small apartment: "You don't have physical space, so you have to create your distance. They are physically always there; you cannot move them out of sight" (2003: 531).

5 The characteristics of "segmenting" and "integrating" are borrowed from Christena Nippert-Eng (1996), who discusses how office workers negotiate the boundary between home and work.

6 Eating arrangements also vary by spatial settings. Some workers are invited to eat with the family at a regular time, but they must eat separately when there are guests. One employer comments, "In front of outsiders, the distinction has to be clear. It's a matter of discipline." By contrast, some families ask the domestic workers to eat separately at home but invite them to sit together when eating out. Another employer explains: "We want people to see that we respect her. She needs dignity in front of others." These cases show distinct ways in which the employers manage the situational definition of "family" across the front and backstage settings.

CONCLUSION

1 Migrants make up some 29 percent of the work force in Singapore; Malaysia has about 16 percent; in the Gulf countries, migrant workers outnumber national workers (Asis 2004: 4).

2 Yasemin Soysal (1994) argues that a model of "postnational membership" has emerged among migrant workers in Europe thanks to the intervention of international political-legal organizations and the emergence of a global discourse on human rights.

3 In Asia, only the Philippines and Sri Lanka ratified the United Nations Convention on the Rights of All Migrant Workers and Members of their Families.

REFERENCES

Abdul Rahman, Noorashikin. 2003. "Negotiating Power: A Case Study of Indonesian Foreign Domestic Workers (FDWs) in Singapore." Ph.D. diss., Curtin University of Technology, Perth, Australia.

Abella, Manolo. 1992. "Contemporary Labour Migration from Asia: Policies and Perspectives of Sending Countries." In *International Migration Systems: A Global Approach*, ed. Mary Kritz, Lin Lean Lim, and Hania Zilotnik, 263–78. Oxford: Clarendon Press.

———. 1993. "Labor Mobility, Trade and Structural Change: The Philippine Experience." *Asian and Pacific Migration Journal* 2(3): 167–249.

Accountancy. 2003. "Technology: Mobile Phones—Pump up the Volume." *Accountancy* 131(1316): 70.

Aguilar, Jr. Filomeno V. 1999. "Ritual Passage and the Reconstruction of Selfhood in International Labour Migration." *SOJOURN: Journal of Social Issues in Southeast Asia* 14(1): 98–128.

Alegado, Dean Tiburico. 1992. "The Political Economy of International Labor Migration from the Philippines." Ph.D. Diss., Hawaii University, Manoa.

Ananta, Aris. 2000. "Economic Integration and Free Labour Area: An Indonesia Perspective." In *Labour Migration in Indonesia: Policies and Practices*, ed. Sukamdi, Abdul Haris, and Patrick Brownlee. Yogyakarta: Population Studies Center Gadjah Mada University. Available at http://www.unesco.org/most/apmrlabo.htm, accessed on 1 March 2005.

Anderson, Bridget. 2000. *Doing the Dirty Work? The Global Politics of Domestic Labour.* London: Zed Books.

Anthias, Floya, and Nira Yuval-Davis. 1992. *Racialized Boundaries: Race, Nation, Gender, Colour and Class and the Anti-Racist Struggles.* London: Routledge.

Appadurai, Arjun. 1996. *Modernity at Large: Cultural Dimensions of Globalization.* Minneapolis: University of Minnesota Press.

Arcinas, Fe R., Cynthia Banzon-Bautista, and Randolf S. David. 1986. *The Odyssey of the Filipino Migrant Workers to the Gulf Region.* Quezon City: University of the Philippines.

Asis, Maruja. 1992. "The Overseas Employment Program Policy." In *Philippine Labor Migration: Impact and Policy*, ed. Graziano Battistella and Anthony Paganoni, 68–112. Quezon City: Scalabrinia Migration Center.

———. 2004. "When Men and Women Migrate: Comparing Gendered Migration in Asia." Paper presented to United Nations Division for the Advancement of

Women (DAW) Consultative Meeting on "Migration and Mobility and How this Movement Affects Women," Malmo, Sweden, 2–4 December 2003. Available at http://www.un.org/womenwatch/daw/meetings/consult/CM-Deco3-EPI.pdf, accessed on 6 February 2005.

Athukorala, Premachandra. 1993. "Improving the Contribution of Migrant Remittances to Development: The Experience of Asian Labor-Exporting Countries." *Migration Review* 24: 323–46.

Bakan, Abigail, and Daiva Stasiulis. 1995. "Making the Match: Domestic Placement Agencies and the Racialization of Women's Household Work." *Signs* 20(2): 303–35.

Balibar, Étienne. 1991. "Is There a Neo-Racism?" In *Race, Nation, Class: Ambiguous Identities*, ed. Etienne Balibar and Immanuel Wallerstein, 17–28. London: Verso.

Barber, Pauline Gardiner. 2000. "Agency in Philippine Women's Labour Migration and Provisional Diaspora." *Women's Studies International Forum* 23(4): 399–411.

Basch, Linda, Nina G. Schiller, and Cristina S. Blanc. 1994. *Nations Unbound: Transnational Projects, Postcolonial Predictions, and Deterritorialized Nation-States*. Langhorne, Pa.: Gordon and Breach Science.

Battistella, Graziano. 1999. "Philippine Migration Policy: Dilemmas of a Crisis." *SOJOURN: Journal of Social Issues in Southeast Asia* 14(1): 229–48.

——. 2002. "International Migration in Asia vis-à-vis Europe: An Introduction." *Asian and Pacific Migration Journal* 11(4): 405–14.

Bourdieu, Pierre. 1977. *Outline of a Theory of Practice*. Cambridge: Cambridge University Press.

——. 1984. *Distinction: A Social Critique of the Judgement of Taste*. Cambridge, Mass.: Harvard University Press.

——. 1987. "What Makes a Social Class? On the Theoretical and Practical Existence of Groups." *Berkeley Journal of Sociology* 32: 1–18.

——. 1991. *Language and Symbolic Power*. Cambridge, Mass.: Harvard University Press.

Brah, Avtar. 1996. *Cartographies of Diaspora: Contesting Identities*. London: Routledge.

Bresnahan, Mary. 1979. "English in the Philippines." *Journal of Communication* 29(2): 64–71.

Brown, Melissa J. 2004. *Is Taiwan Chinese? The Impact of Culture, Power, and Migration on Changing Identities*. Berkeley: University of California Press.

Brubaker, Rogers W. 1989. "Membership without Citizenship: The Economic and Social Rights of Noncitizens. In *Immigration and Politics of Citizenship in Europe and North America*, ed. Rogers W. Brubaker, 145–62. Lanham, Md.: University Press of America.

——. 1992. *Citizenship and Nationhood in France and Germany.* Cambridge, Mass.: Harvard University Press.

Brubaker, Rogers, and Frederick Cooper. 2000. "Beyond Identity." *Theory and Society* 29: 1–47.

Burawoy, Michael. 1976. "The Functions and Reproduction of Migrant Labor: Comparative Material from Southern Africa and the United States." *American Journal of Sociology* 81(5): 1050–87.

Bureau of Official Statistics. 1924. *The First Taiwan Provincial Household Census (1920).* Government-general of Taiwan.

——. 1934. *The 1930 Taiwan Provincial Household Census.* Government-general of Taiwan.

Castles, Stephen, and Mark Miller. 1993. *The Age of Migration: International Population Movements in the Modern World.* New York: Guilford Press.

Castles, Stephen, and Alastair Davidson. 2000. *Citizenship and Migration: Globalization and the Politics of Belonging.* London: Routledge.

Chang, Kimberley A., and Julian McAllister Groves. 2000. "Neither 'Saints' nor 'Prostitutes': Sexual Discourse in the Filipina Domestic Worker Community in Hong-Kong." *Women's Studies International Forum* 23(1): 73–87.

Chang, Mau-Kuei. 2000. "On the Origins and Transformation of Taiwanese National Identity." *China Perspective* 28: 51–70.

Chang Yi-Fun. 1998. "Women and the State: Rethinking the History of the Women's Movement in Taiwan" (Chinese). M.A. thesis, Cheng Chi University, Taipei.

Chant, Sylvia, and Cathy McIlwaine. 1995. *Women of a Lesser Cost: Female Labour, Foreign Exchange, and Philippine Development.* Manila: Ateneo de Manila University Press.

Chao Sho-Buo. 1992. "On the Problem of Foreign Labor" (Chinese). In *Labor Policies and Labor Issues,* ed. Sho-Buo Chao, 143–72. Taipei: Chinese Productive Center.

Chaplin, David. 1978. "Domestic Service and Industrialization." *Comparative Studies in Sociology* 1: 97–127.

Cheng, Lucie. 2003. "Transnational Labor, Citizenship and the Taiwan state." In *East Asian Law: Universal Norms and Local Cultures,* ed. Arthur Rosett, Lucie Cheng, and Margaret Y. K. Woo, 85–106. London: Routledge.

Cheng, Shu-Ju Ada. 1996. "Migrant Women Domestic Workers in Hong Kong, Singapore and Taiwan: A Comparative Analysis." *Asian and Pacific Migration Journal* 5(1): 139–52.

——. 2001. "Serving the Household and the Nation: Filipina Domestics and the Development of Nationhood in Taiwan." Ph.D. diss., University of Texas, Austin.

——. 2003. "Rethinking the Globalization of Domestic Service: Foreign

Domestics, State Control, and the Politics of Identity in Taiwan." *Gender &* *Society* 17(2): 166–86.

Chin, Christine. 1998. *Service and Servitude: Foreign Female Domestic Workers and Malaysian "Modernity Project."* New York: Columbia University Press.

Ching, Leo. 2000. "Savage Construction and Civility Making: The Musha Incident and Aboriginal Representations in Colonial Taiwan." *positions: east asia cultures critique* 8(3): 795–818.

Chiu, Stephen W. K. 2004. "Recent Trends in Migration Movements and Policies in Asia: Hong Kong Region Report." Paper presented at panel, Japan Institute of Labour and OECD, Workshop on International Migration and Labour Markets in Asia. Tokyo, Japan.

Choy, Catherine Ceniza. 2003. *Empire of Care: Nursing and Migration in Filipino American History.* Durham, N.C.: Duke University Press.

Chuo I-Wen. 1993. *Women's Lives in the Ching Dynasty* (Chinese). Taipei: Independence Times Press.

Chu, Jou-Jo. 1996. "Taiwan: A Fragmented 'Middle' Class in the Making." In *The New Rich in Asia: Mobile Phones, McDonalds, and Middle-Class Revolution,* ed. Richard Robinson and David S. G. Goodman, 207–22. London: Routledge.

CLA (Council of Labor Affairs). 1999. *The 1998 Investigation Report on the Management and Employment of Foreign Workers in R.O.C.* Taipei: Executive Yuan, Republic of China.

———. 2004. *The 2003 Investigation Report on the Management and Employment of Foreign Workers in R.O.C.* Taipei: Executive Yuan, Republic of China.

Clifford, James, and George E. Marcus. 1986. *Writing Culture: The Poetics and Politics of Ethnography.* Berkeley: University of California Press.

Cohen, Rina. 1987. "The Working Conditions of Immigrant Women, Live-in Domestics: Racism, Sexual Abuse and Invisibility." *Resources for Feminist Research* 16(1): 36–38.

———. 1991. "Women of Color in White Households: Coping Strategies of Live-In Domestic Workers." *Qualitative Sociology* 14: 197–215.

Colen, Shellee. 1986. "With Respect and Feelings: Voices of West Indian Child Care and Domestic Workers in New York City." In *All American Women: Lines that Divide, Ties that Bind,* ed. Johnnetta B. Cole, 46–70. New York: Free Press.

———. 1995. " 'Like a Mother to Them': Stratified Reproduction and West Indian Childcare Workers and Employers in New York." In *Conceiving the New World Order: The Global Politics of Reproduction,* ed. Faye Ginsburg and Rayna Rapp, 78–102. Berkeley: University of California Press.

Collins, Patricia Hill. 1990. *Black Feminist Thought: Knowledge, Consciousness and the Politics of Empowerment.* London: Routledge.

Constable, Nicole. 1997a. *Maid to Order in Hong Kong: Stories of Filipina Workers.* Ithaca, N.Y.: Cornell University Press.

——. 1997b. "Sexuality and Discipline among Filipina Domestic Workers in Hong Kong." *American Ethnologist* 24(3): 539–58.

——. 1999. "At Home but not at Home: Filipina Narratives of Ambivalent Returns." *Cultural Anthropology* 14(2): 203–28.

——. 2003a. *Romance on a Global Stage: Pen Pals, Virtual Ethnography, and "Mail Order" Marriages.* Berkeley: University of California Press.

——. 2003b. "A Transnational Perspective on Divorce and Marriage: Filipina Wives and Workers." *Identities: Global Studies in Culture and Power* 10: 163–80.

Cooke, Fadzilah M. 1986. "Australian-Filipino Marriages in the 1980s: The Myth and the Reality." Working paper in the School of Modern Asian Studies Centre for the Study of Australian-Asian Relations, Griffith University.

Coser, Lewis. 1974. "Servants: The Obsolescence of the Occupational Role." *Social Force* 52: 31–40.

Crystal, David. 1997. *English as a Global Language.* Cambridge: Cambridge University Press.

Delphy, Christine, and Diana Leonard. 1992. *Familiar Exploitation: A New Analysis of Marriage in Contemporary Western Societies.* Cambridge: Polity Press.

DeVault, Marjorie. 1991. *Feeding the Family: The Social Organization of Caring as Gendered Work.* Chicago: University of Chicago Press.

DGBAS (Directorate-General Budget, Accounting and Statistics). 2002. *Report on the 2000 Population and Housing Survey in Taiwan-Fukien Area, Republic of China.* Taipei: Executive Yuan, Republic of China.

Dikötter, Frank. 1992. *The Discourse of Race in Modern China.* Stanford, Calif.: Stanford University Press.

Dill, Bonnie Thornton. 1988. "Making Your Job Good Yourself: Domestic Service and the Construction of Personal Dignity." In *Women and the Politics of Empowerment,* ed. Ann Bookman and Sandra Morgan, 33–52. Philadelphia: Temple University Press.

Douglas, Mary. 1966. *Purity and Danger: An Analysis of Concepts of Pollution and Purity.* London: Routledge.

Durkheim, Emile, and Marcel Mauss. 1963. *Primitive Classification,* Chicago: University of Chicago Press.

Elmhirst, Rebecca. 2002. "Daughters and Displacement: Migration Dynamics in an Indonesian Transmigration Area." *The Journal of Development Studies* 38(5): 143–66.

Emerson, Robert M., Rachel I. Fretz, and Linda L. Shaw. 1995. *Writing Ethnographic Fieldnotes.* Chicago: University of Chicago Press.

Engels, Friedrich. 1943/1972. *The Origin of the Family, Private Property and the State.* New York: International Publishers.

England, Kim, and Bernadette Stiell. 1997. "They Think You're as Stupid as Your

English Is: Constructing Foreign Domestic Workers in Toronto." *Environment and Planning A* 29: 195–215.

England, Paula, and Nancy Folbre. 1999. "The Cost of Caring." *Annals of the American Academy of Political and Social Science* 561: 39–51.

Enloe, Cynthia. 1989. *Bananas, Beaches, and Bases.* Berkeley: University of California Press.

Espiritu, Yen Le. 1995. "Filipino Settlement in the United States." In *Filipino American Lives*, ed. Yen Le Espiritu, 1–36. Philadelphia: Temple University Press.

——. 2002. "Filipino Navy Stewards and Filipina Health Care Professionals: Immigration, Work and Family Relations." *Asian and Pacific Migration Journal* 11(1): 47–66.

Eviota, Elizabeth U. 1992. *The Political Economy and Gender, Women and the Sexual Division of Labor in the Philippines.* London: Zed Books.

Feith, Herbert. 1980. "Repressive-Developmentalist Regimes in Asia: Old Strengths, New Vulnerabilities." *Prisma* 19(1): 39–55.

Findlay, Allan M., Huw Jones, and Gillian M. Davidson. 1998. "Migration Transition or Migration Transformation in the Asian Dragon Economies?" *International Journal of Urban and Regional Research* 22(4): 643–63.

Fortunati, Leopoldina. 2001. "The Mobile Phone: An Identity on the Move." *Personal and Ubiquitous Computing* 5: 85–98.

Foucault, Michel. 1977. *Discipline and Punish: The Birth of the Prison.* New York: Pantheon Books.

——. 1991. "Questions of Method." In *The Foucault Effect: Studies in Governmentality*, ed. Graham Burchell, Colin Gordon, and Peter Miller, 73–86. Chicago: University of Chicago Press.

Frobel, Folker, Jurgen Heinrichs, and Otto Kreye. 1980. *The New International Division of Labor.* Cambridge: Cambridge University Press.

Gallin, Rita. 1994. "The Intersection of Class and Age: Mother-in-Law / Daughter-in-Law Relations in Rural Taiwan." *Journal of Cross-Cultural Gerontology* 9: 127–40.

Gamburd, Michele Ruth. 2000. *The Kitchen Spoon's Handle.* Ithaca, N.Y.: Cornell University Press.

Garey, Anita. 1999. *Weaving Work and Motherhood.* Philadelphia: Temple University Press.

Gaw, Kenneth. 1991. *Superior Servants: The Legendary Cantonese Amahs of the Far East.* Singapore: Oxford University Press.

Geertz, Hildred, 1961. *The Javanese Family: A Study of Kinship and Socialization.* New York: Free Press.

George, Sheba. 2000. " 'Dirty Nurses' and 'Men Who Play': Gender and Class in

Transnational Migration." In *Global Ethnography*, ed. Michael Burawoy, 144–74. Berkeley: University of California Press.

Gerson, Judith, and Kathy Peiss. 1985. "Boundaries, Negotiation, Consciousness: Conceptualizing Gender Relations." *Social Problems* 32(4): 317–31.

Geser, Hans. 2004. *Towards a Sociological Theory of the Mobile Phone*. University of Zurich. Available at http://socio.ch/mobile/t_geser1.htm, accessed on 30 August 2004.

Glaeser, Andreas. 2000. *Divided in Unity: Identity, Germany, and the Berlin Police*. Chicago: University of Chicago Press.

Glenn, Evelyn Nakano. 1986. *Issei, Nisei, War Bride: Three Generations of Japanese American Women in Domestic Service*. Philadelphia: Temple University Press.

———. 1992. "From Servitude to Service Work: Historical Continuities in the Racial Division of Paid Reproductive Labor." *Signs* 18(1): 1–43.

———. 1994. "Social Construction of Mothering: A Thematic Overview." In *Mothering: Ideology, Experience, and Agency*, ed. Evelyn Glenn, Grace Chang, and Linda Rennie Forcey, 1–32. London: Routledge.

———. 2002. *Unequal Freedom: How Race and Gender Shaped American Citizenship and Labor*. Cambridge, Mass.: Harvard University Press.

Go, Stella. 1993. *The Filipino Family in the Eighties*. Manila: Social Development Research Center, De La Salle University.

Goffman, Erving. 1956. "The Nature of Deference and Demeanor." *American Anthropologist* 58(3): 472–502.

———. 1959. *The Presentation of Self in Everyday Life*. New York: Doubleday/Anchor Books.

———. 1963. *Stigma: Notes on the Management of Spoiled Identity*. New York: Simon and Schuster.

Gregson, Nicky, and Michelle Lowe. 1995. " 'Home'-Making: On the Spatiality of Daily Social Production in Contemporary Middle-Class Britain." *Transactions of the Institute of British Geographers* 20(2): 224–35.

Groves, Julian McAllister, and Kimberly A. Chang. 1999. "Romancing Resistance and Resisting Romance: Ethnography and the Construction of Power in the Filipina Domestic Worker Community in Hong Kong." *Journal of Contemporary Ethnography* 28(3): 235–65.

Hall, John. 1992. "The Capital(s) of Cultures: A Nonholistic Approach to Status, Situations, Class, Gender, and Ethnicity." In *Cultivating Differences: Symbolic Boundaries and the Making of Inequalities*, ed. Michele Lamont and Marcel Fournier, 257–88. Chicago: University of Chicago Press.

Hall, Stuart. 1997. "Old and New Identities: Old and New Ethnicities." In *Culture, Globalization and the World-System: Contemporary Conditions for the*

Representation of Culture, ed. Anthony King, 41–68. Minneapolis: University of Minnesota Press.

Hays, Sharon. 1996. *The Cultural Contradiction of Motherhood*. New Haven, Conn.: Yale University Press.

Hertz, Rosanna. 1986. *More Equal than Others: Women and Men in Dual-Career Marriage*. Berkeley: University of California Press.

Heyzer, Noeleen, Geerje Lycklama a Nijeholt, and Nedra Weerakoon, eds. 1994. *The Trade in Domestic Workers: Causes, Mechanisms and Consequences of International Migration*. Kuala Lumpur: Asian and Pacific Development Center.

Hochschild, Arlie. 1989. *The Second Shift: Working Parents and the Revolution at Home*. New York: Avon Books.

——. 2000. "The Nanny Chain." *The American Prospect* 11: 32–36.

Hollnsteiner, Mary R. 1981. "The Wife." In *Being Filipino*, ed. Gilda Cordero-Fernando, 37–42. Quezon City, Philippines: GCF Books.

Holstein, James A., and Jaber F. Gubrium. 1995. "Deprivatization and the Construction of Domestic Life." *Journal of Marriage and the Family* 57: 894–908.

Hondagneu-Sotelo, Pierrette. 1994. *Gendered Transitions: Mexican Experiences of Migration*. Berkeley: University of California Press.

——. 2001. *Doméstica: Immigrant Workers Cleaning and Caring in the Shadows of Affluence*. Berkeley: University of California Press.

Hondagneu-Sotelo, Pierrette, and Ernestine Avila. 1997. " 'I am Here, but I am There': The Meanings of Latina Transnational Motherhood." *Gender and Society* 11(5): 548–71.

Hsiao Hsin-Huang. 1989. "The Middle Classes in Taiwan: Origins, Formation and Significance" (Chinese). In *Taiwan: A Newly Industrialized State*, ed. Hsin-Huang Hsiao, Wei-Yuan Cheng, and Hou-Sheng Chan, 151–66. Taipei: National Taiwan University.

Hsieh Shih-Chung. 1986. *Stigmatized Identity: A Study on Ethnic Change of Taiwan Aborigines* (Chinese). Taipei: IDN Publisher.

Hsiung, Ping-Chun. 1996. *Living Rooms as Factories: Class, Gender, and the Satellite Factory System in Taiwan*. Philadelphia: Temple University Press.

Hsu Wei-Ching. 2004. "One Mobile Phone, Two Fixed Classes: Evidence from the Practices of Mobile Phone Use by Vietnamese Workers in Taiwan" (Chinese). M.A. thesis, National Chung Hsing University, Taichung, Taiwan.

Hu, Yow-Hwey. 1995. "Elderly Suicide Risks in the Family Context: A Critique of the Asian Family Care." *Journal of Cross-Cultural Gerontology* 10: 199–217.

Huang, Shirlena, Peggy Teo, and Brenda Yeoh. 2000. "Diasporic Subjects and Identity Negotiations: Women in and from Asia." *Women's Studies International Forum* 23(4): 391–98.

Huang, Shirlena, and Brenda Yeoh. 1996. "Ties that Bind: State Policy and Migrant Female Domestic Helpers in Singapore." *Geoforum* 27: 479–93.

———. 2003. "The Difference Gender Makes: State Policy and Contract Migrant Workers in Singapore." *Asian and Pacific Migration Journal* 12(1–2): 75–97.

Hugo, Graeme. 1995. "International Labor Migration and the Family: Some Observations from Indonesia." *Asian and Pacific Migration Journal* 4(2–3): 273–301.

———. 2000. *Indonesian Overseas Contract Workers' HIV Knowledge: A Gap in Information.* Bangkok: United Nations Development Programme, South East Asia HIV and Development Project. Available at http://www.hiv-development. org/publications/Contract%20Workers.htm, accessed on 23 February 2005.

———. 2002a. "Effects of International Migration on the Family in Indonesia." *Asian and Pacific Migration Journal* 11(1): 13–46.

———. 2002b. "Women's International Labour Migration." In *Women in Indonesia: Gender, Equity and Development,* ed. Kathryn Robinson and Sharon Bessell, 158–78. Singapore: Institute of Southeast Asian Studies.

Human Rights Watch. 2004. "Bad Dreams: Exploitation and Abuse of Migrant Workers in Saudi Arabia." Available at http://www.hrw.org/reprots/2004/saudi.0704, accessed on 1 August 2005.

Illich, Ivan. 1981. *Shadow Work.* Boston: M. Boyars.

Illo, Jean Frances. 1995. "Redefining the Maybahay or Housewife: Reflections on the Nature of Women's Work in the Philippines." In *"Male" and "Female" in Developing Southeast Asia,* ed. Wazir Jahan Karim, 209–25. Oxford: Berg.

Israel-Sobritchea, Cayolyn. 1990. "The Ideology of Female Domesticity: Its Impact on the Status of Filipino Women." *Review of Women's Studies* 1(1): 26–41.

Ito, Ruri. 2005. "Internationalizing Reproductive Labor in a Super Aged Society?: Japan's New Immigration Policy and Its Implication on Care Work." Presented at Women's World 2005, 19–23 June 2005, Seoul, Korea.

Jones, Galvin. W. 2002. "The Changing Indonesian Households." In *Women in Indonesia: Gender, Equity and Development,* ed. Kathryn Robinson and Sharon Bessell, 219–34. Singapore: Institute of Southeast Asian Studies.

Jones, Sidney. 2000. *Making Money off Migrants—The Indonesian Exodus to Malaysia.* Wollongong, Australia: Center for Asia Pacific Social Transformation Studies, University of Wollongong.

Kandiyoti, Deniz. 1991. "Bargaining with Patriarchy." In *The Social Construction of Gender,* ed. Judith Lorber and Susan A. Farrell, 104–18. London: Sage Publications.

Kaplan, Elaine. 1987. "I Don't Do No Windows: Competition between the

Domestic Workers and the Housewife." In *Competition: A Feminist Taboo?*, ed. Valerie Miner and Helen E. Longino, 92–105. New York: Feminist Press.

Katzman, David. 1978. *Seven Days a Week: Women and Domestic Service in Industrializing America*. New York: Oxford University Press.

Kibria, Nazli. 1993. *Family Tightrope: The Changing Lives of Vietnamese Americans*. Princeton, N.J.: Princeton University Press.

Kung, Lorna. 2002. "Migrant Workers in Taipei: Biased Central State Policy and Alternative Administration Strategy of Local State" (Chinese). *Taiwan: A Radical Quarterly in Social Studies* 48: 235–85.

Kung, Lydia. 1983. *Factory Women in Taiwan*. Ann Arbor: University of Michigan Press.

Lal, Jayati. 1996. "Situating Locations: The Politics of Self, Identity, and 'Other' in Living and Writing the Text." In *Feminist Dilemmas in Fieldwork*, ed. Diane Wolf, 185–214. Boulder, Colo.: Westview.

Lamont, Michèle. 1992. *Money, Morals and Manners: The Culture of the French and the American Upper-Middle Class*. Chicago: University of Chicago Press.

———. 2000a. *The Dignity of Working Men: Morality and the Boundaries of Race, Class, and Immigration*. Cambridge, Mass.: Harvard University Press.

———. 2000b. "The Rhetorics of Racism and Anti-Racism in France and the United States." In *Rethinking Comparative Cultural Sociology: Repertoires of Evaluation in France and the United States*, ed. Michèle Lamont and Lauront Thevenot, 25–55. Cambridge: Cambridge University Press.

Lamont, Michèle, and Annette Lareaur. 1988. "Cultural Capital: Allusions, Gaps, and Glissandos in Recent Theoretical Developments." *Sociological Theory* 6: 153–68.

Lamont, Michèle, and Marcel Fournier. 1992. Introduction to *Cultivating Differences: Symbolic Boundaries and the Making of Inequalities*, ed. Michele Lamont and Marcel Fournier, 1–20. Chicago: University of Chicago Press.

Lan, Pei-Chia. 2002a. "Subcontracting Filial Piety: Elder Care in Ethnic Chinese Immigrant Households in California." *Journal of Family Issues* 23(7): 812–35.

———. 2002b. "Among Women: Migrant Domestics and their Taiwanese Employers across Generations." In *Global Woman: Maids, Nannies and Sex Workers*, ed. Barbara Ehrenreich and Arlie Hochschild, 169–89. New York: Metropolitan Press.

———. 2003. " 'They Have More Money but I Speak Better English!' Transnational Encounters between Filipina Domestics and Taiwanese Employers." *Identities: Global Studies in Culture and Power* 10: 133–61.

———. 2005. "Surrogate Family, Disposable Labor and Stratified Others: Migrant Domestic Workers in Taiwan." In *Asian Women as Transnational Domestic*

Workers, ed. Noorashikin Abdul Rahman, Brenda Yeoh, and Shirlena Huang, 210–32. Singapore: Marshall Cavendish.

——. Forthcoming. "Legal Servitude, Free Illegality: Migrant 'Guest' Workers in Taiwan," in *Asian Diasporas: New Formations, New Conceptions*, ed. Rhacel Parreñas and Lok Siu. Stanford, Calif.: Stanford University Press.

Lasch, Christopher. 1977. *Haven in a Heartless World*. New York: Basic Books.

Lasen, Amparo. 2002. *The Social Shaping of Fixed and Mobile Networks: A Historical Comparison*, DWRC, University of Surrey. Available at: http://www.surrey.ac.uk/dwrc/, accessed on 30 August 2004.

Law, Lisa. 2001. "Home Cooking: Filipino Women and Geographies of the Senses in Hong Kong." *Ecumene* 8(3): 264–83.

Lee, Anru. 2002. "Guests from the Tropics: Labor Practice and Foreign Workers in Taiwan." In *Transforming Gender and Development in East Asia*, ed. Esther Ngan-ling Chow, 183–202. New York: Routledge.

Lee, Ching Kwan. 1998. *Gender and the South China Miracle*. Berkeley: University of California Press.

Lee, Hey-Kyung. 2005. "Changing Trends in Paid Domestic Work in South Korea." In *Asian Women as Transnational Domestic Workers*, ed. Noorashikin Abdul Rahman, Brenda Yeoh, and Shirlena Huang, 341–63. Singapore: Marshall Cavendish.

Lee Jun-Hsien, Chiang Ho-Chieh, and Shu Mu-Lan. 1999. "The Analysis of the Investment of Taiwanese Capital in the Philippines, Malaysia, Indonesia and Thailand" (Chinese). Presented at the annual conference of Southeast Asian Studies, Academic Sinica, Taipei.

Lee, Powpee. 1995. "Why Don't They Take Actions? A Study on Different Acting Strategies of Foreign Workers" (Chinese). M.A. thesis, Fu-Jen Catholic University, Hsin Chuan, Taiwan.

Lee Yu-Ying. 1999. "'Dreams Come True'—Wedding Photography in Contemporary Taiwan" (Chinese). *Taiwan: A Radical Quarterly in Social Studies* 36: 147–86.

Lie, John. 2001. *Multiethnic Japan*. Cambridge, Mass.: Harvard University Press.

Lin Hsiu-Li. 2000. "Going to Taiwan to Wash Benz: The Daily Practices of Filipina Female Household Workers in Thai Chung" (Chinese). M.A. thesis, Ton-Hai University, Tai Chung, Taiwan.

Lin, Jean Chin-Ju. 1999. *Filipina Domestic Workers in Taiwan: Structural Constraints and Personal Resistance*. Taipei: Taiwan Grassroots Women Workers' Centre.

——. 2000. "The State Policy that Divides Women: Rethinking Feminist Critiques to 'The Foreign Maid Policy' in Taiwan" (Chinese). *Taiwan: A Radical Quarterly in Social Studies* 39: 93–152.

Ling, Richard, and Brigitte Yttri. 2002. "Hyper-Coordination via Mobile Phones in Norway." In *Perpetual Contact: Mobile Communication, Private, Public Performance*, ed. James E. Katz and Mark A. Aakhus, 139–69. Cambridge: Cambridge University Press.

Liu Mei-Chun. 2000. "A Critique from Marxist Political Economy on the 'Cheap Foreign Labor' Discourse" (Chinese). *Taiwan: A Radical Quarterly in Social Studies* 38: 59–90.

Liu Zhong-Dong. 1998. *Women's Medical Sociology* (Chinese). Taipei: Feminist Bookstore.

Lorber, Judith. 1994. *Paradoxes of Gender.* New Heaven, Conn.: Yale University Press.

Loveband, Anne. 2004a. "Positioning the Product: Indonesian Migrant Women Workers in Contemporary Taiwan." *Journal of Contemporary Asia* 34(3): 336–49.

——. 2004b. "Nationality Matters: SARS and Foreign Domestic Workers' Rights in Taiwan." *International Migration* 42(5).

Macdonald, Cameron. 1998. "Manufacturing Motherhood: The Shadow Work of Nannies and Au Pair." *Qualitative Sociology* 21(1): 25–53.

Margold, Jane A. 1995. "Narratives of Masculinity and Transnational Migration: Filipino Workers in the Middle East." In *Bewitching Women, Pious Men: Gender and Body Politics in Southeast Asia*, ed. Aihwa Ong and Michael G. Peletz, 274–98. Berkeley: University of California Press.

Martin, David. 1996. "Labor Contractors: A Conceptual Overview." *Asian Pacific Migration Journal* 5(2–3): 201–18.

Massey, Doreen. 1994. "A Global Sense of Place," in *Space, Place and Gender*, 146–56. Cambridge: Polity Press.

Massey, Douglas, G. Hugo, J. Arango, A. Kouaouci, A. Pellegrino, and J. Taylor. 1998. *Worlds in Motion: Understanding International Migration at the End of the Millennium.* Oxford: Clarendon Press.

McIntosh, William Alexander. 1996. *Sociologies of Food and Nutrition.* New York: Plenum Press.

McKay, Deirdre. 2003. "Filipinas in Canada—De-Skilling as a Push toward Marriage." In *Wife or Worker? Asian Women and Migration*, ed. Nicola Piper and Mina Roces, 23–52. Lanham, Md.: Rowman and Littlefield Publishers.

——. 2004. "Everyday Places: Philippine Place-Making and the Translocal Quotidian." Online Proceedings from Everyday Transformations (the 2004 annual conference of the Cultural Studies Association of Australasia). Available at http://wwwmcc.murdoch.edu.au/cfel/csaa_proceedings.htm, accessed on 6 February 2005.

——. 2005. "Success Stories? Filipina Migrant Domestic Workers in Canada." In

Asian Women as Transnational Domestic Workers, ed. Noorashikin Abdul Rahman, Brenda Yeoh, and Shirlena Huang, 305–60. Singapore: Marshall Cavendish.

Medina, Belinda. 1991. *The Filipino Family: A Text with Selected Readings.* Quezon City: University of Philippines Press.

Mendez, Jennifer. 1998. "Of Mops and Maids: Contradictions and Continuities in Bureaucratized Domestic Work." *Social Problems* 45(1): 114–35.

Miles, Robert. 1989. *Racism.* London: Routledge.

Miles, Robert, and Rodolfo D. Torres. 1999. "Does 'Race' Matter? Transatlantic Perspectives on Racism after 'Race Relations.'" In *Race, Identity and Citizenship: A Reader*, ed. Rodolfo D. Torres, Louis F. Miron, and Jonathan Xavier Inda, 19–38. Oxford: Blackwell.

Ministry of the Interior. 2002. *Report on the Senior Citizen Condition in Taiwan-Fuchien Area.* Taipei: Department of Statistics, Ministry of the Interior, Republic of China.

Mohanty, Chandra. 1991. "Under Western Eyes: Feminist Scholarship and Colonial Discourses." In *Third World Women and the Politics of Feminism*, ed. Chandra T. Mohanty, Ann Russo, and Lourdes Torres, 51–80. Indianapolis: Indiana University Press.

Nayyar, Deepak. 1997. "Emigration Pressures and Structural Change: Case Study of Indonesia." Geneva: International Labour Office, International Migration Papers 20.

NCRFW (National Commission on the Roles of Filipino Women). 1993. *Filipino Women Migrants: A Statistical Factbook.* Quezon City: National Commission on the Roles of Filipino Women.

Nippert-Eng, Christena. 1996. *Home and Work: Negotiating Boundaries through Everyday Life.* Chicago: University of Chicago Press.

Oakley, Ann. 1974. *The Sociology of Housework.* New York: Pantheon.

Ogaya, Chiho. 2003. "Feminization and Empowerment: Organizational Activities of Filipino Women Workers in Hong Kong and Singapore." In *Filipino Diaspora: Demography, Social Networks, Empowerment and Culture*, ed. Mamoru Tsuda, 67–89. Quezon City: Philippine Social Science Council and UNESCO.

Oishi, Nana. 2005. *Women in Motion: Globalization, State Politics, and Labor Migration in Asia.* Stanford, Calif.: Stanford University Press.

Okamatsu, Santaro. 1902. *Provisional Report on Investigations of Laws and Customs in the Island of Formosa.* Kobe: Kobe Herold Office.

Okunishi, Yoshio. 1996. "Labor Contracting in International Migration: The Japanese Case and Implications for Asia." *Asian and Pacific Migration Journal* 5(2–3): 219–40.

Omi, Michael, and Howard Winant. 1994. *Racial Formation in the United States.* London: Routledge.

Ong, Aihwa. 1994. "Colonization and Modernity: Feminist Representations of Women in Non-Western Societies." In *Theorizing Feminism: Parallel Trends in the Humanities and Social Sciences,* ed. Anna C. Herrmann and Abigail J. Stewart, 372–81. Boulder, Colo.: Westview Press.

———. 1999. *Flexible Citizenship: The Cultural Logics of Transnationality.* Durham, N.C.: Duke University Press.

Ozyegin, Gul. 2000. *Untidy Gender: Domestic Service in Turkey.* Philadelphia: Temple University Press.

Palmer, Phyllis. 1989. *Domesticity and Dirt: Housewives and Domestic Servants in the United States, 1920–1940s.* Philadelphia: Temple University Press.

Parreñas, Rhacel Salazar. 2001. *Servants of Globalization: Women, Migration and Domestic Work.* Stanford, Calif.: Stanford University Press.

———. 2005. *Children of Global Migration: Transnational Families and Gendered Woes.* Stanford, Calif.: Stanford University Press.

Paz Cruz, Victoria, and Anthony Paganoni. 1989. *Filipinas in Migration: Big Bills and Small Change.* Quezon City: Scalabrini Migration Center.

Pertierra, Raul. 1992. *Remittances and Returnees: The Cultural Economy of Migration in Ilocos.* Quezon City: New Day Publishers.

Pertierra, Raul, Eduardo F. Ugarte, Alicia Pingol, Joel Hernandez, and Nikos Lexis Dacanay. 2002. *Tex-ing Selves: Cellphones and Philippine Modernity.* Manila: De La Salle University. Available at http://www.finlandembassy.ph/texting1.htm, accessed on 1 July 2005.

Pessar, Patricia. R. 1999. "Engendering Migration Studies: The Case of New Immigrants in the United States." In *Gender and U.S. Immigration: Contemporary Trends,* ed. Pierrette Hondagneu-Sotelo, 20–42. Berkeley: University of California Press.

Pingol, Alicia Tadeo. 2001. *Remaking Masculinities: Identity, Power and Gender Dynamics in Families with Migrant Wives and Househusbands.* Quezon City: University of the Philippines.

Potuchek, Jean L. 1997. *Who Supports the Family? Gender and Breadwinning in Dual-Earner Marriages.* Stanford, Calif.: Stanford University Press.

Pratt, Geraldine. 1997. "Stereotypes and Ambivalence: The Construction of Domestic Workers in Vancouver, British Columbia." *Gender, Place and Culture* 4(2): 159–77.

———. 1999. "From Registered Nurse to Registered Nanny: Discursive Geographies of Filipina Domestic Workers in Vancouver, B.C." *Economic Geography* 75(3): 215–36.

Prothero, Mansell. 1990. "Labor Recruiting Organizations in the Developing World." *International Migration Review* 24: 221–28.

Qayum, Seemin, and Raka Ray. 2003. "Grapping with Modernity: India's Respectable Classes and the Culture of Domestic Servitude." *Ethnography* 4(4): 520–55.

Rabinow, Paul. 1977. *Reflections on Fieldwork on Morocco*. Berkeley: University of California Press.

Raharto, Aswatini. 2002. "Indonesian Female Labour Migrants: Experiences Working Overseas (A Case Study among Returned Migrants in West Java)." Presented at IUSSP Regional Population Conference on Southeast Asia's Population in a Changing Asian Context. Bangkok, Thailand.

Roberts, Dorothy. 1997. "Spiritual and Menial Housework." *Yale Journal of Law and Feminism* 9: 49–80.

Robinson, Kathryn. 2000. "Gender, Islam, and Nationality—Indonesian Domestic Servants in the Middle East." In *Home and Hegemony: Domestic Service and Identity Politics in South and Southeast Asia*, ed. Kathleen M. Adams and Sara Dickey, 157–78. Ann Arbor: University of Michigan Press.

Robison, Richard, and David G. Goodman, eds. 1996. *The New Rich in Asia: Mobile Phone, McDonalds and Middle-Class Revolution*. London: Routledge.

Rollins, Judith. 1985. *Between Women: Domestics and their Employers*. Philadelphia: Temple University Press.

Romero, Mary. 1992. *Maid in the U.S.A.* London: Routledge.

Rothman, Barbara Katz. 1989. *Recreating Motherhood*. New Brunswick, N.J.: Rutgers University Press.

Rudnyckyj, Daromir. 2004. "Technologies of Servitude: Governmentality and Indonesian Transnational Labor Migration." *Anthropological Quarterly* 77(3): 407–34.

Salzinger, Leslie. 1991. "A Maid by Any Other Name: The Transformation of 'Dirty Work' by Central American Immigrants." In *Ethnography Unbound: Power and Resistance in the Modern Metropolis*, ed. Michael Burawoy, 139–60. Berkeley: University of California Press.

Sassen, Saskia. 1996. *Losing Control?: Sovereignty in an Age of Globalization*. New York: Columbia University Press.

——. 1988. *The Mobility of Labor and Capital: A Study in International Investment and Labor Flow*. Cambridge: Cambridge University Press.

——. 1992. *The Global City: New York, London, Tokyo*. Princeton, N.J.: Princeton University Press.

——. 1999. *Guests and Aliens*. New York: New Press.

Satzewich, Vic. 1991. *Racism and the Incorporation of Foreign Labour: Farm Labour Migration to Canada since 1945*. London: Routledge.

Schwartz, Barry. 1968. "The Social Psychology of Privacy." *American Journal of Sociology* 73: 741–42.

Seno, Alexandra A. 2003. "The Boys in the Band." *Newsweek*, September 22.

Shieh, Gwo-Shon. 1994. *"Boss" Island: The Subcontracting Network and Micro-Entrepreneurship in Taiwan's Development*. New York: Peter Lang.

Sibayan, Bonifacio. 1991. "The Intellectualization of Filipino." *International Journal of the Sociology of Language* 88: 69–82.

Sibley, David. 1995. *Geographies of Exclusion: Society and Difference in the West*. London: Routledge.

Skeldon, Ronald. 1992. "International Migration within and from the East and Southeast Asian Region: A Review Essay." *Asian and Pacific Migration Journal* 1(1): 19–63.

Skolnick, Arlene S. 1992. *The Intimate Environment: Exploring Marriage and the Family*, 5th ed. New York: Harper Collins.

Soysal, Yasemin Nuhoglu. 1994. *Limits of Citizenship: Migrants and Postnational Membership in Europe*. Chicago: University of Chicago Press.

Spaan, Ernst. 1994. "Taikong's and Calo's: The Role of Middlemen and Brokers in Javanese International Migration." *International Migration Review* 27(1): 93–113.

Suzuki, Nobue. 2000. "Between Two Shores: Transnational Projects and Filipina Wives in/from Japan." *Women's Studies International Forum* 23(4): 431–44.

Tarcoll, Cecilia. 1996. "Migrating 'For the Sake of the Family?' Gender, Life Course and Intra-Household Relations among Filipino Migrants in Rome." *Philippine Sociological Review* 44(1–4): 12–32.

Teng, Emma J. 2004. *Taiwan's Imagined Geography—Chinese Colonial Travel Writing and Pictures, 1683–1895*. Cambridge, Mass.: Harvard University Asia Center.

Thorne, Barrie. 1993. *Gender Play: Girls and Boys in School*. New Brunswick, N.J.: Rutgers University Press.

Thornton, Arland, and Hui-Sheng Lin. 1994. *Social Change and the Family in Taiwan*. Chicago: University of Chicago Press.

Tirtosudarmo, Riwanto. 1999. "The Indonesian State's Response to Migration." *SOJOURN: Journal of Social Issues in Southeast Asia* 14(1): 212–27.

Tolentino, Roland. B. 1996. "Bodies, Letters, Catalogs: Filipinas in Transnational Space." *Social Text* 14(3): 49–76.

Torpey, John. 2000. *The Invention of the Passport: Surveillance, Citizenship and the State*. Cambridge: Cambridge University Press.

Tronto, Joan C. 1993. *Moral Boundaries: A Political Argument for an Ethic of Care*. New York: Routledge.

Tsai, Pan-Long, and Ching-Lung Tsay. 2001. "Economic Development, Foreign Direct Investment and International Labor Migration: The Experiences of Japan, Taiwan and Thailand." *Prosea Research Paper* 51: 1–36.

Tsay, Ching-Lung. 1992. "Clandestine Labor Migration to Taiwan." *Asian and Pacific Migration Journal* 4(4): 613–20.

——. 1999. "International Labor Migration and Regional Transition: An Analysis of the Development in Thailand" (Chinese). Presented at the annual conference of Southeast Asian Studies, Academic Sinica, Taipei.

Tseng Yen-Fen. 2004. "Expressing Nationalist Politics in the Guestworker Program: Taiwan's Recruitment of Foreign Labor" (Chinese). *Taiwanese Journal of Sociology* 32: 1–58.

Tung, Charlene. 1999. "The Social Reproductive Labor of Filipina Transmigrant Workers in Southern California: Caring for Those Who Provide Elderly Care." Ph.D. diss. University of California at Irvine, Irvine.

United Nations. 2002. *International Migration 2002*. New York: United Nations Population Division, Department of Economic and Social Affairs.

Uttal, Lynet. 1996. "Custodial Care, Surrogate Care, and Coordinated Care: Employed Mothers and the Meaning of Child Care." *Gender and Society* 10(3): 291–311.

Veblen, Thorstein. 1912/1994. *The Theory of the Leisure Class: An Economic Study of Institutions*. New York: B. W. Huebsch.

Wallerstein, Immanuel. 1991. "The Construction of Peoplehood: Racism, Nationalism, Ethnicity." In *Race, Nation, and Class: Ambiguous Identities*, ed. Etienne Balibar and Immanuel Wallerstein, 71–85. London: Verso.

Walzer, Michael, 1983. *Spheres of Justice: A Defense of Pluralism and Equality*. New York: Basic Books.

Wang Chih-Hung. 2004. "Dis/placed Identification and Politics of Space: The Consumptive Ethnoscape around Tao-Yuan Railroad Station" (Chinese). Presented at the Conference on Globalized Migration/Migrant Workers and Social Changes. Shih Hsin University, Taipei.

Wang, Horng-Luen. 1999. "In Want of a Nation: State, Institution and Globalization in Taiwan." Ph.D. diss., University of Chicago.

Wee, Vivienne, and Amy Sim. 2005. "Hong Kong as a Destination for Migrant Domestic Workers." In *Asian Women as Transnational Domestic Workers*, ed. Noorashikin Abdul Rahman, Brenda Yeoh, and Shirlena Huang, 175–209. Singapore: Marshall Cavendish.

Weix, G. G. 2000. "Inside the Home and Outside the Family: The Domestic Estrangement of Javanese Servants." In *Home and Hegemony: Domestic Service and Identity Politics in South and Southeast Asia*, ed. Kathleen M. Adams and Sara Dickey, 137–56. Ann Arbor: University of Michigan Press.

Wieviorka, Michel. 1994. "Racism in Europe: Unity and Diversity," in *Racism, Modernity and Identity*. London: Polity Press.

Williamson, Oliver. 1981. "The Economics of Organization: The Transaction Cost Approach." *American Journal of Sociology* 87(3): 548–77.

Wolf, Diane Lauren. 1992. *Factory Daughters: Gender, Household Dynamics, and Rural Industrialization in Java*. Berkeley: University of California Press.

Wolf, Margery. 1970. "Child Training and the Chinese Family." In *Family and Kinship in Chinese Society*, ed. Maurice Freedman, 37–62. Stanford, Calif.: Stanford University Press.

——. 1972. *Women and the Family in Rural Taiwan*. Stanford, Calif.: Stanford University Press.

——. 1975. "Women and Suicide in China." In *Women in Chinese Society*, ed. Margery Wolf and Roxane Witke, 111–14. Stanford, Calif.: Stanford University Press.

Wong, Sau-Ling. 1994. "Diverted Mothering: Representations of Caregivers of Color in the Age of 'Multiculturalism.'" In *Mothering: Ideology, Experience, and Agency*, ed. Evelyn Nakano Glenn, Grace Chang, and Linda Rennie Forcey, 67–94. London: Routledge.

Wrigley, Julia. 1995. *Other People's Children: An Intimate Account of the Dilemmas Facing Middle-Class Parents and the Women They Hire to Raise their Children*. New York: Basic Books.

Wu Ting-Fong. 1997. "Cultural Struggle in the Leisure Life of 'Foreign Workers'" (Chinese). M.A. thesis, Tung Hai University, Taichung, Taiwan.

Wu Bi-Na. 2003. "ChungShan—The Formation of a Filipino Migrant Workers' Community Space in Taipei" (Chinese). M.A. thesis, National Taiwan University, Taipei.

Wu Mei-Yao. 2004. "Rupture of Hegemonic Space: Sunday Gathering of Foreign Workers in Taipei Railway Station" (Chinese). M.A. thesis, National Chung Hsing University, Taichung, Taiwan.

Yamanaka, Keiko. 2003. "Feminized Migration, Community Activism and Grassroots Transnationalization in Japan." *Asian and Pacific Migration Journal* 12(1–2): 155–87.

Yamanaka, Keiko, and Nicola Piper. 2003. "An Introductory Overview." *Asian and Pacific Migration Journal* 12(1–2): 1–19.

Yea, Sallie. 2005. "When Push Comes to Shove: States of Vulnerability, Personal Transformation, and Trafficked Women's Migration Decisions." *SOJOURN: Journal of Social Issues in Southeast Asia* 20(1): 67–95.

Yeoh, Brenda, and Shirlena Huang. 1998. "Negotiating Public Space: Strategies and Styles of Migrant Female Domestic Workers in Singapore." *Urban Studies* 35(3): 583–602.

——. 1999. "Singapore Women and Foreign Domestic Workers: Negotiating Domestic Work and Motherhood." In *Gender, Migration and Domestic Service*, ed. Janet H. Momsen, 277–300. London: Routledge.

——. 2000. "'Home' and 'Away': Foreign Domestic Workers and Negotiations of Diasporic Identity in Singapore." *Women's Studies International Forum* 23(4): 413–29.

Yeoh, Brenda, Shirlena Huang, and Joaquin Gonzalez III. 1999. "Migrant Female Domestic Workers: Debating the Economic, Social and Political Impacts in Singapore." *International Migration Review* 33(1): 114–36.

You Jian-Ming. 1995. "Taiwanese Employed Women under Japanese Rule" (Chinese)." Ph.D. diss., National Taiwan Normal University, Taipei.

Young, James Philip. 1980. "Migration and Education in the Philippines: An Anthropological Study of an Ilocano Community." Ph.D. diss., Stanford University, Stanford, Calif.

Zerubavel, Eviatar. 1981. *Hidden Rhythms: Schedules and Calendars in Social Life.* Chicago: University of Chicago Press.

——. 1991. *The Fine Line: Making Distinctions in Everyday Life.* Chicago: University of Chicago Press.

Zolberg, Aristide. 1991. "Bounded States in a Global Market: The Uses of International Labor Migrations." In *Social Theory for a Changing Society*, ed. Pierre Bourdieu and James Coleman, 301–24. Boulder, Colo.: Westview Press.

INDEX

PEI-CHIA LAN

is Associate Professor of Sociology at

National Taiwan University.